The Portuguese Revolution and the Armed Forces Movement

Rona M. Fields

The Praeger Special Studies program—
utilizing the most modern and efficient book
production techniques and a selective
worldwide distribution network—makes
available to the academic, government, and
business communities significant, timely
research in U.S. and international economic, social, and political development.

The Portuguese Revolution and the Armed Forces Movement

PRAEGER SPECIAL STUDIES IN INTERNATIONAL POLITICS AND GOVERNMENT

Praeger Publishers   New York Washington London

Library of Congress Cataloging in Publication Data

Fields, Rona M
    The Portuguese revolution and the Armed Forces Movement.

    (Praeger special studies in international politics and
government)
    Includes bibliographical references.
    1. Portugal—History—Revolution, 1974-
2. Portugal—Politics and government—1974-
3. Portugal. Movimento das Forcas Armadas.   I. Title.
DP680.F48   946.9'042   75-19785
ISBN 0-275-55610-7

Excerpts from William Minter, PORTUGUESE AFRICA AND THE WEST
(Penguin African Library 1972) pp. 20, 24-25, 32-33, 68-69, 79-80,
copyright © William Minter, 1972, appear in this volume on pp. 17, 21,
24-25, 29, 45, and 57. Reprinted by permission of Penguin Books, Ltd.,
and Monthly Review Press, Inc.

PRAEGER PUBLISHERS
111 Fourth Avenue, New York, N.Y. 10003, U.S.A.

Published in the United States of America in 1975
by Praeger Publishers, Inc.

Printed in the United States of America

in memory of my mother Kate

whose life and love inspired my own

PREFACE AND ACKNOWLEDGMENTS

In June 1974 I was invited to speak at the Medical Faculty of the University of Lisbon. I had for a number of years been doing research on political prisoners, concentrating on the effects of torture and other psychologically destructive processes commonly used against prisoners and other institutionalized persons. I had also worked at developing rehabilitation procedures. Through Amnesty International's Medical Commission I met other mental health professionals who had themselves been political prisoners in Portugal. After the events of April 1974, Dr. Alfonso Alburquerque, a psychiatrist and colleague on the Medical Commission, had arranged the conference at which I spoke.

I had planned a very brief stay in Portugal. However, when I became aware of the enormous enthusiasm that the revolution had engendered throughout Lisbon, I decided to stay a while and learn more.

When I returned to Clark University, I realized that we Americans had very little access to current, accurate information on events in Portugal, and I began to design studies of the current history and causes of the revolution. In December 1974 I returned to Portugal and began interviewing members of the MFA and the Cabinet. I was astounded and delighted at their willingness to see me and to spend hours in interview sessions. Political party leaders were equally generous with their time. As a result there are more contributors to this study than could ever be mentioned.

Jose and Eduarda Fernandes and their family, my hosts, guides, and interpreters in Portugal, gave generously of their time and hospitality. Engineer Maria de Lourdes Pintassiglo, who for a very hectic seven months was Minister for Social Affairs in the Portuguese government, and her executive assistant, Ana Vicente, gave hours of their precious time to provide me with background information, sociological and health data and, best of all, their friendship. Commander Jorge Correia Jesuino and Lt. Commander Botelho Leal, Minister for Social Communications and Chief of Cabinet, respectively; Major Costa Martins, Minister for Labor; and Dr. Gouveia Perreira encouraged and aided my research, gathered materials for me, and allowed me to participate with them in their U.S. tour.

Journalist Chris Reed of the British press and Mitsukazu Shibou of the Japan Afro-Asian Writers' Association were extremely helpful.

General M. J. Costello, Irish Military Historian, provided me with information on the economic and military condition of Portugal prior to the revolution.

    On the other side of the Atlantic, Milea Froes and Beth Rendeiro, Clark students, gave me injections of enthusiasm, translating help, and lessons in Portuguese. Beth's father, Chris Rendeiro, was extremely helpful in recommending me to his contacts in Portuguese political parties. I received considerable encouragement through correspondence with two eminent sociologists, A. McClung Lee and Morris Janowitz, both expert in the methodology and subject matter of this study.

    George and Charlotte Gray of WGCY-AM, New Bedford, Massachusetts, provided me a base in their Portuguese language radio station, as well as their valuable friendship.

    The unexciting but difficult work of making my research readable was considerably aided by my friend and colleague Dr. Harold Moody of Clark University, who patiently reviewed the manuscript for everything from grammar to tables; Lynn Olson and Gloria Solari, who typed it; my daughter Miriam, who did some typing, brought me coffee, and gave her comments; my son Marc, who did the initial editing; Shawn and Cathy, who gave me all kinds of encouragement through their filial loyalty; and finally my father, William Katz, whose generous support of this and my other research projects, as well as the inspiration he provides, makes it all possible.

CONTENTS

LIST OF TABLES, FIGURES, AND MAP

Figure

Map

The helicopters swept low over the stadium. The people, elbow to elbow and waving banners, looked up and reached to collect the red carnations being showered on them from the skies. On May 1, 1975, a celebration in Lisbon sponsored by the Intersindical, the National Congress of Trade Unions, and four other political parties marked the conclusion of a week of celebrations. A week earlier on April 25 the people of Portugal, after 48 years of one-party rule, had gone to the polls to elect a constitutional assembly.

On April 25, one year before, the Movimento das Forcas Armadas (Armed Forces Movement, MFA), proclaiming a leftist revolution in Portugal, had called for a new socialist state in metropolitan Portugal and the decolonization of Portuguese Africa.

The revolution had been nearly bloodless, with six people killed by a contingent of the fascist political police. * The six were among tens of thousands of civilians who flocked into doorways and streets to cheer the MFA. Although the MFA had used both loudspeakers and the national broadcasting station to ask people to stay in their homes for fear of actions by PIDE/DGS and other fascist groups, the people of Lisbon wanted personally to witness and participate in the revolution.

Tortured political prisoners were freed on the day the revolution began, and their torturers and imprisoners locked up. On election day one year later, there were 1,246 confessed torturers occupying the prisons and another 250 prisoners who, although classified as political prisoners, had committed offenses against the state of an economic or violent nature.[1] For the first time in 50 years it was not illegal to hold membership in opposition political parties in Portugal.

During this first year--from April 25, 1974 to election day on April 25, 1975--the Portuguese nation attempted to achieve the objectives set forth in the original MFA program, in spite of three attempts to force the MFA out by the use of armed force.

At the same time, the evolution of political parties proliferated. In July 1974 there were 80 groups identifying themselves as political parties. By the time of the elections in 1975, there were only 12

---

*PIDE--International and State Defense Police, established in 1945. DGS--its successor, Directorate General of Security, established under Caetano in 1969.

parties on the ballots with three others having been suspended for "undemocratic behaviors jeopardizing the political process." The overwhelming majority of the parties were leftist.

Simultaneously three new nations emerged on the African continent out of former Portuguese colonies. Guinea-Bissau took its place at the United Nations in June 1974; within months, FRELIMO* had been recognized as the provisional government for Mozambique; in January 1975, agreements with the three national liberation groups in Angola marked the initiation of a transitional government for a new state in that colony as well. The African liberation movements and the Armed Forces Movement had thus presented to the world two symbiotic revolutions--revolutions that had at the same time fused and transcended the objectives of African nationalism and Western socialist democracy.

The revolution in Portugal also had a unique characteristic that is contrary to most theories of revolution. It was a leftist revolution, not a coup, by what might be expected to be the most right-wing institution of a fascist society, the military. In terms both of normal social organization and of normal political socialization, this was an impossibility, because all military institutions are predicated on the conservation of the power structure and on the supposition that it must be defended from prospective attack.

Military organizations normally operate on the assumption that human nature must be hierarchically patterned for internal control and order, and that institutions must constantly be ready to guard society against the natural perversity of humankind. Studies of political socialization, furthermore, would seem to indicate that persons socialized through authoritarian structures are unable as adults comfortably to function in a democratic fashion. [2]

How is it, then, that career officers in the Portuguese military organized themselves along democratic lines and managed successfully to overthrow a government, organize a socialist state, decolonize the oldest imperial power in Western Europe, and ensure free elections--elections in which, by the use of a secret ballot, a majority of the population voted for a socialist political and economic system? Of the eligible citizens, 92 percent voted in the election, only 7 percent cast either blank or spoiled ballots, and 38 percent voted for the Socialist Party--a party which did not even exist in Portugal prior to April 25, 1974.

Cynics say that the revolution was a rebellion by career officers dissatisfied when reserve officers were granted equal pay and promotion privileges. Others insist the revolution was entirely a

---

*FRELIMO--the acronym for the Mozambiquen Liberation Movement first styled by Eduardo Mondlano in his 1964 writings.

product of the outlawed Communist party's infiltration into the military. The MFA, on the other hand, has defined itself clearly enough without reference to these aspersions, and I intend to examine their definitions with reference to their actions. This study is an attempt to analyze the background of the MFA revolution, its process, development, and personality, during the first year of the provisional government. In this context, I will also explore the dynamic interaction between the two symbiotic revolutions I have mentioned.

I conducted this study as a participant observer during four crisis periods of the first year of the Portuguese provisional government. The first research field work was done during the cabinet crisis in July 1974, when the MFA and President Antonio de Spinola clashed on the selection of a leftist, Vasco Goncalves, for Prime Minister. The conflict at this time was far more than a matter of choosing personalities: It was a contest over reform versus revolution. Chapters 5 and 6 provide a detailed analysis of this process and its background.

My second participatory observation was during December 1974-January 1975, the crucial period for resolving the question of Angolan independence. In Chapters 2 and 3, I discuss the interdependency both in economics and population in this period between Angola and Portugal--an interdependency much greater than that in the other colonies.

The third period of field research took place during April-May 1975, the month of constitutional assembly elections and the subsequent inflated struggle between the Socialist and Communist parties. I discuss this period in Chapters 4, 5, and 7. The epilogue summarizes my fourth period of field research during the crisis which resulted in the fifth and sixth governments during June-September 1975.

As revolutions and the literature which analyzes them proliferate during the twentieth century, a peculiar problem arises. Although researchers aim for "generalizability," the most useful research on revolutions must, of necessity, be particular. All revolutions, from the Russian example of 1917-20 to the current revolution in Portugal, are considerably different not only from each other, but also from the Marxian model itself. In Chapter 8 I will examine the unique combination of phenomena which define the Portuguese revolution as the most comprehensive example of contemporary leftist revolutions.

While preparing his study of Cuba, Listen Yankee, C. Wright Mills had forecasted not only the success of the then small, revolutionary movement in Cuba, but also the growing impatience of the Cuban people with U.S. support for Batista's repressive regime.[3] Critics of Mills were quick to point out that he took a partisan position, and actually supported the insurgents. When as a result the perennial question of objectivity took center stage, the important message of the book was lost to many social scientists, and Mills himself returned to writing social theory. Since those days, participant observation research has become respectable, and even "client advocacy" writing has become fairly established. Advocacy works such as Michael Harrington's The Other America form bases for social policy decision making and action.[4]

The particular value of participant observation for policy research is, of course, that over the bridge formulated by the researcher between the perspective of the participants and the scientific theory, communication is possible and understanding enhanced. Occasionally journalists are able to present the participants' perspective clearly. Too often, however, the final product is distorted as time, space, and the sociohistorical inclinations of journalists package the perspective to meet media needs. Chapter 7 examines the Western journalistic presentation of the Portuguese revolution and the impact that that presentation has had on the revolution itself.

If this study suggests that I share the enthusiasm of the MFA for Portugal's new situation, it is an accurate impression. I am glad to acknowledge the value decision that lies at the root of all social research: We study what interests and excites us. We proceed with enthusiasm as sleuths and with dedication as aficionados. If we succeed, we infect others with our own excitement.

NOTES

1. The figures on prisoners were given by Brig. Otelo Servaia Carvalho at a press conference in Lisbon on April 27, 1975. One year earlier, in June 1974, similar figures had been provided by Dr. Alfonso Alburquerque at a meeting of the Amnesty International Campaign to Abolish Torture Medical Commission in Holland. Dr. Alburquerque, himself a former torture victim, had interviewed former PIDE agents who were identified by others as torturers and who themselves admitted to having performed these acts.

2. Gordon Allport, The Nature of Prejudice (New York: Doubleday-Anchor, 1958).

3. C. Wright Mills, Listen Yankee (New York: McGraw-Hill, 1960).

4. Michael Harrington, The Other America (New York: Macmillan, 1962).

The Portuguese Revolution and the Armed Forces Movement

On the eve of the first anniversary of the MFA revolution, an estimated 100,000 people turned out onto Avenida Liberdade, parading to the Rossio, singing, chanting, honking horns in tribute to their liberators--the MFA. The celebration lasted into the morning and people laughingly recalled that only a year before that very avenue was described as "the avenue of liberty that ends with the penitentiary." (Ironically, Avenida Liberdade has its terminal point at the penitentiary.)

The 200 leaders of the Armed Forces Movement for whom this spontaneous celebration was a tribute had undergone an intensive struggle for political socialization as individuals and as a group since September 1973 when, in small, secret cadres, career officers began meeting together to plan a revolution. Among them were many senior officers who had entered the military when military careers were still the prerogative of an elite class and ensured a high social status. Others--sons of the struggling petty bourgeoisie, the small farmers, the industrial workers--had entered after 1958, when the military academies were opened to persons from all strata of society without tuition. For them the military academy had represented the only possible route for socioeconomic mobility and education. It is important to note here that the traditionally elite status of military officers in Portuguese society had declined considerably by 1958, and that the scions of affluent families were pursuing their higher education in universities in Portugal and abroad. The reason for opening admission to the academy, then, was the dearth of officer candidates.

While access to military leadership was liberalized, serious attempts to change the political and economic focus of the Salazarist regime were continually and increasingly suppressed. When the

1

April 25 revolution swept Portugal, journalists and scholars in the rest of the world were taken by surprise, largely because of the heavy mantle of secrecy which had for years shrouded the history of sporadic rebellions among workers, students, and military personnel.[1] In fact disaffection had been growing rapidly as the prolonged African wars, combined with the archaic economic policies of an unpopular government, led the country further away from its twentieth-century neighbors in France and the rest of Western Europe. In spite of the fact that the price for political divergence before the revolution had been indeterminate prison sentences, torture, or death, opposition movements had flourished.

The induction of draftees into the colonial wars had introduced an additional focus for dissension. By 1973, when the MFA began organizing, the army consisted of 210,000 men, with draftees inducted for four-year terms. In July 1973 the Defense Ministry of the Caetano administration announced that draftee officers would be equal in pay and promotional status to career officers. This decree provided a pretext which the military officers could use without fear of reprisals to meet together for discussion. It was to prove the major instrument for disguising the real objectives and organization of the MFA.

On March 15, 1974, an MFA meeting at the Military Academy in Lisbon was attacked by the Portuguese Legion and PIDE/DGS, who arrested seven officers that night and another 33 the following night. This attack and the regime's deposing of General Antonio de Spinola and General Francisco da Costa Gomes from their positions on the general staff, provided further cover for MFA meetings. The authoritarian state which carefully censored all publications, imprisoned all suspected dissenters, and deposed military commanders for insubordination to the civilian authorities, nonetheless accepted as logical and legitimate the prospect of self-interest organizing by military officers. Perhaps "acceptance" is not an accurate description of the authorities' attitude. As one officer put it, "The regime couldn't afford to arrest all of us, and there was no way that their spy network could thoroughly infiltrate our very close, personal network, so they had to let us meet and then hope for the best."

At first, all of the officers involved in the MFA were career men. However, their career commitments were not exclusive, and many of them had completed studies for licensures in various fields and, in many cases, advanced professional degrees. Unlike the American officers described by Janowitz in his classic study of the U.S. military,[2] most of the Portuguese officers, and particularly the naval officers, were products of universities as well as the service academies. In addition to the managerial and administrative skills acquired through their service education, their advanced degrees included engineering, medicine, philosophy, law, economics, languages, history, psychology, government, geography, and agronomy. (The "university officers"--those draftees whose university degrees made them officer candidates--were less thoroughly schooled in preparation for their equivalent pay and rank.) Furthermore, in addition to their formal and service education, career officers had attended special NATO staff and command schools in various of the Western European countries, so their background was cosmopolitan as well as intellectual. This was especially true of naval officers, for whom educational requirements were always higher than in the other services.

Although there were a few draftee officers who had joined the MFA before April 25, 1974, command power, despite the July decree, rested firmly with the widely educated career officers, and it was this group who took primary responsibility for planning the revolution.

Portuguese military officers, like those of other countries, were indoctrinated to be apolitical. As Janowitz described it, "According to the definitions of military honor, the professional soldier is 'above politics' in domestic affairs. In an authoritarian society-- monarchical or totalitarian--to be above politics means that the officer is committed to the status quo."[3] When MFA leaders talk of having had a "guilt complex," and having become "politically socialized through it," they are reflecting the special circumstances of their mandate to be above politics. The apolitical ideal is a particularly unrealistic one when it is applied to persons whose range of experience extends so far beyond the narrow confines of military history, tactics, strategy, and technology--the usual curriculum of service academy education. It was even more of a contradiction in Portugal, where military officers had consistently been the unopposed candidates for President, and even the few opposition candidates had also been military figures.

As the officer corps became more representative of the general population, it was sure to reflect the variety of political opinions, beliefs, and attitudes present in the society. And, since the Portuguese military spent considerable time living with or near their families, particular class and local issues were never far from their minds. In addition, the political nature, structure, and operations of NATO could not help but arouse political consciousness in even the most technologically oriented officers. As a result, while the authority system of the totalitarian government was waning along with the physical strength of its leaders, Salazar and Tomas, the military was being politicized to an extraordinary degree. Janowitz explains how such a process works:

> The transformation of political beliefs from im-
> plicit commitments and loyalties to a more ex-
> plicit ideology relates directly to the strain on
> military honor. To what extent have the growing
> limitations on effectiveness of honor as an or-
> ganizing concept of the military profession been
> accompanied by an increase in emphasis on ex-
> plicit ideology? Ever since the writings of Max
> Weber, social research has stressed the theme
> that modern rationality and industrial efficacy
> weaken traditional authority. Since honor is an
> essential component of traditional authority, the
> growth of rationalism in the military establish-
> ment means the growth of a critical attitude, not
> only in technical and administrative matters, but
> towards the purposes and ends of one's profes-
> sion. [4]

The military had in 1961 been blamed and ridiculed for the loss
of Goa, Danao, and Diu (territories on India's west coast) to the Indian army. The constitution had been changed to further restrict
popular electoral processes, and General Humberto Delgado, the popular leader of an opposition party (Directorio Democrata Social) had
already aroused considerable support among the military, students,
intellectuals, and the working class. His political commitment represented a new direction for regaining honor. The events which followed in the wake of the African wars provided increasing impetus
for taking his path.

As early as 1964, Alvaro Cunhal, a law professor, leader of
the Portuguese Communist Party, and eventually Minister without
Portfolio in the provisional government, had written that the only
possible means of liberation from fascist control would be through
the activist efforts of the military. The political tract in which he
predicted this likelihood (and in fact developed the thesis into a plan
of action not too dissimilar from that which was actually followed)
was only published in Portugal after the revolution.

But the politicization of the military would not in itself have
sufficed to trigger a revolution. What was needed was an immediate
cause, and this the MFA found in Africa, where colonial wars had
for decades been the focus of their humiliation.

It was the ongoing debacle of the African wars that gave sus-
tenance to the revolutionary aspirations of military and civilians
alike.

No one today can estimate accurately the number of officers
who were initially involved in planning the revolution. Nor would it

be possible to name any individual or committee as the initiator of
the plans. This is not because of any high degree of MFA secrecy,
but because the antifascist movement was so widespread that when it
evolved into an organization, there were already communication net-
works, representatives, and liaison personnel. The first revolutionary prime minister, Brigadier General Vasco Dos Santos Goncalves,
is recognized as the main organizer of the MFA to have been not
only the theoretician of the revolution, but also the defender of its
leftward political course. His experience is in some ways typical,
however, for like many of the other MFA leaders who had entered
the service during the 1940s and 1950s, he served as a senior officer during the African campaigns.

In one sense it was in Africa that the MFA was born. In the
course of their administrative functions, some of the senior officers
stationed there had met with leaders of the various liberation movements, and these contacts, however brief, had probably engendered
some respect for the fascist regime's African enemies. In addition,
all military personnel serving in Africa were aware of the rhetoric
and accomplishments of these movements. Even in metropolitan Portugal, groups supporting the liberation movements managed to circulate pamphlets, newspapers, and speakers underground, and Portuguese citizens who had spent time abroad were further informed by
the foreign press of developments in Africa.

The influence of the insurgent groups in stimulating the evolution of a leftist military organization among officers of the colonial
army is not directly traceable. Perhaps it is more accurate to say
that the economic exploitation of the African colonies and of metropolitan Portugal itself had produced the necessary conditions for revolution in both places at the same time. The revolutions were thus
mutually dependent, or symbiotic.

The wars for independence in Africa may be considered a sufficient but not a necessary cause for the revolution in Portugal. The
Portuguese military had been fighting and losing a colonial war for
13 years. There is considerable historical precedent for an army
coup to depose the political leadership of a country under such circumstances. Witness, for example, the periodic attempts by the
German General Staff to depose the Nazi regime at times when defeat seemed inevitable.

But in these and other attempts at military coups under a dictatorship, the military group itself was either without a political
ideology or was even further to the political right than the regime it
was trying to depose.

In Portugal the situation was very different. The nature and
direction of its revolution, like those of the African revolutions, resulted from reaction to a political system that was equally repressive

to the homeland and the colonies. As an MFA senior officer mentioned in an interview, "We knew that they [the FRELIMO] couldn't
win and we couldn't win--after all, we were all Portuguese."

In Portuguese Africa, the major sources of income are owned
by British, American, West German, and French interests. During
the past century, Portugal played a role in the international arena not
dissimilar to its role in the slave trade. After having carried out the
early explorations and established major trade bases in Africa, her
interests were taken over through purchase and armed conflict by
British, German, French, and later American mercantile elites. In
both Africa and Portugal, national and private income--concentrated
in a small ruling class--was derived through a contemporary slave
trade, the export of unemployed, destitute workers to neighboring
countries.

When Salazar resigned in 1968, Marcelo Caetano assumed
power in the midst of an already doomed military struggle to retain
the overseas provinces, the Portuguese African colonies. The armed
forces had not unanimously nor consistently supported the Salazarist
regime or its African policies. When Henrique Galvao hijacked the
Portuguese luxury liner Santa Maria in 1961, he was articulating the
aggravation of an already organized opposition among military officers. This opposition, led by General Humberto Delgado, attempted
first to overthrow the government through election in 1958 and then,
having failed to do that, by organizing underground.[5] Delgado's
assassination was planned by the Salazar government as early as
1962, and he and a companion were lured to their deaths on February
13, 1965 by PIDE agent Ernesto Lopes Ramos.[6]

In November 1970, the Armed Revolutionary Action group began a campaign of sabotage with explosions aboard ships bound for
the African wars. It also destroyed aircraft on the ground, shut off
Lisbon telecommunications during the May 1971 NATO conference,
and blew up an ammunition dump in Portugal. This group, led by a
woman physician, Isabel DoCarmo, was made up of students, soldiers, and workers to the political left of the Communist Party.

By 1973, Portugal had the distinction of having the lowest per
capita income in Western Europe, the highest rate of inflation, and a
34 percent illiteracy rate. The army was comprised of 210,000 men,
with draftees being inducted for four years (the longest period of
induction for any NATO country). Soldiers in Mozambique, called
upon to massacre whole villages, were alienated from the colonials;
they had stopped fighting in Guinea months before the revolution, and
Angola, they knew, would present the most difficult problem of ex-
trication.

The several hundred military officers who led this disgruntled
army had wide political differences among them and varied military

experiences, but they shared a commitment to end the colonial wars and see their country through to elections. They were well aware that the officers involved in the attempted army coup of January-February 1962 were still in prison; Delgado had become a martyr for them as well as for the larger population. After attempts to organize for better salaries, pensions, and promotions were either ignored by Caetano or dealt with by marginal and token measures, dissension widened. They began to organize in secret cells in each service in the fall of 1973. Liaison persons were carefully selected, and each cell elected representatives to the next level of authority. Out of the nearly one thousand officers who were members of the movement, 20 were elected to coordinate the planning. The coordinating committee began drafting a program, and this too was done democratically, through elected committees.

Because of the superior education and experience of these officers, the government's attempts to keep them apolitical conflicted increasingly with their knowledge of the world and their experience of disintegration in Portugal and disaster in the colonial war. Since most of them were between 30 and 45, their personal experiences of fascism as a political ideology was that of a dying, distant system. The fascist youth organizations had atrophied by the 1950s, and the idealism of youth was therefore without a model. The army was in effect adrift and awaiting direction. An MFA naval commander described the situation as follows:

> I believe that fascism in Portugal fell because it was rotten, like a ship that is so rotten it sinks. No one wanted to sail it because it was rotten. Everything was rotten, political power, economic power. Even with censorship, without freedom of the press, everyone knew what was going on. Even people at the beginning, youth who believed in fascism, gradually lost their faith. And, what else? If not fascism, what else?[7]

The MFA was initially composed of a representative congress consisting of approximately 200 officers and a coordinating commission, which was a decision-making executive consisting of 20 officers elected by the other representatives. Repeated tours of service together in Africa had provided officers within each service, and even across service lines, with intimate knowledge about each other's political proclivities and leadership capacities. Suggestions about organization and nominations for representation therefore were made fluidly and without regard to rank. This would have been impossible had there not already been a relatively high level of articulation of grievances by military personnel.

In drafting their revolution, the Portuguese officers had numerous indigenous models to choose from. In Portugal itself, there had been military coups both to the right and to the left of existing regimes. Why did the April 1974 coup succeed where others had failed?

There is no doubt that the failure of the 1962 military coup was as much a product of the strength of Salazar's regime as the success of the 1974 coup was the product of the weakness of the Caetano regime. Even the Portuguese capitalists had become restive under the wild inflation and depletion of national resources in the colonial wars. General Antonio de Spinola had been a popular general, both with his troops and with the public. He had had some experience as a business administrator and a good deal of combat experience. He was also a fanatically patriotic man who had come to the conclusion that his country was destined for collapse unless drastic reforms were undertaken--not the least of which was self-determination for the African colonies. At a time when publication of books critical of the regime or Portuguese traditions were banned and their authors arrested (as in the celebrated case of the three Marias' New Portuguese Letters[8]), Spinola published his book, Portugal and the Future. [9]

The book was extremely critical of the Caetano regime's policies in Africa, economic failures, political oppression, and corruption. Around February 1974, Spinola at the behest of the MFA confronted Caetano with the fact that dissension was rife and that he, Spinola, had been approached to take over the leadership of the country and would probably do so. Caetano agreed to make some changes, including replacing Admiral Tomas as president with Spinola. Whether it was a double cross by Caetano or the first command action ever taken by the aged Admiral Tomas as president remains uncertain. What is certain is that Spinola and the then head of the Joint Chiefs of Staff, General Francisco Costa da Gomes, refused to swear loyalty to the regime's policies and in March were both fired by Tomas.

THE COUP

On March 15, the Portuguese Legion (an elite corp similar to the Nazi Sturm Arbend) broke into the Army Military Academy in Lisbon, where an MFA emergency meeting was being held, and arrested seven officers. The following night they arrested another 33 at an army post in Caldas da Rainha. At that time, final plans for the coup had not been adopted, and the arrested officers were not privy to any information or key to any planning. The arrest of these officers could not frustrate the coup itself. In fact, during March and April, while PIDE was busily arresting civilians who might create disturbances with or through the Communist Party on May Day, the MFA was meeting openly to "plan a demonstration of solidarity with their imprisoned colleagues." By the third week in April PIDE caught up with the coup and issued warrants for three-quarters of the coordinating committee on April 24. Brigadier Otelo Carvalho gave his personal account of this hectic period.

> On the 16 of March, I was the only one of the cen-
> tral nucleus that was not arrested . . . only after
> this date did I take on my shoulder responsibility
> for planning and conduct of operations.
> We had knowledge, through General Spinola
> that on the 14 of March a deputation of Generals
> . . . would ask us to void the Manifesto and the
> logical consequence would be the discharge of
> Generals Spinola and Costa Gomes. . . . We
> made a small plan of operations in which partici-
> pated Lt. Col. Garcia dos Santos, Major Casa-
> nova, Major Monge, Lt. Gerdes, myself . . .
> Major Azevedo. This plan was very weak. . . .
> On the 12th I went with Capt. Vasco
> Lourence to the house of General Spinola. . . .
> On the 13th, in the afternoon, we got to-
> gether with the officers of the unit that we had
> included in the plan of operations in order to
> give instructions about their intended missions.
> We verified . . . that the plan was not per-
> formable and it was I who assumed the responsi-
> bility of putting it aside.

Carvalho revealed that the coup was originally to have taken place the night of March 13-14 in order to directly intervene on Caetano's in-tention to publish the manifesto discharging Generals Spinola and Costa Gomes. The latter had refused to take the new loyalty oath in-vested by Admiral Tomas as the means for undercutting prospective military mutiny over the colonial wars. However, because the plan for the mid-March coup was put aside, there was a split in the rebels' ranks with Majors Monge and Casanova and Captain Marques Ramos taking part in an abortive march on Lisbon and subsequently being arrested. However, in the process of trying to contact his colleagues during that hectic weekend, Carvalho witnessed the anticoup opera-tions, and considered that:

> While I was at the Encarnacao, together with
> Major Miquelina Simoes who had accompanied
> me during the whole night, I had the opportunity

of verifying the nature of the military command
which had been developed to oppose the Caldas
formations. This gave me enormous possibili-
ties for preparing myself psychologically, and
knowing the materials . . . of the enemy . . .
all of which served greatly for the final planning
of the 25th of April. [10]

Shortly before 11 P.M. April 24, 1974, a signal song was
broadcast on radio throughout Portugal, and the officers led their
troops to their posts. The first song, Grandola, told of a village in
Alentejo, and the brotherhood of the workers through struggle.
Shortly after midnight a second signal song was broadcast which indicated that army units had taken over the radio and television stations in Lisbon.

THE AFRICAN REVOLUTIONS

African resistance to the Portuguese colonization was always
present. However, it had persisted largely on a tribal basis and as
such had given no recognition to the larger issues of nationhood. In
Guinea, local resistance to colonial rule was not overcome until 1936.
Some authorities, in fact, place the effective subjugation of Guinea
and the Cape Verde Islands as having been in 1945 with the establishment of a Portuguese monopoly of trade and shipping through the internationally financed trust Companhia Uniao Fabril (CUF). [11]
In Angola, the struggle of the Dembos area persisted from 1907
to 1910, the Bakango country had revolted again in 1913 and the
Bailundu from 1902 to 1904. In Mozambique there was constant resistance, and it was only in southern Mozambique that the Portuguese ever really established complete control. The northern area
was the first to be liberated in the 1960s.
Nationalism was slow to emerge, partly because of the under-
development of Portuguese Africa, and partly because of the ruthless
fashion with which protests were oppressed and isolated. Local
authorities, both bureaucratic and police, assumed great and clandestine powers, and were responsible for issuing secret orders to
murder hundreds of people. These orders seem never to have been
questioned or punished by higher authorities. Modern nationalism
seems to have arisen among Africans and mulattos living in towns
and working on the docks or plantations who somehow had got an education. They organized groups like the Liga Africana, which was established in Lisbon in 1923 and hosted W. E. B. Dubois's Third Pan-
African Congress. It was conservative in style and composed only

of educated people, but it stood for African unity against colonial
rule. In 1930 Salazar's regime put an end to it by declaring it illegal. Similar groups founded as social or mutual aid associations
developed in the African countries themselves. These included the
Liga National Africana (Angola), the Associacao Regional des
Naturais de Angola, and the Centro Associativo dos Negros de
Mozambique. The first was banned in 1950 after only two issues of
its magazine had been published. (They had formed as a literary
discussion group in 1948.) The Liga National Africana, which had
been formed in 1919 as an association primarily of assimilados (those
who had passed the literacy and other requirements for this legal
status), was defused in the 1950s when it began to move toward more
contact with the African masses, and its elected leadership was replaced by officers selected by the governor general. The Mozambique organization met a similar fate.

These were scattered, short-lived, issue-oriented organizations which died when their leaders were imprisoned, massacred,
or exiled. Their existence, however, shows that the war for liberation was taking place in all three of the colonies in a fragmented,
sporadic fashion prior to 1961, when it came to the attention of the
world as a result of events in Angola.

Ongoing contact with the African liberation movements provided both the future members of the MFA and opposition political
forces in metropolitan Portugal a revolutionary model that was contemporary and appealing--that of a liberation movement. Where the
earlier organizations for enhancing the participation of assimilados
in the governance of the colonies had failed of achievement, the liberation struggles had united masses behind them and not only accomplished the rapid development of native institutions in their liberated zones, but captured the attention and sympathy of the rest of
the world.

One important characteristic of the liberation movement model
which was adopted by the MFA was its pragmatic nature. The
strength of liberation movements is that they do not operate out of
a preformed political ideology. There are disadvantages in this.
Often a movement not based on ideological consensus fragments after
the immediate victory. A good example of this is the Irish Republican movement, which fragmented so badly after the treaty with Britain in 1922 that civil war ensued. But a movement can still relate to
the needs of its constituency more realistically and personally than
can an ideologically based program.

The direction of the movement was strongly colored by the
leftist idealism of the majority of the participants. Even those who,
like General Spinola, would be placed at the far right of the movement spectrum, saw the necessity--as Spinola said in an interview

in Expresso--for "democratizing, socializing, and setting free."
Spinola went on to describe the movement as he understood it:

> I judge myself sufficiently identified with the
> spirit of the Movement to be able to state that
> there was never the intention of forging a
> political instrument for immediate action, but
> rather of finding a formula that would allow the
> definition of the nation to be made by itself to
> self-determine a constitution to be a signature
> of a free and legitimately formed Sovereign
> state--in sum, a nation built in freedom. [12]

Spinola's position, in the lexicon of European political ideologies,
reflects in general the ideology of the social democrats.

The far left of the political spectrum represented among the
MFA membership was to the left of the Moscow-oriented Portuguese
Communist Party. But it is essential, in understanding the thinking
and planning of the MFA as it developed, to recognize that there
were no ideological debates or examinations of ideological models.
As a liberation movement, it had set itself three goals: elimination
of fascism, decolonization, and maximum self-determination. For
all of these goals they looked for models to Africa.

It would be misleading to suggest that the MFA was or is an
imitation of the African liberation movements. Nor, on the other
hand, was it born in emulation of the Cuban revolution or of the
French Revolution. It would be fair to say that the MFA drew inspiration from all of revolutionary history and thinking, appraised
its own circumstances, and did their planning in the context of the
reality of the Portugal of 1974.

On April 25, 1974, members of the Armed Forces Movement
believed that, within less than a year, they would be out of the business of government and have restored the dignity of the military as
the defenders of the freedom of their citizenry rather than the tools
of a stagnating, imperialist strategy. To this end, they had already
discreetly informed some exiled opposition political leaders, including Dr. Mario Soares and Dr. Alvaro Cunhal, that they would soon
be requested to return home and develop a pluralistic socialistic state.

NOTES

1. Ronald H. Chilcote, Portuguese Africa (Englewood Cliffs,
N.J.: Prentice-Hall, 1967); Amnesty International, 53 Theobald's
Way, Amnesty International Report on Torture (London: Duckworth

Press in association with Amnesty Publications, 1973); interviews conducted with former political prisoners by this author.

2. Morris Janowitz, The Professional Soldier: A Social and Political Portrait (New York: The Free Press Paperback, 1960; London: Macmillan, 1971).

3. Ibid., p. 233.

4. Ibid., p. 235.

5. Chilcote, op. cit.

6. Ministry of Mass Communications, Portugal: Freedom Year One, 1926-1975 (pamphlet) (Lisbon: March 1975).

7. From an interview with an MFA naval officer in December 1974.

8. Maria Velho da Costa, Maria Isabel Barrena, and Maria Theresa Horta, New Portuguese Letters (Lisbon: Estudios Cor, 1973).

9. General Antonio de Spinola, Portugal e o Futuro: Analise da Conjunctura Nacional (Portugal and the Future) (Lisbon: Arcadia, 1974).

10. Expresso, interview, January 4, 1975.

11. Lars Rudebeck, Guinea-Bissau: A Study of Political Mobilization (Uppsala, Sweden: Scandinavian Institute of African Studies, 1974).

12. Expresso, interview, January 4, 1975.

Political leaders in Portugal are fond of describing themselves as a "mixed-blooded people," and refer to their history to explain their nonracist attitudes and policies. Africans, of course, would hotly contest their claim to being nonracist. An examination of the history of Portugal and of Portuguese behavior in Africa makes it apparent that, despite the seeming contradiction, both views are correct.[1]

BACKGROUND

Roderick, the last Visigoth king in what is now Portugal, was defeated in 711 by the Moors. His kingdom collapsed. During the next 300 years, Islam spread over the Iberian peninsula, across the Pyrenees, and throughout the southern shore of the Mediterranean beyond the Caspian Sea. For the next 100 years, from 1055 onward, Portuguese royalty of the houses of Braganza and Burgundy began to reestablish Portugal as a Christian country, finally taking Lisbon in 1147. During another century of warfare against the Moors, the Portuguese dynasty began colonizing the land and establishing law, language, and institutions.

Nor did the Portuguese stop with driving the Moors from Portugal itself. In a series of wars they pursued the Moors to fight and lose at Tangiers. The Portuguese royalty then formed shaky alliances through marriage and common cause with the houses of Castile, Leon, and Aragon. The Portuguese fear that, unchecked, the Spanish influence would extend to conquest and subjugation, proved justified: Spain dominated Portugal for nearly 100 years.

In the thirteenth and fourteenth centuries there were major alliances between Portugal and England. The first of these, a

commercial treaty enacted in 1294, initiated Portuguese naval activity under Genoese and Venetian guidance. In 1386, by the Treaty
of Windsor, England and Portugal became permanently allied, and
King John of Portugal married Philippa, the daughter of England's
John of Gaunt.

In 1433 the Portuguese navy, under King Henry the Navigator,
first rounded Cape Bojador to a long series of explorations along
the coast of Africa. Soon afterward Portuguese became the first
Europeans to import slaves from the west African coast. They began almost inadvertently. Moslems held North Africa, and the
Portuguese wanted not only to secure the products of the Sudan, but
also to gain allies there for an attack on Islam from the flank and
rear. When, in 1441, the two captains of the expedition which
reached Cape Blanc, Tristao and Goncalves, captured 12 Africans
to take back as trophies to Lisbon, Lisbon merchants recognized
the commercial value of the slave trade and for that purpose financed
Portugal's subsequent expeditions.

Before the century ended traders had explored Cape Verde,
sailed south across the equator, were at the mouth of the Congo, and
sailed around the Cape of Good Hope and up the east coast to India.
By 1510, by conquest, threat, and treaty, 2,000 miles of the east
African coast had been brought under Portuguese hegemony. On the
west coast the Portuguese had established forts and trading posts
from Cape Blanc to what is now Angola. By the mid-1500s slave
traffic was so heavy that it is estimated that slaves comprised 10
percent of Lisbon's population.[2]

The exploration and conquest of the New World set up further
demands for the slave and mining wealth of Africa. The Spanish,
who were precluded from the slave trade by a series of papal bulls
and treaties in the latter part of the fifteenth century, were in urgent
need of manpower for their colonies. Since Indians had not proved
satisfactory slaves, they commissioned the Portuguese to provide
them 4,000 African slaves a year. Until the latter part of the six-
teenth century, when other countries entered the market, the Portuguese had a virtual monopoly on the trade. The West African
slave trade spanned a period of 400 years, during which the Portuguese government--through a royal monopoly--profited directly
from the trade on a per unit basis. With the discovery of gold and
diamonds and the growth of sugar industries in Brazil, that country
alone imported 10,000 slaves a year.

In four centuries Portugal shipped an estimated 5 million
slaves to the Western Hemisphere.[3] The Guinea Coast, Angola,
and the adjacent Congo, the most fertile region in Africa, was,
through the Portuguese exploration and exploitation, the ethnic
source of most of today's Afro-Americans. It is both appropriate
and ironic that on the last weekend of July 1974, a ship named after

Henry the Navigator carried back to Portugal the first 1,100 Portuguese colonists leaving the new nation state of Mozambique.

The course of expansion brought the people of Western Europe into contact with peoples of vastly different cultures. Those hostile contacts provided a base for feelings of competitiveness and superiority. In the Iberian peninsula, on lands reconquered from the Moslems, free Christian peasant communities were encouraged by grants of greater land freedoms than existed in the northern lands from whence they came. Side by side with them were Islamic communities subjected to almost slave conditions. This servitude was the model for that later imposed by Spanish and Portuguese conquerors on the Indians of the New World, and was quite in keeping with the conditions of warfare between Christian and Islamic countries during the medieval period. Besides the enslavement of each other by conquest, both groups had already enslaved Africans for domestic labor.

MERCANTILISM AND RACISM

Even while the Portuguese were involved in the exploitation of Africans through the slave trade, mercantilism rather than racism was the motivating influence. Only later, when the Portuguese began to push inland and colonize in Africa, did the basis for racism become evidenced. In order to justify the extension of Portuguese civilization on the African territory, the Portuguese had to perceive their culture superior and themselves as a race capable of bringing order and profit out of the "chaos" and primitiveness of the territory. Racism is a widely used and variously defined term. Dante Puzzo's description is instructive:

> Racism [he says] is a modern conception. Prior
> to the sixteenth century there was nothing in the
> life and thought of the West that can be described
> as racist. To prevent misunderstanding a clear
> distinction must be made between racism and
> ethnocentrism. . . . The moral self sufficiency
> of the nation state proved of salient importance.
> For, in the circumstances engendered by the
> struggle for empire, it gave powerful impetus
> to the natural tendency of nationalism to become
> chauvinism. And chauvinism, perverting to its
> uses the new sciences, could become and where
> conditions were propitious, did become racism.
> The interaction between colonialism and this

nationalism provided the necessary milieu for
the emergence and development of racism. [4]

The object of Portuguese native policy in Africa was to produce assimilated Portuguese out of the African natives. This, not
unlike the earlier objectives of the English in Ireland, is the typical
goal of colonial racism, which denies the legitimacy and integrity of
indigenous cultures and political systems in order to legitimate their
subjugation. [5] William Minter says about this:

> To become an assimilado involved, until shortly
> after the beginning of the war in Angola, a con-
> siderable procedure. An applicant had to prove
> his ability to speak and write correct Portuguese;
> show that he had a certain income, submit a num-
> ber of documents and certificates and finally, pay
> a fee. . . . The Portuguese settler who might be
> illiterate and unable to satisfy the requirements
> himself did not have to worry about such a test:
> he was already a Portuguese citizen. [6]

There is no question that the racialism of Portuguese Africa is
manifested most particularly in the economic sphere, and that despite Caetano's belated attempt to apply the Nazi eugenic thesis in
his warning to his fellow Portuguese in Africa, skin color has not
had a particularly strong social impact on the metropolitan Portuguese in terms of miscegenation, entrance into professions, and
housing. In that sense, there has always been less racist overtone
in Lisbon than in New York, Chicago, or London. In the African
colonies themselves, it has been commonplace for the white Portuguese settler to engage in sexual relations with native African women,
and the children of such matches are brought up in the socioeconomic
class and household of the father regardless of the marital status of
the parents. The Portuguese settler, in fact, takes some pride in
his mistos children. One told me, "I have planted my seed in the
soil of this place and it will grow and continue here long after I myself am gone." [7] If the settler is economically successful, his
mistos children as well as his other children are likely to return to
Portugal itself for their education. If he is less successful, all of
his children will receive their education in the African province. [8]

Marcelo Caetano, Salazar's hand picked successor, was Minister for the African Colonies in 1945. In repeated visits to those
colonies, his speeches reflected a degree of racism comparable with
that of Rhodesian and South African leaders:

> On one point only should we be rigorous with re-
> spect to racial separation: namely, marital or
> casual sexual mixing of blacks and whites, the
> source of serious disturbances in social life, and
> of the serious problem of race mixing. Serious
> I say, if not from the biological point of view, so
> controversial and on which it's not for me to take
> a position, then at least from the sociological
> point of view. [9]

It is apparent that despite the prolonged and continuous struggle for
democracy in metropolitan Portugal itself, despite the Portuguese
tradition of individualism and humanism, despite the mixture of
bloods which characterized the Portuguese people ethnically, it is
the tradition of imperialism, racism, fascism, despoliation, and
corruption which has most often characterized the Portuguese
presence in Africa.

PORTUGUESE DEMOCRACY AND DICTATORSHIP

As members of the Armed Forces Movement are fond of point-
ing out, Portugal and the Portuguese people have a tradition of
freedom and democracy. Even more relevant to their revolution,
they claim, is the tradition of individualism and humanism which is
in contrast to that of their neighbors, the Spaniards. This tradition,
however, has been obscured by 50 years of dictatorship, which make
the April 25, 1974 revolution and its subsequent events so much of a
shock and puzzlement to Western political analysts. Here I want to
outline that lost tradition.

The nineteenth century in Portugal saw a series of attempts to
achieve a constitutional republic. These attempts made the period
from 1820 to 1861 one of ongoing civil strife.

Under King Louis I in the 1860s, the country was ruled in a
pseudo parliamentary system by two political parties, the Conservative and the Liberal, which held office in rotation. In 1881 the
formation of the Republican Party marked the real beginning of a
system of elected representation and party politics. Sporadic revolts, strikes, and conspiracies during the reign of Carlos I led to
his appointment of a prime minister, Joao Franco, who in 1906 oppressed the parliamentary government, gagged the press, and
punished all opposition to his dictatorial regime. On February 1,
1908, the king and the crown prince were assassinated in the streets
of Lisbon, and although the new king put an end to Franco's reign,
he was forced to flee to England when, in October 1910, insurrection
flared up again in Lisbon.

On October 5, 1910, a provisional government proclaimed the Republic of Portugal, which proceeded to a frontal attack on the Catholic Church. Religious orders were expelled, their property was confiscated, and religious teaching in the primary schools was forbidden. In 1911 there were enactments separating church and state, and the constituent assembly adopted a liberal constitution and elected a president, Dr. Manuel de Arriaga. Royalist plots, however, created unrest among the workers, who were disappointed when the revolution failed to bring them relief from long hours and low wages. In January 1912, a serious general strike broke out in Lisbon. The city was put under military rule and thousands of syndicalists were imprisoned. The radical outbreaks continued.

On November 28, 1914, the Portuguese National Assembly voted to join Great Britain and France in war against Germany, but General Pimenta de Castro, representing a pro-German faction in the army, led an insurrection which lasted until May 1915. At that point President Arriaga resigned and Bernardino Machado became president. In 1916 Germany declared war on Portugal after the Portuguese had seized German vessels in port at Lisbon. In 1917, another general sympathetic with the German cause, Sidionio Pais, led an insurrection, deposed the president, and took office himself. One year and ten days later he was assassinated and the democratic regime was reestablished.

In a land which was still 65 percent illiterate, the democratic system could hardly be expected to function smoothly, and throughout the early years of the century the average duration of governments was about four months. Insurrections and coups were as numerous as changes in the cabinets, and the already perilous economic situation went from bad to worse. During the 1920s, unrest provoked a succession of changes, and in 1926 an army movement inspired by Mendes Cabecadas and led by General Gomes da Costa overthrew the democratic regime. Machado (again President) and the cabinet of Antonio Mara da Silva were thrown out, political parties were broken up, and parliament was again dissolved.

In February 1927 insurrection against the military dictatorship broke out in Oporto and Lisbon. The uprising was described as "Communist" but was really inspired by a group of intellectual reformers. It was, in any case, defeated. In 1928, General Antonio Oscar de Fragosa Carmona was elected president. His regime proved little different from its predecessors, except that it was led by the military rather than by civilian politicians. On April 27, a 40-year-old professor of economics, Antonio de Oliveira Salazar became Minister of Finance with extraordinary powers. He solved the financial muddle by economy and strict accountancy, and before long was the dominant figure in Portugal.

The National Union Party was founded in 1930, the only party allowed by the government. On July 5, 1933, Salazar became Premier and virtual dictator. In 1935, a new constitution provided that a president would be elected for a seven-year term, a cabinet would be selected by the president and responsible to him alone, a national assembly would be elected by heads of families possessing a certain degree of education, and there would be a corporate chamber with advisory powers representing occupations.

In January of the following year an insurrection led by the General Confederation of Labor and the Communists was suppressed and the leaders were imprisoned. The first national assembly of the new regime met on January 10, 1935. Salazar, to achieve stability by employing massive systems of repression, remained in office for 40 years. His system was then maintained under the dictatorship of his former associate, Marcelo Caetano.

The 48-year history of the fascist state and the resistance movements which took various actions against it is a picture of an ongoing action and reaction, repression and rebellion, and continual political maneuvering. Viewed in this perspective, the MFA revolution was neither outside the context of Portuguese history, nor an improbability in the context of Portuguese political sophistication. (See Appendix A.)

AFRICA UNDER COLONIALISM

Forced labor was the characteristic system for the exploitation of the African population in Portuguese Africa. It is most specifically this system which exemplifies the economic racism of that society and which became the basis of disaffection through which the liberation movements gained masses of adherents. The Labor Regulation of 1899 put it like this:

> All natives of Portuguese overseas provinces are subject to the moral and legal obligation of attempting to obtain through work the means that they lack to subsist and to better their social conditions. They have full liberty to choose the method of fulfilling this obligation, but if they do not fulfill it, public authority may force a fulfillment. [10]

By making unemployment a crime, the regime was able to legislate forced labor on plantations and industries, thus providing cheap, noncompetitive labor not only in the Portuguese provinces, but also in the mines and plantations of Rhodesia and South Africa.

The export of cheap labor, in fact, was so widespread that an American reporter remarked in 1958, "Something like two-thirds of the mature, able-bodied men of Southern Mozambique are employed in foreign territories."[11]

A final element of the relationship between Portugal and her overseas provinces is the economic sphere. Minter contends that metropolitan Portugal has a consistent trade deficit which is offset primarily by a strong surplus with the overseas provinces. He goes on to say:

> The income created for Portugal by Angola and Mozambique comes mainly from export of primary commodities and African labour; secondarily from their role in transport for South Africa, Rhodesia, Zambia and the Congo. Angola exports coffee, diamonds, iron ore and oil to world markets. Mozambique's most important exports are all agricultural: cashew nuts, sugar, tea, sisal.
>
> Portugal profits not only from the income gained by Angola and Mozambique but also from the pattern of trade established with them.
>
> But these advantages for particular Portuguese interests depend on cooperation with particular interests from other Western countries. The Benguela Railroad and the Angola Diamond Company are under the control of British, South African and Belgian financial interests. . . . In Mozambique, Sona Sugar Estates, the largest producer of sugar in the country, is British owned. . . . Indeed, in Portugal itself there is substantial foreign command of the economy. The largest producer of Wolfram is a former British company, recently acquired by the Angola American Corporation of South Africa. The main producer of tires is controlled by General Tire and Rubber of Ohio. The public transport system of Lisbon is run by a British company; SACOR, which runs the principal petroleum refinery in Portugal, is two thirds controlled by French interests.[12]

Guinea-Bissau

Guinea-Bissau, the first independent nation state born out of the Portuguese African colonies, was also the oldest of the colonies.

It was perhaps the first of the provinces to manifest the cumulative after-effects of the peculiarly Portuguese brand of racism, and its liberation movement was the model for the other liberation movements. The leader of that movement, Partido Africano da Independencia de Guinea e Cabo Verde (PAIGC), was Amilcar Cabral, who showed a precise understanding of the economic issues involved in liberation:

> If we wish to place the fact of imperialism within
> the general trajectory of the evolution of the
> transcendental factor which has changed the face
> of the world, namely, capital and the process of
> its accumulation, we can say that imperialism is
> piracy transplanted from the seas to the dry land,
> piracy reorganized, consolidated and adapted to
> the aim of exploiting the natural and human re-
> sources of our people.[13]

PAIGC was first organized in Bissau in 1956 with its principal support among urban workers. Leadership came from a group of assimilados who formed a larger percentage of the population here than in the other two colonies. Organization of the workers resulted in several strikes, the bloodiest of which was a dock strike that took place in August 1959 and paralyzed the port of Bissau. It was broken with extreme brutality by the Portuguese military, and although no casualty figures were ever released, Cabral estimated them to be very high.

Cabral was born in Bafata, Cape Verde Islands, of mixed African and Portuguese ancestry. Educated as an agronomist in Lisbon and later employed as a census officer for the Portuguese colonial government, he organized PAIGC and dedicated himself to guerrilla warfare.

Cabral's anticapitalist convictions did not reflect an uncritical adaptation of Marxist theory and strategy. He recognized its shortcomings when applied to the nature of peasant society in Guinea. In a way which was to become characteristic of the other Portuguese African liberation movements and of the MFA itself, Cabral understood that "the people are not fighting for ideas. They are fighting for material benefits, to live better in peace, to see their lives go forward."[14]

Among the 36,000 troops required to maintain control of the one-third of Guinea-Bissau not under PAIGC control by 1970 were many future leaders of the MFA. It was in Guinea that General Spinola, who became the first president of the provisional government, obtained his major experience in governing a colony during its liberation struggle. Out of his experiences in that colony, he wrote the book that went farther than any other publication had gone before criticizing Portuguese colonial policy and the conditions of the armed forces. It was through his experience in Guinea, also, that Spinola was to develop his political thesis for the evolution of the colonies into a kind of partnership status with Portugal. Other MFA leaders, while posted in Guinea, did academic studies of the movement and had interactions with PAIGC leaders--either while the latter were imprisoned or in the process of negotiations.[15] The effectiveness of Cabral's instruction, then, extended far beyond his African constituency, and well into the forces of oppression originally marshaled to subdue them.

Cabral was in close touch with the leaders of Movimento Popular de Liberacao de Angola (MPLA) and Frente de Liberacao de Moçambique (FRELIMO Mozambique). In addition, in 1961 he had played an important part in the development of Organizacaos Nacionalistas das Colonias Portugueses (CONCP), which coordinated the nationalist movements. PAIGC was organized so effectively that, even after the arrest of its leaders in Bissau commencing on March 13, 1962, the network of organization continued to extend throughout the country.

PAIGC had the constant support of Conakry, which borders Guinea on one side, and limited support from Senegal, bordering on the other side. In 1973 systematic guerrilla warfare began in the north, where dense forests and numerous waterways made guerrilla action feasible. By 1965 half of Guinea was under PAIGC control, and local institutions for food production, education, health services, and trade had been established by the organization. By 1970 PAIGC claimed control of three-fifths of Guinea, although aerial bombardment and counterattack by Portuguese military was frequent. Exports of rice and palm oil helped pay for the import of necessary trade goods, and by 1970, 20,000 students were enrolled in the schools. Like the other African colonies, Guinea under PAIGC had a voice and impact in the Organization of African Unity, relations with its neighboring African states, and contacts for weapons and training in North Africa and Eastern Europe.[16]

Between April and July of 1972, elections had been held in the liberated area of mainland Guinea. With the minimum voting age at 15, 600,000 eligible voters were registered. They elected regional councils which then selected a third of their number to sit with members nominated by PAIGC in the National Council. Cabral set the date for announcement of independence of mainland Guinea for early 1973. There was an opposition party as well as local opposition groups.

Mozambique

The first Mozambiquan nationalist movements had been organized among the exiles who were exported as workers to surrounding countries.

Frente de Liberacao de Mozambique (FRELIMO) formed as a
coalition of Unido Nacional Democratica de Mozambique (UDENAMO),
organized in Rhodesia in 1960; Mozambique African National Union
(MANU), formed in East Africa along the models of the Tanganyikan
and Kenyan parties, TANU and KANU; and Unito Africana de Mozambique Independente (UNAMI), organized in Malawi. When Tan-
ganyika became independent in 1961, all three parties set up headquarters in Dar es Salaam. The three movements merged in 1962,
met in a congress and worked out a program of action, political organization, training, and mobilization of world opinion.

FRELIMO objectives were to form an independent government
representing the majority of the population, which was African and
colored.

The first group of 250 guerrilla fighters was trained in Al-
geria. FRELIMO began education programs among the refugees in
Tanzania and sent large numbers of scholarship students abroad.
Its first action was on September 24, 1964, with attacks in four
provinces. FRELIMO forces remained in two of those provinces
fighting and living in the jungle. Soon they began training inside
Mozambique itself, and by 1967 FRELIMO had approximately 8,000
troops armed and active. Minter says:

> From 1967-70 FRELIMO forces in Cabo Delgado
> and Niassa provinces moved to larger scale at-
> tacks on Portuguese posts and air bases. Mueda,
> the site of the massacre years before and now one
> of Portugal's major airbases in the area, was hit
> several times. . . . Heavier weapons and pre-
> experienced fighters as well as control of base
> areas inside Mozambique, made possible such in-
> tensification of the combat.
>
>   In the liberated areas production of food crops
> increased, while the forced cultivation of cotton
> was abandoned. People marvelled at having
> enough to eat. Some cash crops such as cashew
> nuts and peanuts were cultivated, and traded by
> FRELIMO across the border for farm tools,
> cloth and other necessities. FRELIMO nurses
> and medical aides set up a system of first aid
> posts and clinics; primary schools were set up

> inside Mozambique and in the refugee camps.
> Administrative structures for the liberated areas
> were established for the Portuguese to play on
> latent tension between northerners and southern-
> ers and the contradiction between those who
> understood the necessity of a protracted war of
> liberation and those who expected an immediate
> victory. In March, 1968, a new front was opened
> up in Tete province, adjacent to Zambia, a front
> of crucial strategic importance. In July, 1968,
> the second party congress, held inside Mozam-
> bique . . . solidified the direction and unity of
> the movement. [17]

FRELIMO, along with MPLA and PAIGC, drew support from
a variety of organizations and states. In 1970, at an international
conference in Rome, they received support from the Vatican.
The various Black African countries surrounding the Portuguese
colonies (Congo, Tanzania, Zaire, Zambia) and the Zimbabwe
movement in Rhodesia (ZANU) participated and supported the movement by raising issues in the international arena. U.S. groups as
diverse as the Black Panthers and the Congressional Black Caucus
took favorable positions and offered one or another kind of support.

In addition, the massacre of whole villages and the tortures
and penalties imposed on the native population generated support
from sources which normally take a dim view of leftist revolutionary
movements, among them various Roman Catholic and Protestant
missionaries, many of whom were expelled from Mozambique for
their outspokenness in denouncing atrocities committed by government troops against the native population:

> The missionaries also had severe criticism to
> make as regards the compromise policies of
> the Mozambican hierarchy: "The Church in
> Mozambique renounces its prophetic mission,
> since it fails to proclaim openly that the people
> in that country is fully entitled to its own iden-
> tity. It also fails to proclaim basic human
> rights and permits missionaries to be bound
> by laws agreed upon by the Holy See and the
> Lisbon government, according to which their
> activities must correspond with the African
> country's complete nationalization (the policy
> of 'Portugalization'). Nor does the Church
> speak out against the socioeconomic system

in effect in Mozambique, nor against the stealing
of land from the Africans, the huge landed estates
and the privileges. Nor does it denounce violence
and war, thus submitting to the view of the Portuguese (government) instead of acting as a middle
man between the two parties, as it ought to do."
Other expelled missionaries spoke on Italian
radio. They told of villages that had been "wiped
out" by acts of war and reprisal: "Viriano,
Juvano, Viola and Chilimani are now nothing but
names that recall huts consumed by flames,
children burned alive, girls raped, men pitilessly
murdered, women disembowelled." They described the means employed in perpetrating these
atrocities: airplanes, helicopters, chemicals
that destroy harvests, flamethrowers to burn the
forests--in order to drive out the guerrillas.

In addition there are the tortures perpetrated
in the prisons, called "places of political regen-
eration," where all those who express disagreement with the government are locked up. At
Macailba, for instance, 35 Protestant pastors
were imprisoned; two of them died from the
tortures they had to endure.

"The more sensitive, more educated and
more politically aware sector of the population
hasjustly rebelled," the missionaries stated.
"And so was formed the Front for the Liberation
of Mozambique."[18]

The fact that diverse tribes and adverse terrain were united
under a democratic leadership first into a nonstate nation and then
into a nation state, suggests great efficiency. The matter was accomplished, moreover, within 13 years of the commencement of
organization. Furthermore, the organization developed institutions
and structure and is not a novice to government as it commences its
nationhood.

We Stay! (FICO), a right-wing political party, emerged in
Mozambique after 1974; a white Portuguese newspaper owner and
millionaire businessman of Beira, Mozambique, Engineer Jorge
Jardin, is the organizer. Born in 1918, he qualified as an agronomist at Lisbon University. Beginning in 1946, he served in a number of increasingly important posts under the Salazar regime. After
quarreling with Salazar, he moved to Beira 22 years ago and built
up newspapers and a model farming estate. Since then he has acted

as a go-between with Dr. Banda of Malawi, President Kaunda of
Zambia, and the Swaziland government. He was also involved in a
plot to overthrow President Nyerere of Tanzania.

Jardin states his goals as the defeat of FRELIMO and the creation of a conservative, capitalist, multiracial society in Mozambique,
or an Independent Dominion (UDI) for the whites in Mozambique. He
is trying to mobilize the flechas (arrows), the black soldiers recruited to fight FRELIMO. He estimates there are between 30,000
and 50,000 of them, some of whom are deserters from FRELIMO,
others of whom participated in the massacres at Wirriyamu. In
addition, he is recruiting mercenary officers of the Fifth Commando
Unit who had experience in the Congo against Lumumba and a group
called the Dragons of Death composed of former paratroopers and
commandos. Prospects are good for support and even direct aid
from the governments of Rhodesia and South Africa, both of which
have expressed wariness about new nations on their doorsteps.

With such a powerful reactionary figure at work, FRELIMO
may not yet have fought its last battle.

Angola

The war for liberation came to the attention of the world
through events in Angola in 1961. The struggle here is also the last
to be resolved. For one thing, there are more Portuguese settlers
involved in Angola, greater economic stakes, and three different
competing and often conflicting liberation groups.

The Movimento Popular de Liberacao de Angola (MPLA) was
the largest of the three Angolan liberation movements, and the
oldest. Dr. Agostinho Neto, an intellectual, led the movement for
a decade. Daniel Chipenda, former professional soccer player in
Portugal who has the friendship of heads of state in Zambia, Zaire,
Tanzania, and Congo, contested Neto's leadership in 1974 and in 1975
organized his own splinter group which then joined with Uniao por
Total Independencia o Angola (UNITA). The other group, Frente
Nacional Liberacao Angola (FNLA), formed and headquartered in
Zaire, is led by Holden Roberto.

It would be comforting to think that the knottiest colonial question of all, Angola, had been resolved by the January 15, 1975 Independence Agreement worked out between the president and prime
minister of the provisional government (both MFA leaders) and the
leaders of the three Angolan liberation movements. (See Appendix
B.) It climaxed eight months of intensive fighting among these liberation groups, which had intensified even after Admiral Rosa
Coutinho, the MFA leader, had taken the place of the former
Salazarist administrator, Marques.

The racial connotations of the Angolan struggle are the product of the past 20 years. They are typified by the division of Luanda, the capital city, which is divided into two sections, the "Asphalt" (white) and the "Red Clay" (black) sections. In the last 20 years, the black unskilled population of Luanda has gradually moved to the outskirts of the city--70 percent of the inhabitants of Luanda live in musseques (suburban ghetto shantytowns). The whites who had lived in these musseques were merchants, they were expelled and their shops robbed and burned.

Many of the Angolans now leading the liberation movements were among the young intellectuals of the late 1950s who expressed their patriotism and leftist idealism in literature. They founded the magazine Mensagem, which was subsequently suppressed by the authorities. Then, when the Sociedade Cultural of Angola welcomed the membership of this element, it too was suppressed. Between 1959 and 1964, PIDE stepped up its activities and any legal expression of dissent became impossible, and in 1964, the governor closed the cultural society, the Association of Natives of Angola, and the Portuguese Society of Writers.

In 1956 the MPLA was founded clandestinely with the support of whites and blacks, some connected with the Communist party and some with the progressive Portuguese movements. In 1961 Galvao hijacked the Santa Maria and announced that he would head for Angola, there to prepare the liberation of Portugal. On February 4, a group of 20 Angolans assaulted the prison of Sao Paulo de Luanda to set free the prisoners that were scheduled to be sent to the concentration camp of Terrafal. Many were killed and a wave of repression followed.

The year 1961 really marks the beginning of the armed struggle in Angola. The MPLA opened its first political military region in the north and Holden Roberto, heading the Unitae dos Povos de Angola (UPA), began a wave of terrorism in the region of the coffee plantations and extended it to the zone of the cotton plantations. The MPLA had had support and freedom of movement in neighboring Congo. However, in 1963 they were expelled from the Congo and began operating from Zaire with increasing success. They were particularly effective in Luanda.

From its initiation, MPLA attempted to bring the conditions of Angolan exploitation and the contradictions enacted by the colonial authorities to the attention and action of the international arena. For this reason, operations have been aimed at maximal publicity and issues of international law.[19] For instance, in February 1961 their raid on the central prison in Luanda coincided with the presence of large numbers of foreign journalists gathered to report on Galvao's seizure of the Santa Maria. The combined incidents raised interna-

tional legal issues and finally caused the United Nations Security
Council, at the request of Liberia, to place Angola on its agenda.
In the meeting of March 15, 1961, a draft resolution was introduced
calling on Portugal to introduce reforms in conformity with the previous year's resolution on the granting of independence to colonial
countries and peoples. The Security Council resolution also man-
dated a subcommittee to study the situation. The resolution failed
with six abstentions from Latin American and European countries
against five positive votes, including that of the United States.

The same day that the Security Council voted, Holden Roberto
(FNLA) and his group attacked the Portuguese in northern Angola.
Fighting continued with savage reprisals. On April 20 the General
Assembly passed Resolution 1603 (XV) by a vote of 73 to 2, with 9
abstentions, reaffirming the Security Council resolution of the previous month. In June the Security Council voted again and adopted
the resolution by a vote of 9 to 2 with 2 abstentions.

> The Special Committee on Territories under
> Portuguese Administration completed its re-
> port in August 1962. It declared "that the
> danger lies, on the one hand, in Portugal's
> insistence there can be no change in its rela-
> tionship with the Territories which it consid-
> ers are integral parts of its national territory,
> and, on the other, in the complete disregard
> for the legitimate aspirations of its indigenous
> populations." As representatives of the Afri-
> can nationalist movements had expressed
> willingness to negotiate with Portugal over the
> terms and timing of independence, the Commit-
> tee concluded that the onus for lack of any peace-
> ful solution fell on Portugal. . . . The Com-
> mittee also concluded that the arms furnished
> to Portugal by her allies were of aid to her in
> suppressing the people of Angola. It, there-
> fore, recommended that the General Assembly
> "should consider and adopt measures aimed at
> immediate discontinuance of such assistance
> and a complete embargo on further sales and
> supplies of such weapons."20

MPLA had made an effective impact in the international arena
through relationships formed with the governments of surrounding
nations and through advocates in the United Nations. Their battle
for independence did not consist of terror tactics in Lisbon, and it

had involved only one incident, in the early part of the campaign, of
international skyjacking.   It did involve maintaining coordination
with underground political dissidents in Portugal and abroad and developing institutions to nationalize and educate the native population
to join the struggle in the territory itself.   Perhaps the single major
impediment to success was the split between MPLA and the other
Angolan movements, which delayed recognition by the Portuguese
Provisional Government until the end of January 1975.

Holden Roberto, who organized UPA in 1961, went on to form
the Angolan Government in Exile (GRAE), a government-in-exile recognized in 1963 by the Organization of African Unity.   American and
other supplies were funneled through the armies of Morocco, Tunisia, and Congo to FNLA, his guerrilla movement.   In 1968 the
Military Commission of the Organization of African Unity withdrew
recognition of GRAE's status as a government in exile and Jonas
Savimbi broke away and formed UNITA.   Initially, GRAE's great
impact was not only on other African states, but also on America
and North African Arab countries.   It was dissolved after the formation of UNITA and had no official part in the new provisional government.

Jonas Savimbi (former Minister for Foreign Affairs of Holden
Roberto's GRAE, from whom he says he separated because of lack
of accomplishment of democratic objectives),[21] organized UNITA.
Savimbi, son of a Protestant pastor, received a degree in political
science in Lausanne, but chose to live near his people and to fight
by their side in the Liso region.   His prestige and popularity are
vast.   He established himself there ten years ago and only left in
October 1974, in order to visit some African capitals for conferences with the leaders of the other liberation movements, Agostinho
Neto and Holden Roberto.

Savimbi was accused by the magazine Afrique Asie of treason,
of attachment to and complicity with the Portuguese colonial armed
forces in their combat against the MPLA.   UNITA called the charge
a maneuver of its enemies, including the MPLA and "its Soviet
friends."

UNITA, which arose as a movement open to all Africans, developed primarily in Luso and Silva Porto, counted also on the support of certain tribes from southern Angola.   It proposed the organization of a government of African majority, the purposes of which would
be to organize general elections in the spirit of the Universal Declaration of the Rights of Man for a national constitutional assembly
elected through direct and secret vote of all citizens older than 18;
to promote an authentically African and Angolan culture and to fight
"against obscurantism"; to energetically combat tribalism as a latent
enemy of national unity; to guarantee the emancipation of Angolan

women; and to guarantee the equality of all Angolans before the law
without any discrimination."22 Its basic thrust was for national independence without dependence on external aid. As a result Savimbi
refused foreign aid for fear of outside control--which, UNITA
claims, happened with the FNLA aid, and in certain circumstances,
with the MPLA.

UNITA is essentially a movement of farmers and country people who are more concerned with pragmatics and reality than with
revolutionary theory. Today it includes many white elements from
among the small and medium bourgeoisie: merchants principally,
for whom UNITA stands as a guarantee of peace and security. As
time passes, UNITA proposes to defend the interests of the less
protected classes, and it has with time moderated its attitude toward
capitalism. On the other hand, UNITA attacked the provisional government for proposing its own participation in security and policing,
stating that security is a job of the liberation movements themselves.

Holden Roberto organized the FNLA after the dissolution of his
Uninao de Africa Portuguese (UPA) organization. Many whites chose
at the last minute to be part of this movement to guarantee their interests as a privileged class. FNLA resulted from a division of
the former UPA over issues of foreign involvements. It has always
defined itself as an African and rightist movement, and is supported
indirectly by the United States, via Mobutu in Zaire.[23]

Holden Roberto denounced (in the magazine Noticia) "tenden-
tiously Soviet maneuvers in the interior of Angola" and stated that
the "FNLA already has at this moment forces of combat and sufficient means to provoke a military defeat to the demoralized Portuguese Army, but we have agreements of peace which we will respect
as long as the Portuguese government respects them too."[24] Force
of arms is the great argument of the FNLA. Its representative in
Luanda, Val Neto, claims they have 20,000 well-armed, well-
trained, disciplined men ready to fight.

FNLA reputedly receives help from China, Romania, and
Zaire,[25] and it avoids references to aid from the United States. Of
all delegations that were opened in Luanda, the FNLA office seems
to be the most militarily defended. Yet FNLA claims that it
brought to Luanda only the necessary number of soldiers for the
protection of its headquarters. Moreover, because most FNLA
soldiers speak French, suspicions have been raised that the group
employs foreign mercenaries. According to some observers, the
FNLA was the initiator of many disturbances which occurred in
Luanda since April 25, 1974. The FNLA communicated from
Kinshasa through the radio program "Vez de Angola Livre," and
announced in Luanda: "The junta has before it three alternatives:
either punish the extremists, assuming their responsibilities; accept

our petition of formation of brigades in order to restore peace, security and order, or declare itself incapable and resign."

RACE AND NATIONALISM

Racial policy and nationalization of resources are two of the major problems facing Angola. The population is believed to include 350,000 to 450,000 white Portuguese settlers of whom over 200,000 are leaving. About 25 percent of them were born in Angola and the others are long-time residents. It is the second largest European population (next to South Africa's) on the continent. As of spring 1975, no more than 20,000 Angolans had left; many of them, after a brief time in Lisbon or Brazil, returned to Angola. The Europeans, consistent with colonial policy, have been the technicians, managers, or financiers who have made the sophisticated capitalist economy operative.* How will the new government deal with this population?

None of the leaders of the three movements have been calling for radical economic reforms. They see progress in agriculture as being best promoted by cooperatives rather than collectivization. But it is expected that Dr. Augustinho Neto will be in favor of nationalizing the rich oil fields of Cabinda, the diamond mines, and the coffee plantations.

Because of the nature of the war in Angola, the extensive involvement of foreign capital (to be discussed further in Chapter 3), and the involvement of foreign military support, the prospects for developing a workable coalition government--even in accordance with the January 1975 agreements--seem gloomy.

Perhaps the vital symbiotic relationship between the struggles of the liberation movements in Guinea-Bissau, Mozambique, and Angola with the development of a viable liberation movement in metropolitan Portugal had gone unnoticed because scholars and journalists tended to study and/or report either one or the other end of the related entities. There is a tendency to view the link between a European Center power and its colonial periphery as a unilateral

---

*The estimates on emigration of whites from the former colonies vary considerably. There is no doubt that the pace of emigration out of Angola quickened in April 1975 and by mid-June estimates ran to 80,000 emigrants from Angola alone. By the end of August, over 100,000 emigrants were already taxing the limited resources of the Provisional Government in Lisbon. Another 200,000 white Angolans are estimated to be seeking transportation back to Portugal or to Brazil.

direction line, rather than the umbilical cord-like connection which transmits change in two directions simultaneously.[26]

NOTES

1. Cf., D. M. Abshire and M. A. Samuels, eds., Portu-guese Africa: A Handbook (New York: Praeger, 1969); deOliveira Marques, History of Portugal, vol. 1 (New York and London: Columbia University Press, 1972); James Duffy, Portugal in Africa (Baltimore, Md.: Penguin African Library, 1963).

2. de Oliveira Marques, op. cit., says: "In truth there is no reliable source for evaluating the impact of slaves on the growth of population (in Lisbon), yet it seems improbable that slaves ever exceeded one-tenth of the total population. . . ." (p. 167).

3. H. V. Livermore, A New History of Portugal (London: Cambridge at the University Press, 1967).

4. Dante A. Puzzo, "Racism and the Western Tradition, " Journal of The History of Ideas (1964): 579-86.

5. Leonar B. Liggio, "English Origins of American Racism" (Paper presented at the Columbia University Symposium on Irish Studies, February 1974).

6. William Minter, Portuguese Africa and the West (London: Penguin African Library, Penguin Ltd., 1972), p. 20.

7. Communication from confidential interview with an An-golan colonist returned to Portugal in 1974. Similar statements were made by returned Mozambiquan colonists in interviews by the author in Lisbon in 1974 and 1975. At an early time, miscegenation had been official policy in the colonies.

8. Communication from returned colonists substantiated by David Abshire, op. cit., pp. 101-103.

9. Marcelo Caetano, Alguns Discorsos e Relatorios: Viegen Ministerial a Africaem 1945 (Lisbon: Agencia Geral das Colonias, 1946).

10. African Labor Regulation issued in 1899. This decree and its aftermath are discussed at length by Henry W. Nevison, A Modern Slavery (London and New York: Harper & Brothers, 1906). The decree was countermanded in 1960, but the latter was never enforced. Cf. Minter, op. cit.

11. Marvin Harris, Portugal's African Wards (New York: American Committee on Africa, 1958), p. 29.

12. Minter, op. cit., pp. 32-33.

13. Quoted by Basil Davidson, The Liberation of Guinea: Aspects of an African Revolution (Baltimore, Md.: Penguin, 1969), p. 83.

14. Ibid., p. 83.

15. Communication through interviews with MFA officers by author in 1974 and 1975. These officers had been stationed in Guinea and Mozambique prior to the April 25, 1974 revolution. My impression is that this circumstance was more characteristic of the interaction and effect of Cabral's PAIGC and Mondlane's FRELIMO than it was related to the Angolan groups. In fact, MFA officers tended often to quote from the writings of these two leaders.

16. Lars Rudebeck, Guinea-Bissau: A Study of Political Mobilization (Uppsala: Scandinavian Institute of African Studies, 1974).

17. Minter, op. cit., pp. 68-69.

18. IDOC/IPS International news service, published out of New York, with offices in Buenos Aires, Rome, and New York. May 1974 issue. These statements were made during the period just prior to the revolution in Portugal, when considerable world opinion had been focused on the debate about whether an entire Mozambiquan village had been destroyed, or, as the Caetano government claimed, such a village had never existed in the first place. The missionaries in this account had been imprisoned and subsequently expelled for having made public statements about the atrocities they had witnessed in that and other similar episodes.

19. "Angola on the Eve of Independence," Vida Mundial, December 26, 1974.

20. Minter, op. cit., pp. 79-80.

21. Vida Mundial, op. cit.

22. Ibid.

23. Ibid.

24. Noticias (Lisbon), December 1974.

25. Vida Mundial, op. cit.

26. Phillippe Schmitter, writing on the April 25, 1974 revolution in Portugal, said, for instance:

> To my knowledge no scholarly or journalistic
> observer of Portugal foresaw the overthrow of
> Marcelo Caetano, least of all the rapid and com-
> plete collapse of authoritarian rule in Portugal.
> Quite the contrary, the mini-boom in Portuguese
> studies of 1972-73 produced several supposedly
> objective and documented essays by North Amer-
> ican social scientists which emphasized the dy-
> namic, reformist and presumably viable qualities
> of the Caetano regime. Marxist and/or radical
> scholars despite their more critical scrutiny of
> the data and their more or less perennial wishful
> thinking about the imminent maturation of contra-

dictions also failed to predict the overthrow of
Caetano, much less the extent and profundity
of political change which has so far accompanied
it. . . .

"Retrospective and Prospective Thoughts About the Liberation of
Portugal," paper prepared for the Mini-Conference on Contemporary
Portugal, Yale University, March 28-29, 1975.

Whether calculated in terms of housing, emigration, commerce, health, agricultural production, or inflation, conditions in Portugal as of April 25, 1974 were the worst in Europe. Despite a steady growth in gold reserves and foreign investment capital, which some scholars used as indicators of the success of Caetano's "Social State" program, the conditions of daily life for 8 million Portuguese people were terrible.

Table 3.1, an Organization for Economic Cooperation and Development (OECD) survey, indicates the seriousness of Portugal's economic problems. Private consumption per capita, for example, was lower only in Turkey and Yugoslavia, and Portugal trailed every European country. These economic conditions did not occur by chance. Their presence was due to structural distortions which were exacerbated by short-run economic pressures from outside Portugal.

STRUCTURAL DISTORTIONS

Many authorities point to the economic and financial drain of the prolonged African wars as the main cause of the economic decline of Portugal.[1] However, taken in the longer range perspective, other factors have been more important contributors to these debilitating conditions.

While the entire economic and social system had been designed with the sole purpose of sustaining the Salazarist regime, it actually contained the seeds of disaster in its workings. Harry Makler describes the foundations of Salazar's system of gremio, the state-controlled guild system, and its relative political efficacy in an excellent study of that "corporatist" system:

> Salazar introduced corporatism in 1933 as part
> of his Estado Novo . . . a state organized and
> regulated system of interest representation in
> which various constituencies . . . grouped on
> the basis of their occupations or vocations are
> organized into a limited number of singular,
> compulsory, noncompetitive, hierarchically
> ordered and functionally differentiated cate-
> gories . . . granted a representational monop-
> oly and autonomy in exchange for observing
> certain controls on their selection of and
> articulation of leaders and on their intercor-
> porate relations. . . . [2]

Makler goes on to define the corporate state as:

> State corporatism is . . . the antiliberal, de-
> layed capitalist, authoritarian, neo-mercantilist
> state in which territorial subunits are tightly
> subordinated to central bureaucratic power;
> . . . party systems are dominated or monopolized
> by a weak single party; executive authorities are
> ideologically exclusive and more narrowly re-
> cruited . . . the regime reserved the right to in-
> tervene . . . as the arbitrator and regulator of
> production, wages, and labor relations . . .
> created patronal guilds (gremios) in each indus-
> trial, agricultural and commercial sector to
> join, contribute and abide by the decisions of
> the gremio. [3]

Through this system, the price of goods produced in Portugal
could be controlled to maintain export sales and corporate profits.
The basic cost of production was kept low by the gremio system,
which controlled wages, strikes, and jobs. At the same time, the
power to make decisions in self-interest were vitiated by the regime's
system which provided the sociopolitical controls. Makler cites how
the regulations embodied in Decreto-lei No. 23049, Artigos 1-3, and
Decreto-lei No. 24715, Artigo 13, accomplished this purpose:

> The regime secured the power of these corporate
> organizations by (a) officially recognizing them
> as the legal representatives of their respective
> sectors and as having a monopoly and formal ac-
> cess to various government councils, (b) stipulating

TABLE 3.1

Basic Statistics: International Comparisons

				Australia	Austria
Population		Mid-1972	Thousands	12959	7487
	Net average annual increase	1962-72	%	1.93	0.49
Employment	Total civilian	1971	Thousands	5425	3176
	Agriculture		(	8.00	17.30
	Industry[7]		(% of total	38.80	41.90
	Other		(	53.20	40.80
Production	GDP[4] per head	1971	$[8]	3170	2210
GDP by sector:	Agriculture	1971	(	7.20[2,15]	6.00[11]
	Industry		(% of total	38.10[2,15]	49.00[11]
	Other		(	54.70[2,15]	45.00[11]
GDP[4,23] annual volume growth		1971	(%	3.00[15]	5.60
		1966-71	(	5.00[15]	5.20
Indicators of living standards					
	Private consumption per head	1971	$	1880	1230
	Public expenditure on education	1970	% of GNP	4.00[9]	4.60[2]
	Dwellings completed, per 1000 inhabitants	1971	(	11.00	6.00
	Passenger cars, per 1000 inhabitants	1970	(	306	162
	Television sets, per 1000 inhabitants	1971	(Number	227[13]	213
	Telephones, per 1000 inhabitants	1971	(	324	207
	Doctors, per 1000 inhabitants	1970	(	1.18[19]	1.85
Gross fixed investment[23]	Total	1967-71 average		26.50[15]	28.00
	Machinery and equipment		(	11.70	12.10
	Residential construction		(% of GDP[4]	5.10	15.8[28]
	Other construction		(	9.70	-- [28]
Gross saving		1967-71 average	% of GDP[4]	25.70	28.50
Public sector[30]	Total current revenue	1971	% of GDP[4]	29.50	37.00
Wages/Prices	Hourly earnings[32]	Annual increase 1966-71	(	6.90[34]	8.50[16]
	Consumer prices		(%	3.70	3.80
	GDP[4] deflator		(	4.60	3.80
Foreign trade	Imports[46]	1971	($ million[8]	5870[15]	5060
			(% of GDP[4]	14.50	30.70
	Exports[46]		($ million[8]	6310[15]	5030
			(% of GDP[4]	15.70	30.50
Balance of payments	Current balance	1967-71 average	% of GNP	-3.20[15]	-0.30
Official reserves[47], end-1972: % of imports					
of goods in 1972			%	129.90	52.60
Change		May 1973-May 1974	Mill. SDRs	-365	-204
Net flow of resources to developing countries[50]		1972	% of GNP	0.96	0.54
Export performance[53]	Growth of markets[54]	1971-72	(%	16.70	17.90
		1960-61 to 1970-71 (average)	(	--	11.50
	Gains or losses	1971-72	(%	10.90	4.80
	of market shares[55]	1960-61 to 1970-71 (average)	(	--	-1.50

Belgium	Canada	Denmark	Finland	France	Germany	Greece	Iceland	Ireland	Italy
9711	21848	4992	4624[1]	51700	61669	8866	209	3014	54344[3]
0.52	1.61	0.72	0.29	0.96	0.82	0.48	1.39	0.63	0.67
3788	8079	2338	2139	20518	26673	3275	79[13]	1063	18700
4.40	7.50	10.90	21.20	13.40	8.40	37.30	18.80[13]	26.50	19.50
44.20	31.00	37.20	35.20	38.60	50.10	24.60	36.80[13]	30.90	44.10
51.40	61.50	51.90	43.60	48.00	41.50	38.10	44.40[13]	42.60	36.40
2980	4340	3510	2450	3180	3550	1190	2920	1530	1880
3.90	4.40	7.50	13.70	6.00[11,13]	2.80[11]	19.50	--	16.40	11.50
43.80	37.00	38.70	42.30	48.40[11,13]	53.50[11]	30.50	--	35.60	40.50
52.30	58.60	53.80	44.00	45.60[11,13]	43.70[11]	50.00	--	48.00	48.00
3.70	5.50	4.00	2.30	5.10	2.70	7.60	9.90	3.80	1.50
5.00	4.40	4.90	5.20	5.70	4.70	7.50	1.90	5.10	5.00
1810	2480	2080	1280	1870	1910	810	1860	1040	1210
5.40[2]	9.10[2]	7.00	6.30	4.70	3.50	2.00[2]	4.30	4.90[2]	4.20[2]
4.40[22]	8.90[22]	10.10	10.80	9.30	9.00	14.00	6.60	5.10	6.30
211	312	219	137	245	237	22	200	122	187
216[13]	349	277	230	227	299	10[2]	196	164	191
224	468	356	270	185	249	137	360	109	188
1.55[2]	1.41[2]	1.45[18]	1.02	1.33	1.69[2]	1.55[2]	1.41	1.09[2]	1.80
20.80	21.70[24]	23.30	24.10	26.10	25.40	27.20[25]	29.20	23.40	19.90
9.00	8.00	11.90	8.80	11.70	11.80	10.50	8.60	11.60	8.20
4.80	4.20	11.40[28]	5.60	6.50	5.30	7.40	5.50	4.20	6.10
7.00	9.50	--	9.70	7.80	8.30[29]	9.40	15.10	7.70	5.60
24.60	22.50	18.50	29.10	27.30	27.20	22.00[25]	--	20.40	23.30
35.50	35.70	44.60	37.60	37.70	38.40	27.40[13]	33.30[18]	34.20	33.70
8.70	7.90[34]	11.70[35]	10.70	10.20[36]	8.30[34]	8.80[34]	12.90[37]	12.10[34]	10.10[38]
3.50	3.70	6.30	5.30	4.90	3.00	2.10	12.00	6.50	3.40
4.00	3.80	5.70	5.90	5.20	4.20	2.50	13.40	7.10	4.40
12020	19550	5350	3190	26180	43900	2090[13]	290	1960	18670
41.60	21.10	30.70	28.10	16.10	20.20	22.30	48.00	43.30	18.50
12670	21020	5080	2970	27390	47010	1000[13]	250	1640	19770
43.90	22.70	29.10	26.10	16.80	21.60	10.70	41.40	36.30	19.60
1.90[21]	0.00	-2.60	-1.30	-0.30	0.90	-3.70	-5.50	-3.30	2.20
25.00[21]	32.00	17.00	23.70	37.70	59.80	44.10	36.70	53.60	31.50
-407[21]	79	-257	21	-2872	2533	-124	-17	-35	-573
1.12	0.95	0.57	--[51]	1.06	0.67	--[52]	--[51]	--[51]	0.46
19.80	18.30	19.70	21.10	18.80	18.60	14.70	--	22.40	19.50
11.50	13.50	10.30	10.60	9.60	10.80	11.50	--	8.50	10.90
10.20[21]	-4.10	-0.30	3.90	6.60	-0.20	16.80	--	0.50	3.10
0.50[21]	-2.00	-1.60	-2.00	1.00	1.00	0.30	--	1.20	2.80

(continued)

TABLE 3.1 (continued)

			Japan	Luxem-bourg
Population		Mid-1972	Thousands	106960[6]	347
Net average annual increase		1962-72	%	1.19	0.78
Employment Total civilian		1971	Thousands	51140	148
Agriculture			(	15.90	10.20
Industry[7]			(% of total	36.00	47.30
Other			(	48.10	42.50
Production GDP[4] per head		1971	$[8]	2150	3180
GDP by sector: Agriculture		1971	(	5.90[11]	4.10[13]
Industry			(% of total	44.30[11]	56.90[13]
Other			(	49.80[11]	39.10[13]
GDP[4,23] annual volume growth		1971	(%	6.30	0.70
		1966-71	(	11.30	3.40
Indicators of living standards					
Private consumption per head		1971	$	1120	1760
Public expenditure on education		1970	% of GNP	4.00[2]	4.90[2]
Dwellings completed, per 1000 inhabitants		1971	(	14.40[13]	5.30[13]
Passenger cars, per 1000 inhabitants		1970	(	85	267
Television sets, per 1000 inhabitants		1971	(Number	222	208[13]
Telephones, per 1000 inhabitants		1971	(	282	346
Doctors, per 1000 inhabitants		1970	(	1.11[2]	1.03[2]
Gross fixed investment[23] Total		1967-71 average		37.80	24.20[25]
Machinery and equipment			(	31.30[27]	7.30
Residential construction			(% of GDP[4]	6.50	16.90[28]
Other construction			(	-- [27]	--
Gross saving		1967-71 average	% of GDP[4]	39.10	30.20[25]
Public sector[30] Total current revenue		1971	% of GDP[4]	22.30	35.70[13]
Wages/Prices Hourly earnings[32]		Annual increase 1966-71	(	15.20[39]	..
Consumer prices			(%	5.70	3.30
GDP[4] deflator			(	4.70	5.10
Foreign trade Imports[46]		1971	($ million[8]	20720	730[13]
			(% of GDP[4]	9.20	70.90
Exports[46]			($ million[8]	27010	850[13]
			(% of GDP[4]	12.00	81.80
Balance of payments Current balance		1967-71 average	% of GNP	1.30	--
Official reserves[47], end-1972: % of imports of goods in 1972			%	78.20	--
Change		May 1973-May 1974	Mill. SDRs	-2241	--
Net flow of resources to developing countries[50]		1972	% of GNP	0.93	-- [51]
Export performance[53] Growth of markets[54]		1971-72	(%	14.80	--
		1960-61 to 1970-71 (average)	(	10.10	--
Gains or losses of market shares[55]		1971-72	(%	4.30	--
		1960-61 to 1970-71 (average)	(	7.90	--

Netherlands	Norway	Portugal	Spain	Sweden	Switzer-land	Turkey	United Kingdom	United States	Yugo-slavia[17]
13330	3933	8590	34365	8127	6385	37010	55877	208842	20770
1.22	0.78	-0.41	1.06	0.72	1.20	2.49	0.45	1.14	0.99
4604	1497[13]	3033	12442	3860	3063	(13639)[13]	24329	79120	7651[5]
6.90	13.90[13]	31.10	28.60	7.80	7.20	(71.50)[13]	2.70	4.30	50.40
38.00	37.30[13]	36.30	37.50	37.60	47.50	(11.80)[13]	45.70	(31.00)	49.60
55.10	48.80[13]	32.60	33.90	54.60	45.30	(16.70)[13]	51.60	(64.70)	
2820	3350	760	1070	4410	3780	350	2430	5130	760
6.20[13]	5.30	16.20	13.50	4.40[11]	6.40[10]	30.20[12]	2.90[14]	2.90[11]	19.30[13]
42.00[13]	37.80	44.30	34.40	39.30[11]	49.60[10]	25.70[12]	43.50[14]	33.10[11]	41.10[13]
51.80[13]	56.90	39.50	52.10	56.20[11]	44.00[10]	44.10[12]	53.60[14]	63.90[11]	39.60[13]
4.50	5.00	6.20	4.50	0.20	3.80	7.90	1.60	2.50	--
6.10	4.60	6.60	5.70	3.50	3.80	6.30	2.30	2.50	--
1610	1780	580	720	2390	2230	260[13]	1510	3230	390
7.00[18]	5.90	2.00	2.20[2]	8.20	4.10[2]	3.70[18]	5.50[2]	5.40[2]	4.30[18]
10.40	9.80	2.90[13]	9.10	13.20	10.70	4.80[13]	6.70	8.30	6.10
194	193	47	71	279	221	4	213	432	35
243	229	40[13]	132	323	222	3	298	449	100
280	307	92	151	557	509	18	289	604	40
1.19	1.37	0.85	1.34[2]	1.30[2]	1.59	0.44	1.18[9]	1.49[2]	1.10
26.70	28.20	18.00	24.10	23.00	27.80[49]	--	19.30	16.60[26]	--
12.60	13.90	8.00	12.60	8.30	9.50	--	9.40	7.00[26]	--
5.20	5.10	3.00	3.90	5.10	7.10	--	3.40	3.30	--
8.90	9.20	7.00	7.80	9.60	11.20	--	6.50	6.30	--
26.20	28.00	20.40	22.70	22.80	28.90[49]	--	19.40	17.30	--
42.50[13]	47.30	24.00	22.60	49.10[31]	27.10[2]	--	38.60	30.50	--
9.20[40]	9.90[41]	10.20[33]	12.30[42]	9.00[43]	6.10[44]	--	7.80[45]	5.50[20]	14.70
5.30	5.50	7.80	5.40	4.60	3.80	10.00	5.70	4.50	9.10
5.30	5.70	3.80	5.50	4.80	5.10	7.70	5.60	4.40	--
17710	5360	2130	5610	8410	8240	990[13]	28750	62440	3750
47.50	41.00	31.50	15.40	23.50	34.50	7.70	21.50	5.90	23.90
17700	5130	1650	5840	8770	8090	620[13]	30650	56220	2860
47.50	39.30	24.50	16.00	24.50	33.80	4.80	22.90	5.30	18.20
-0.50	-0.80	2.80	-0.10	-0.30	1.50	-0.70	0.60	0.00	--
27.90	30.30	105.90	75.80	19.70	75.90	92.60	20.30	23.70	22.50
-130	75	175[48]	649[48]	-274	-277	429[48]	150	431	171
1.42	0.37	(2.15)	--[52]	0.66	0.58	--[52]	1.11	0.64	--[52]
19.90	19.60	--	19.10	18.80	19.20	19.70	14.50	16.70	--
11.10	10.20	--	10.60	10.50	11.10	10.80	9.80	9.80	--
-2.00	8.30	--	6.90	-2.50	-0.10	11.70	-6.80	-5.60	--
0.80	0.50	--	3.40	-0.10	-0.30	-4.20	-2.90	-2.10	--

(continued)

TABLE 3.1 (continued)

Note: Figures within parentheses are estimates by the OECD Secretariat.

[1]Does not include total net migration between Finland and the other Nordic countries.
[2]1969.
[3]Total resident population.
[4]GDP in purchasers' values.
[5]Private and socialized sector.
[6]From 1972, including Okinawa prefecture.
[7]According to the definition used in OECD Labor Force Statistics: mining, manufacturing, construction, and utilities (electricity, gas, and water).
[8]At current prices and exchange rates.
[9]1967.
[10]The estimates for GDP by sector for Switzerland have been published in "La Vie economique," November 1969.
[11]GDP at market prices.
[12]Net domestic product.
[13]1970.
[14]Including stock appreciation.
[15]Fiscal year--beginning July 1st.
[16]Monthly, wage earners.
[17]National source.
[18]1968.
[19]1966.
[20]Manufacturing, gross earnings per production worker.
[21]Including Luxembourg.
[22]Dwellings started.
[23]At constant (1963) prices.
[24]Excluding transfer costs of land and existing assets.
[25]1966-70.
[26]Government and government enterprise expenditure on machinery and equipment is included in government current expenditure.
[27]"Other construction" included under "machinery and equipment." Work in progress on heavy equipment and ships for the domestic market are included in fixed asset formation.
[28]"Other construction" included in "residential construction."
[29]Including transfer costs of land.
[30]General government.
[31]Including depreciation.
[32]Industry.
[33]Monthly.
[34]Manufacturing.
[35]Including bonuses.
[36]Hourly rates in manufacturing.
[37]Hourly wages rates, unskilled workers.
[38]Hourly rates in manufacturing, excluding family allowances.
[39]Monthly earnings in manufacturing. Cash payments including bonuses, regular workers.
[40]Hourly rates in industry, males.
[41]Males.
[42]Manufacturing, including salaried employees.
[43]Mining and manufacturing, males.
[44]Hourly rates.
[45]Hourly rates in manufacturing, males.
[46]Goods and services, excluding factor income.
[47]Including reserve position in the IMF and special drawing rights.
[48]April 1973-April 1974.
[49]1965-69.
[50]According to the Development Assistance Committee (DAC) definition. Including flows to multilateral agencies and grants by voluntary agencies.
[51]Not Development Assistance Committee member.
[52]Considered as a developing country for purposes of DAC reporting.
[53]Values, percentage change. Figures are subject to many limiting factors. For an explanation see OECD Economic Outlook, simple definition, December 1970, pp. 65, 69.
[54]The growth which would have occurred in a country's exports if it had exactly maintained its share in total OECD exports to each of 19 broad geographical zones.
[55]The difference between the growth rates of markets and exports.

Sources: Common to all subjects and countries, except Yugoslavia (for special national sources see above): OECD: Labour Force Statistics, Main Economic Indicators, National Accounts, Balance of Payments, Observer, DAC and Statistics of Foreign Trade (Series A); Office Statistique des Communautes Europeennes, Statistiques de base de la Communaute; IMF, International Financial Statistics; UN, Statistical Yearbook.

that decisions taken by the gremio were applicable to all enterprises regardless of whether
they were members or not, and (c) allowing
them the right to impose membership on other
employers in the same sector . . . the regime
also assured its control . . . by requiring that
they comply with the country's labor code, submit periodic reports for ministerial ratification, and solicit approval from the Ministry of
Corporations of candidates proposed for gremio
office.

Moreover, industrial elites, particularly
some of the large, Lisbon-headquartered con-
sortia (e.g. Companhia Uniao Frabric [CUF],
Champalimand Group, Portuguese do Atlantico
group), were able to pursue their interests via
direct contact and alliance with different sectors of the state apparatus, including the military. [4]

Since many gremios were controlled by the larger firms, many
of these foreign-owned, the bourgeoisie, both the petite and managerial sectors, found themselves at the mercy of financial and industrial interests as the rate of inflation, at 16 percent in 1971, rose to
30 percent between March 1973 and 1974, with an extraordinary jump
to an annual rate of 72 percent in the month of February. Historian
Douglas Wheeler describes the erosion of support for the Caetano
regime:

It is a truism in Portuguese politics that without
significant middle class support no Government--
whether democratic or dictatorial--can survive
for long. Salazar's New State (1932-1968) consolidated itself in the 1930's. In some respects, this
strangely time-resistant "constitutional oligarchy"
represented a middle and upper class reaction to
the failures of a turbulent parliamentary regime,
the first Republic, 1910-26. Salazar built his New
State upon a behind the scenes coalition of middle
and upper class interest groups, both rural and
urban, which features southern landowners, big
business, the Church, and the armed forces officer corps. [5]

In this manner, the economy, controlled by external forces,
still lacked a growth direction--at least in the minds of the industrial

elite. To them, the only solution was to enter the Common Market.
But because of the Salazar-Caetano regime, Portugal could not qual-
ify for membership. Thus, paradoxically, it was individuals from
the industrial class who both attempted to depose Caetano in order
to return to a Salazarist control of wages as well as appealed for a
progressive government which would assure Common Market entry. [6]
As Wheeler says:

> An increasing number of businessmen now asked:
> if the Premier tells us that we cannot restore free-
> doms until the African wars are finished, if we
> cannot go into partnership with the Common Market
> unless we democratize, why not find a way to do just
> this? The importance of Western Europe in Portu-
> gal's trade, now clearly outweighed the African
> colonial trade; in 1973, only 15% of Portugal's ex-
> ports went to Africa. [7]

If the economic life of metropolitan Portugal itself resembled
a colonial economy--with wages, prices, and distribution controlled
by a foreign market, and foreign investment increasingly the major
factor in its industrialization--then the economy of the overseas
territories which served as providers of raw materials and consumers of manufactured goods from Portugal was totally colonial. These
countries also provided raw materials and cheap labor for non-
Portuguese industry, primarily for Great Britain. [8]

The exact proportion of foreign ownership of Portuguese companies is still unclear. Banks, insurance companies, and investment houses were allowed to operate as unfettered private enterprises rather than as guilds within the gremio system. There was no
consistency in regard to interest rates, qualifications for loans,
capitalization minimums, or any of the usual safeguards for financial
institutions. Some companies existed only on paper, insurance reserves were often missing and unaccounted for, and in some cases
their own office buildings were fully mortgaged as well.

Because of the ownership of Portuguese businesses by major
British multinational companies, the most important exports, refined sugar, canned fish, cork, olive oil, and wine, have not been
sold at genuine international free trade prices. Britain's investments
in Portugal and the Portuguese colonies date back to the eighteenth
century, and the proportion of British investment and trade monopoly
in metropolitan Portugal was a steady 26 percent from the 1920s to
1974. While West German investment surpassed that of Great Britain during the 1960s, British firms own the public transportation
system for Lisbon, they play the major role in the production and

export of port wine, tinned fish, and olive oil, they own seven automobile assembly plants, and until 1968 they were the major Portuguese producer of wolfram (when South African financial interests
took over).[9]

British capital is also heavily involved in Portuguese Africa
as well as the home country. They are the major interests in sugar
production in Mozambique with their Sena Sugar Estates and Spence
and Pierce, Ltd., as well as many other combinations with South
African and Rhodesian investors. Portuguese Africa was also a
prime target for many of the multinationals prior to the 1960s, and
increasingly so since 1962. The multinationals' involvement in
Africa is primarily in the exploration and distribution of natural resources such as oil and minerals, as is illustrated in Tables 3.2
and 3.3. The interconnections of U.S., British, and South African
financial interests can be exemplified by the case of a South African
bank subsidiary operating in Angola and Mozambique which is also
partly owned by both British investors and by Chase Manhattan Bank.[10]
This kind of "external impulsion," described by Organization for Economic Cooperation and Development (OECD) surveys as the basis of
the Portuguese economy, is directed by foreign investors to the extraction of natural resources from Africa, and only secondarily to
the development of industry in metropolitan Portugal.[11]

Prior to the 1900s foreign investment capital was not welcomed
in metropolitan Portugal, but was directed so heavily toward African
resources that the Portuguese financial advantages from trade with
the African colonies decreased markedly through the decade of the
1960s. Minter points out how foreign investments increased:

> Even in the initial stages of Portuguese coloniza-
> tion, major enterprises were under foreign con-
> trol. In Angola, the Benquela Railway and the
> Angola Diamond Company are under the control
> of the British, South African and Belgian finan-
> cial interests . . . the Mozambique and Niassa
> Companies, with British, French and German
> capital, has responsibility for economic develop-
> ment and even government control over much of
> the country.[12]

Since these foreign-owned Portuguese firms preferred to
specialize in raw materials so that the production of finished goods
could take place in the developed homeland, the rather specialized
pattern of exports was developed both in terms of the kinds of goods
exported and the country to which they were exported. Table 3.4
indicates the degree of relative specialization in 1972. Of particular

TABLE 3.2

Investment in Angola

Resources	Oil	Diamonds	Sulphur	Iron
National origin of company	United States	United States South Africa	United States Great Britain	West Germany
Estimated investment (millions of dollars)	130	Unknown	75	Unknown
Beginning in year	1966	Pre-1960	Unknown	Pre-1960
Companies	Gulf Oil	Diversa Inc. (Dallas) Diamond Dist., Inc. (New York)	Tennecol, Inc.	Fried-Krupp

Source: Compiled by the author.

TABLE 3.3

Investment in Mozambique

Resources	Oil	Hydroelectric Energy	Columbo (classified as a strategic metal)	Butane Gas
National origin of company	United States	South Africa	United States and Great Britain	United States
Estimated investment (millions of dollars)	45	--	Unknown	10
Beginning in year	1968	--	1966	1948
Companies	Sunran Kelly Getty Clark Hunt Tenneco	--	--	Gulf Pan-American

Source: Compiled by the author.

interest is the fact that all three of the largest groups of commodity exports are in the raw material, or more importantly, relatively un- processed material group, and that they constitute well over half of total exports. On the other hand, over a third of all imports were in the machinery and transport equipment group.

TABLE 3.4

1972 Foreign Trade

(by commodity groups, millions of U.S. dollars)	
Exports	
Goods classified chiefly by material	458.2
Food and beverages	229.5
Basic materials	180.4
All other	425.7
Total exports	1293.8
Imports	
Machinery and transport equipment	759.7
Basic materials	443.5
Goods classified chiefly by material	392.5
All others	631.5
Total imports	2227.2
Trade deficit	933.4
(by country, billions of escudos)	
Exports	
United Kingdom	10.6
Escudo Area	6.6
United States	4.4
All other	23.2
Total exports	44.8
Imports	
Germany	10.6
United Kingdom	8.4
Escudo Area	7.4
All other	46.8
Total imports	73.2
Trade deficit	28.4

Source: OECD Report, 1973.

As might be anticipated from our discussion of British-owned firms in Portugal, for the purpose of capturing raw materials, a large percentage of exports from Portugal went directly to England, with exports to the escudo area second. Paralleling West Germany's investment interest in Portugal, more goods were imported from West Germany than any other country, with imports from the United Kingdom and the escudo area slightly lower.

> Great Britain is also . . . Portugal's most important trading partner; in 1968 she was ranked first in imports from Portugal (nearly twice as much as the second ranking USA) and second only to West Germany in exports to Portugal. . . . In spite of competition from West Germany and the United States, Britain's joint membership with Portugal in the European Free Trade Association provides continuing advantages for British interests. [13]

Portugal has not, for the past 200 years at least, operated in a genuine international free trade market. Instead, major exportable products, refined sugar, canned fish, cork, olive oil, and wine, have been traded with major multinational British companies at far below the prices these products bring when marketed by other producing countries such as Italy, France, and Spain. The gremio system, by allowing foreign-owned companies to set industrial policy, aided and abetted these distortions: Wages were maintained at subsistence levels; export prices were set unrealistically low for the overall profit maximization of multinational companies (which resulted in low profits for domestically owned firms, the dispersal of the profits of multinationals to other countries, and a damaged terms of trade by selling materials at artificially low prices and buying machinery at market prices).

In addition to these distortions, Portuguese society had changed drastically between 1950 and 1970. Partly because of the utilization of raw materials from the colonies, partly because of international financing, and partly because of the failure to develop the agricultural sectors, the economy shifted from a share-cropped agrarian society to an industrial capitalist economy. There had been an increase in industrial workers of only 5 percent between 1900 and 1950, but from 1950 to 1970 the industrial labor force increased 18 percent. This shift resulted not only in the depletion of agricultural production, but more importantly for our analysis, new bases for organizing political opposition to the Salazar regime. [14]

Ironically, the collapse of the agricultural economy, while it alienated and pauperized the peasantry, also served to forestall anarchy or revolution because of the pressures toward emigrant labor in France, West Germany, Britain, and Canada. For many years, remittances from the young emigrant laborers had provided the major source of spendable income for families of subsistence farmers remaining in Portugal. In many of the rural areas, the workforce consisted of women, young children, and old men, since the young men had either emigrated to work, or had gone to the African wars as draftees. [15]

Between 1960 and 1970, continental Portugal's population decreased by 200,000 as a direct result of emigration. As of 1974 the estimated number of emigrant Portuguese workers in Europe alone was 1,100,000. Emigration rates, which had exceeded 70,000 for 1973, decreased by almost 50 percent in 1974. [16] Since 1974 was marked by an economic recession in the Common Market, which absorbed the majority of Portuguese emigrant labor, this factor alone may account for the decrease. However, it is possible that the April 1974 revolution raised the economic expectations of the working class and especially of the agricultural workers. It is also possible that the rapidly changing and often traumatic political circumstances of 1974 provided a rationale for husbands and fathers to remain at home. The number of emigrant Portuguese has never, in fact, been reflected in the figures for workers abroad. Many of the emigrants, especially those to the United States and Brazil, have been permanent or long-term residents abroad.

The structural distortion of this massive shift in the Portuguese economy did more than force many young men abroad. As people moved to the urban areas where the industrial jobs were to be found, extreme housing shortages developed. At the beginning of the decade of the 1960s, the estimated housing shortage was approximately 500,000 units--one out of every four Portuguese families was without a dwelling of its own. [17] The shortage worsened after that period. Although 35,000 units were constructed each year of the decade, it was not sufficient because of the shift in population as well as the formation of new family units. Actually, the construction program was one of the poorest in Europe, with only 4.3 units built per 1,000 persons per year during the decade. In addition, much of the existing housing was so dilapidated as to constitute a safety and health hazard, as discussed in the next section.

SHORT-RUN ECONOMIC PRESSURES

In addition to the structural distortions which created pressures throughout the economy, additional pressures were imposed

by short-run economic events. Unfortunately, many of the precise
causes and effects cannot be evaluated at this time simply because
the extent of various changes is not known at this time. As the OECD
states: "In this report [July 1974] as in previous ones, it is again
necessary to stress the radical inadequacies of the Portuguese statistical system, short-term data in some cases not becoming available
until after a delay of over a year."[18]

Certain short-run pressures, however, are self-evident and
can be stated without contradiction. The annual OECD review of Portugal for 1974 presents a view of the economic status of the country
just prior to April 25:

> Prior to the events of April, the Portuguese
> economy has been facing difficult problems, both
> of a structural and a short-term nature. Admit-
> tedly, the economy had achieved a high rate of
> growth in recent years, the steep rise in domestic
> activity being mainly due to the expansion of in-
> vestment and exports. But in 1973, pressure on
> prices was mounting at an increasing rate and,
> as far as can be judged from the statistics avail-
> able, the purchasing power of households de-
> clined somewhat, since the growth of wages did
> not offset, at least in the latter part of 1973 and
> the beginning of 1974, the rise in the cost of liv-
> ing. Disposable income was affected too, by the
> smaller increase in emigrants' remittances, a
> factor linked with the slowdown in activity in cer-
> tain host countries.[19]

Tables 3.5 and 3.6 describe the crucial relationships between
wages and prices. The data on wages are bound to underestimate the
effect of the decline on families since there were no accurate records
on unemployment and underemployment. The workers' strikes which
preceded the MFA takeover, therefore, were acts of sheer despera-
tion rather than indications of greater liberalism on the part of the
Caetano regime in dealing with dissension. The OECD survey points
out that:

> It is not possible with the available statistics to
> make a precise analysis of the recent trend of
> wages. The data to hand suggests that in 1973
> wage rates rose on an average a little faster than
> the price index, thus showing a small margin of
> increase in purchasing power of households. In

TABLE 3.5

Consumer and Wholesale Prices

(percentage change on corresponding period of previous year)

	1971	1972	1973	1973 II	1973 III	1973 IV	1974 I	1974 II
Consumer prices								
Six main towns[b]	10.1	11.2	12.5	9.8	13.8	16.4	23.0	
Lisbon	11.9	10.7[a]	12.9	10.4	13.6	17.6	23.8	26.0
Food	8.1	9.9	9.2	4.3	10.4	16.2	23.2	31.2
Nonfood products	15.3	11.6	16.4	16.1	16.6	18.8	25.1	21.3
Clothing and footwear	6.1	9.1	25.6	27.1	26.3	30.4	35.7	31.7
Rents	..	19.4[a]	18.4	17.4	19.1	19.4	29.5	18.3
Miscellaneous services	8.3	6.7	13.0	12.4	12.8	16.1	16.9	
Lisbon (excluding rents)	8.4	8.8	11.5	8.5	12.2	17.5	22.3	21.1
Wholesale prices--Lisbon	2.0	5.9	11.1	8.0	11.2	17.1	25.2	
Food	5.0	6.8	5.1	0.6	4.5	12.3	20.8	
Manufactured goods	3.1	6.9	10.7	9.4	10.0	13.0	12.1	
Primary products other than food	-1.3	6.4	25.3	17.8	26.4	42.4	29.3	
Fuels and lubricants	0.8	0.0	16.9	17.7	17.7	21.5	29.2	
Drink and tobacco	-2.2	6.3	18.2	15.4	20.3	21.3	25.3	

[a]As from 1972 a new method of calculating rents has been used.
[b]Average of the indexes for the six main towns weighted by their populations.

Source: National Statistics Institute, Monthly Bulletin of Statistics.

TABLE 3.6

Nominal and Real Wages

(percentage change on corresponding period of previous year)

	1970	1971	1972	1973	1973 I	1973 II	1973 III	1973 IV	1974 I
Nominal wages									
Wages in agriculture									
Men	11.2	13.0	12.2	13.1	11.8	12.7	12.1	15.6	20.8
Women	9.7	15.5	11.4	15.8	17.4	13.6	13.3	18.8	21.3
Wages in industry and transport									
Lisbon	11.8	10.8	8.5	11.8	9.1	12.6	15.2	18.6	19.8
Porto	10.4	13.4	12.7	7.4	8.2	6.6	9.8	14.6	19.0
Wages in civil construction[a]	15.0	14.5	13.7	15.3	12.7	14.7	16.3	17.7	--
Real wages[b]									
Wages in agriculture									
Men	6.1	2.5	1.2	0.5	1.8	2.8	-1.3	-0.7	-1.7
Women	4.6	4.8	0.5	2.9	6.9	3.6	-0.3	2.1	-2.2
Wages in industry and transport									
Lisbon	5.2	-1.1	-2.0	0.3	-0.7	2.1	1.4	0.8	-3.2
Porto	7.2	5.2	1.5	-1.3	-0.1	-0.9	-1.2	-0.5	-2.2
Wages in civil construction[a]	9.6	3.9	2.5	2.5	2.6	4.7	2.4	1.1	--

[a]Average daily wage in selected occupations.
[b]Deflated by the consumer price indexes for the respective towns.

Source: Information sent by the Portuguese authorities to the OECD. Ministry of Labour report on short-term trends.

Daily Wages in Selected Occupations[a]

(escudos)

	1968	1971	1972	1973
Agriculture (general workers)				
Men		75	84	95
Women		43	48	61
Metals and metalworking				
Electricians	96	129	142	178
Foundry workers, etc.	70	96	110	122
Rubber				
Male operatives	65	95	103	120
Female operatives	32	55	58	69
Plastics products				
Male operatives	61	93	105	118
Female operatives	29	45	52	58
Construction				
Bricklayers, etc.	64	90	106	117
Laborers	50	71	81	96

[a]The figures for each year represent the average of the wages quoted at end–March, end–June, end–September, and end–December.

Source: Monthly Bulletin of Statistics.

absolute terms, this was still one of the lowest
among the OECD countries, with very large differences between wages for a man and for women.
In rural areas the daily wage for a man was approximately $3.40, and for a woman, $2.50; in
the plastics industry, the daily wage for a man
was approximately $4.70 while that for a woman
only about $2.30.[20]

As the 1974 OECD survey further points out, household consumption, which had risen in 1970 and 1971, slowed in 1972 and even
further in 1973 in combination with the deterioration in the purchasing power of households. The decline in real income, along with a
decline in remittances from Portuguese workers in foreign countries, hurt many consumers and families in a deep sense. Of this,
the OECD report observes:

> Retail prices also rose rapidly in 1973, the rise
> accelerating from the third quarter onward. The
> retail price index for the city of Lisbon shows that
> prices of food continued to rise rapidly in 1973,
> but that the higher rate of increase is mainly due
> to other items in the index . . . for the second
> year in succession there was a particularly sharp
> rise in rents. . . . Similar increases seem to
> have taken place in their sectors: thus for fish
> and fish preserves there was a sharp rise in re-
> tail prices compared with wholesale prices towards
> the end of 1973, and in the case of dried cod, some
> dealers would seem to have laid in speculative
> stocks. . . . The scale of the problem is such
> that it was specifically taken into account in the
> Government's programme published on the 15th
> of May, 1974.
>   The moderate rise, in terms of annual aver-
> ages in the purchasing power of household actually
> conceals a steady deterioration over the year as a
> whole. During the last quarter of 1973, almost all
> workers probably suffered a decline in purchasing
> power, and in the first months of 1974, this trend
> was accentuated as the rise in the cost of living
> index accelerated over the country as a whole.[21]

Thus, the wage-price disaster played an important part in in-
tensifying the struggle of the working class for survival and further

wreaked havoc on the already disenchanted petite bourgeoisie by re-
ducing sales and, through the mismanagement of the financial sector,
preventing recourse to normal business finance.

Yet some scholars who viewed the scene did not perceive these
facts as portending upheaval. Phillippe Schmitter, for instance, observed:

> There is nothing in the period immediately pre-
> ceding the April coup to suggest imminent col-
> lapse or even acute difficulties . . . the short
> term aggregate performance of the regime and the
> Portuguese economy was, if anything, relatively
> impressive in 1972 and 1973. . . . By Western
> European standards for the period, the compara-
> tive performance was poor--but evenly so. [22]

Perhaps the economic indicators selected by political econo-
mists like Schmitter are insufficient reflections of the manner by
which these conditions are translated into the perceptions of the ordinary inhabitants of Portugal. He cites Gross National Product as
another criterion for evaluation of the strength of the Caetano regime:

> G.N.P. was still growing; employment was rising;
> wages, especially in the agricultural sector,
> seemed to have been increasing; internal services
> were at an all time high; receipts from emigrants
> were coming in greater and greater quantities;
> the stock market was booming; government reve-
> nues had gone up to 19.3% of G.N.P. in 1973 and
> were budgeted to increase by 22% in 1974; mili-
> tary expenditures were still increasing in abso-
> lute terms but decreasing as a proportion of total
> government expenditures (if the 1974 budget can
> be treated in this manner). [23]

As the budget for military expenditures increased in the overall proportion of governmental expenses from 1966 through 1968,
arrangements were made to combine the debt due on an international
loan from the United States with the costs of weaponry purchased
from the United States which in the long run managed to disguise and
thus distort that increase into 1973. [24] Table 3.7 illustrates this.

Increased tourism during the 1960s also accounted for some of
the growth rate. Construction investment, both indigenous and foreign capital, was consigned to building condominiums and luxurious
resort-hotels. Along with the other declines of 1973, there was a

25 percent drop in the rate of tourism. Even tourism showed a slow-down having dropped in 1973 to below 1971 levels and continuing to decline into 1974. The first three months of 1975 reflected a 63.5 percent increase in U.S. tourists over the number for the same period in 1974. However, that merely emphasized the discrepancy again when, during the second quarter of 1975, tourism receded in almost the same proportion.[25]

TABLE 3.7

Budgeted Military Expenditures as a Percentage of
Total Central Government Budgeted Expenditures

	Percent	Escudo Amount
1958	22.4	514
1961	36.5	4,907
1962	38.5	5,710
1963	37.3	5,853
1964	38.3	6,552
1965	40.9	7,390
1966	41.3	8,100
1967	41.9	9,785
1968	42.4	10,696
1969	40.7	11,292
1970	39.9	12,346
1971	36.5	10,760
1972	33.4	11,550
1973	30.0	13,070
1974	27.6	14,630

Sources: Anvario Estatistico, various issues; OECD, Economic Survey: Portugal, various issues.

In summary, although the Portuguese economy may have ex-perienced a steady growth for some time, in the latter half of 1972 and throughout 1973 it went into a sudden decline, and fell even further during the first quarter of 1974. Schmitter's use of GNP, stock market prices, and other macro-economic measurements can be seen as irrelevant to the people who would soon support the revo-lution. With employment down and prices up, the real condition of Portugal, in terms of the circumstances of its citizenry, had reached a new low. With or without the revolution of April 25, collapse was certainly not far away.

SOCIAL CONDITIONS

A kind of slave labor economy persisted in continental Portugal and the overseas territories. The Labor Regulation of 1899 had continued to be applied to the native populations of Angola and Mozambique until the April 25th revolution.

> All natives of Portuguese overseas provinces
> are subject to the moral and legal obligation
> of attempting to obtain through work the means
> that they lack to subsist and to better their
> social condition. They have full liberty to
> choose the method of fulfilling their obligation,
> but if they do not fulfill it, public authority
> may force a fulfillment. [26]

The subsistence farming which characterized indigenous African culture was thus made illegal. So, of course, was unemployment. The recruitment of forced workers in Angola was in practice during the 1950s and 1960s when it became something of an international scandal through the writings of Basil Davidson,[27] Gwendolyn Carter,[28] and John Gunther.[29] Marvin Harris[30] documented the practice in Mozambique. Local officials in Mozambique recruited for the South African mines an average of 100,000 workers a year. Minter describes the effects of this conscription:

> The result of this labor migration to South
> Africa and . . . to Rhodesia, is that something
> like two-thirds of the mature able-bodied men
> of Southern Mozambique are employed in for-
> eign territories. . . . As the men do not earn
> enough to buy food for their families at home,
> and cannot take their families with them to the
> mines, the food must be grown by those who
> stay at home. It is very "efficient" manage-
> ment. Otherwise the South African mine-
> owners might have to pay subsistence for fam-
> ilies and not just single men, and it might not
> be so profitable to extract the gold for the
> world's money markets.
>   If the African worker does not go to South
> Africa, he may end up working on a sugar or tea
> plantation . . . [as contract labor]. . . . Fail-
> ure to fulfill one's obligation under the contract,
> or other offenses may lead to conviction in court,
> and to a sentence of unpaid "correctional labor."[31]

The system, with some minor variations, less harshly applied
and considerably less punitively managed, applied in metropolitan
Portugal as well. It was found after the revolution that government
officials had been making profits by contracting Portuguese workers to
the factories of West Germany, France, and Luxembourg.[32] Because
the so-called social security system of Salazarist Portugal offered
no unemployment benefits, aid to dependent children, or minimum
assistance, the subsistence farmer, the unemployed worker, the or-
phaned child, and the sick and aged had no recourse for income. Social security and health benefits operated only in accordance with the
prior job status of the individual, length of time worked, and on job
payments. Funds invested by the Ministry were supposed to have been
available to employ persons on public works projects. However, the
funds had "vanished" by the time of the reorganization of the government which followed the revolution.[33] With no recourse to public
assistance or even to survival through their agricultural enterprise,
millions of Portuguese people emigrated to work in Western Europe
and North America. Their remittances home did not do as much to
support their families as they did to support the balance of trade
deficits of the Portuguese government.

The families of draftees were in extreme financial duress. A
soldier totally incapacitated by war injuries would receive a small
pension; for those who were not totally disabled, there were no pensions and no jobs.

A minority of the emigrant laborers brought their families with
them--especially those who went to work in France. But the women
were homesick and the children confused by the change of languages
and cultures; having gone from rural Portugal to urban, industrial
France, they often became alienated from both cultures. In many
Portuguese villages, the only adults to be seen before the revolution
were women and old men. Although child labor was illegal, the children were essential field hands until they too could go off to work in
France or West Germany.[34] It was a common saying of women in
rural Portugal that "they marry because they want to be alone."

There are no reliable statistics for unemployment rates of the
Portuguese population prior to the revolution. Most Portuguese
stopped their education average in primary school, and a third of the
population remained illiterate.

Salazar's concordat with the Vatican reestablished the influence
of the Church in civic matters. Portugal did not allow divorce or
family planning (contraception and abortion). In the rural areas,
priests were often the only literate figures in the community. Although Bishop of Oporto, Bishop Ferreira Gomes, was exiled for
expressions of dissent from the regime's colonial policies, few other
priests joined his protest. In fact, the Church in Spain far exceeded

the Portuguese Church in social and political action in behalf of its people. Fear of communism was an overriding principle guiding the behavior of individual clerics and the conservative policies of the hierarchy.

Health conditions in Portugal reflected the contradiction between its status as an industrial European nation and its similarity to the underdeveloped countries. Portugal had a high incidence of diseases which were long ago eradicated in the more advanced countries. Table 3.8 details disease statistics for a typical year, 1970.

TABLE 3.8

Mortality Rates for Some Infectious Diseases, 1970
(selected European countries, per 100,000 inhabitants)

Type	Portugal	Netherlands	Sweden	France	Italy
Diphtheria	0.2	--	--	0.0	0.05
Tetanus	1.6	0.05	--	0.5	0.4
Whooping cough	0.14	0.0	0.0	0.1	0.1
Poliomyelitis	0.02	--	0.0	0.0	0.0
Measles	2.9	0.1	0.01	0.05	0.3
Respiratory tuberculosis	14.6	0.8	3.1	7.1	6.1
Enteritis and other diarrheas	29.0	1.5	1.5	1.1	5.4

Sources: Annuaire de Statistiques Sanitaires Mondiales OMS (1970), Health Statistics, National Institute of Statistics, 1970.

In cardiovascular diseases and motor vehicle accidents, areas of mortality which reflect a highly industrialized society, Portugal outranks the Netherlands and France in the former, and Italy, the Netherlands, and France in the latter. Cardiovascular diseases reflect social conditions arising from pollution, anxieties, nutritional defects, and communicable infections. Motor vehicle mortalities reflect on mechanization, poor safety regulation, life style, and possibly provide another index of suicide and emotional disturbance. Table 3.9 summarizes these data.

Population shifts from rural to urban areas extended poverty. The lack of government-supported low-rent housing for the urban poor created living conditions which exacerbated vulnerability to communicable diseases and safety hazards. More than 60 percent of the population of Portugal did not have access to a sewage system, or even a hygienic system of garbage removal. Gastrointestinal disorders, both parasitic and infectious, reach epidemic proportions quickly under these circumstances. Table 3.10 summarizes sanitary conditions.

TABLE 3.9

Indicators of Mortality from Other Causes
(per 100,000 population)

Indicators	Portugal (1973)	Italy (1974)	Netherlands (1974)	France (1974)
Cardiovascular disease	438.6	446.0	374.3	402.4
Malignant tumors	137.1	184.0	194.8	211.5
Motor vehicle accidents	28.9	24.9	24.0	25.4

Sources: Health Statistics, National Institute of Statistics (1973), Annuaire de Statistiques Sanitaires Mondiales, OMS (1971).

The rates of infant mortality reflected poor hygienic conditions, lack of prenatal care, inadequate housing, nutritional deficiencies, and low educational levels. The life expectancy of Portuguese women reflected high rates of maternal mortality. Statistics gathered by a women's group in 1975 suggest that illegal abortions have been at the rate of 150,000 per year, and that the conditions under which they are performed have contributed heavily to maternal mortality rates.[35] Table 3.11 summarizes these figures as of 1972-73.

A report published by the Ministry of Social Affairs in March 1975 reviewed the distribution of health care facilities, mortality rates, pharmaceuticals, and the functioning of available health care facilities. The findings proved even worse[36] than reported:

It is easy to guess the consequences of the fact that only one in five Portuguese has the use of a kitchen, a toilet and a bath in his house.
In Portugal [in 1971] . . . there were 800,000 accidents among 3.5 million workers.
Lack of infrastructures for hygiene and protection of the environment are not the only deficiencies responsible for the poor health conditions

of the Portuguese.   The lack of adequate and
efficient health care is also very marked.[37]

TABLE 3.10

Summary of Hygienic Conditions in Metropolitan Portugal
(1970)

	Percentage of Population Served
Water supply	
Supplied to home	40
Good conditions	25
Irregular conditions	10
Poor conditions	5
Supplied by public fountains	27
No supply	33
Urban sewage disposal	
By sewage system	17
Good conditions	10
Poor conditions	7
By collective septic tanks	0.3
Without sewage disposal	82.7
Urban garbage removal	
With collection and treatment	14
With collection, no treatment	25
Without removal	61
Public swimming pools	
Number inventories	118
With adequate treatment	29 (25%)
Without adequate treatment	89 (75%)
Housing	
Possessing kitchen, toilet, and bath	20
With deficient conditions	20
With unacceptable conditions	60
Number of new dwellings necessary in the next ten years (according to the Administration for Urbanization Services)	800,000

Source: Inquiry by MUD (1970), published by Ministry for
Social Communications, March 1975.

TABLE 3.11

Infant and Maternal Mortality

Indicators	Portugal (1973)	Nether- lands (1971)	Sweden (1971)	France (1971)	Italy (1971)
Infant mortality (per 1,000 live births)	44.83	12.10	11.10	17.10	28.50
Mortality in group 1-4 years (per 100,000 popu- lation)	290.80	83.30	41.80	79.20	91.00
Maternal mor- tality (per 1,000 live births)	0.59	0.13	0.08	0.22	0.52
Life expectancy at birth					
Males	64.70	71.10	72.00	69.00	68.70
Females	71.10	76.90	77.60	76.70	74.90
Life expectancy at 1 year					
Males	67.00	71.00	72.00	69.10	69.90
Females	73.10	76.70	77.30	76.70	75.90
Proportion of deaths at over 50 years	0.76	0.85	0.88	0.84	0.82

Sources: Health Statistics, National Institute of Statistics (1973), Annuaire de Statistiques Sanitaires Mondiales, OMS.

The report points out that the distribution of health care facilities in Portugal is asymmetrical. Coimbra, a university town, has a
ratio of nearly one doctor for every person in the population. Nonetheless, patients have to make appointments weeks in advance for
medical treatment. In a large part of the countryside, particularly
in the area north and east of Lisbon, there are no local physicians,
oftentimes not even a road from a village to a highway bus stop.

A young woman student at the Institute of Economics described
the medical care facilities in her home village (located in Guarda
District) as consisting of one doctor in a town several kilometers distance from her own village. It was said in the village that their doctor

has two prescriptions, "If you are under forty he tells you, 'don't worry, you're young and will recover.' If you are over forty, he says, 'well, you're going to die one day anyway, so there's no point in worrying about whether it will be this illness or another one!'"[38]

Specialist services are hard to find in Portugal. There are fewer than 900 psychiatrists, none of whom are located outside of the major cities--Lisbon, Coimbra, and Porto (or their suburbs). Because of a chronic nursing shortage, persons have been recruited who are semiliterate and have had minimal on-the-job training. Most of the nursing and medical specialists have received their training outside of Portugal--many of them in Britain.[39]

The Institute for Psychology, the only institution for training clinical psychologists in Portugal, is located in Lisbon and is a private institution with higher tuition rates than the university itself. The shortage of health specialists and their distribution are exemplified in the mental health profession.

The report from the Ministry for Social Affairs goes on to discuss these problems of distribution of health services:

> It is undeniable that in some sectors the health services have achieved notable results, as is the case, for example with the infectious diseases preventable by vaccination. Smallpox was eradicated more than 20 years ago and results for the diseases included in the National Vaccination Plan begun in 1965 have been highly satisfactory, especially for diphtheria, poliomyelitis, and whooping cough.
>
> Progress in the control of tuberculosis has also been favorable, although the rates of incidence are still high when compared with international statistics, above all for morbidity.
>
> Nonetheless, when we study the indices of infant mortality, maternal mortality, unassisted births (29.5%) or deaths without medical certification (3.2%), as well as the number and distribution of medical professionals in the country, we must conclude that the country does not possess adequate operational facilities. Such facilities must be evaluated in terms of their efficacy in promoting the health of the individual throughout his life--in the intrauterine period, in infancy, in the pre-school and school periods, in sports, at work and in old age. The problem is aggravated in certain areas because of regional asymmetry.[40]

Poor health conditions and endemic poverty form the pieces of a vicious circle that permeated all aspects of social life. The adherence to an archaic laissez-faire economic system prohibited any kind of social planning or social action in the public domain. This philosophy is especially apparent when we examine the health maintenance facilities, their utilization, and geographic placement.

Out of these data, one can project "typical" examples of the day-to-day existence of the Portuguese people during the past 50 years. Such a case in the rural sector might read as follows:

Parents, Maria (age 32) and Jose (age 34) share a four-room, dilapidated, ancient bungalow, with her parents (age 60 and 61), and their six children, ranging in age from 12 to 3. Maria suffers from periodic enteritis, and has lost three of her babies (she had 9 pregnancies) between the ages of birth and five years. Jose's employment history includes work in factories and on construction jobs in France where he spent periods of up to a year at a time. His earnings pay the rent on the family's house and the small plot of land, which primarily serves to provide their own vegetables and includes a small grape field. Maria's father tends the grapes, and with the help of relatives in the village, yearly manages to produce a small quantity of wine which, when sold through the cartel, may provide just enough money for each person in the family to purchase a pair of shoes, and perhaps a sweater or blanket. Maria's parents both suffer from blood pressure disorders. Her mother has already had a stroke which has left her lame and hard of hearing. Maria has an ovarian cyst, but can't afford to have it removed, so she endures considerable pain, and often, lonely and worried, falls into fits of depression. The children attend school when they are well and the two oldest children, both boys, hope to become carpenters. However, there is a real problem about sending them for vocational training since they would have to live away from home and that is costly. Jose plans to return to work in France in hopes of earning the necessary funds. However, if he leaves again, only his aging father-in-law can properly care for the crops, and that may mean a semistarvation diet for the whole family in the coming year. Prices are constantly rising, and although Jose did his army service 14 years before, he fears that if the conditions worsen in Africa, since he is under 45, he may be called up for service again. Maria's eldest brother and his family emigrated to the United States many years ago. They occasionally receive letters and money from him, and when this happens it is possible to get medical treatment for the aging parents--maybe some painkilling prescriptions or extraction of rotted teeth. The children are docile and obedient generally. However, it is evident that the daughters, age seven and nine, are frequently depressed and uncommunicative. Maria wants to send them to a convent school where they will receive better instruction, but she needs them at home to help with the younger children and the chores. Also, where would the money come from?

Or, we might hypothesize an urban family, the daSilvas' household. Their lives and problems in 1970 would probably be something like this:

Ana-Maria (age 32) and Joao (age 32) were born in a village in Vila Real Province. They have an apartment in Lisbon, with a kitchen of their own, a bathroom, two bedrooms--a total of four rooms. They have four young children ages ten, seven, five, and two. Ana-Maria has had one miscarriage and one stillbirth. Joao works in a big chemical manufacturing plant. His wages have not increased in the eight years he has kept the same job. If they hadn't been so fortunate in obtaining the apartment 11 years ago, when Joao got out of the service, they would have had to return to their village or he would have had to work as an emigrant in France. Both of them finished secondary school and Ana-Maria had found a job immediately in a bank office and sent most of her pay home to help educate the six younger children in her family. She continued working until their first child was born. Her earnings never rose beyond $25 a week, but she shared a room with her cousins in her aunt and uncle's apartment in Lisbon until she married. That way, she could send half her pay home and pay a quarter of it to her relatives for room and board. She ended up sometimes with $20 a month for herself. Out of this she had to pay for transportation and lunches. The three older children are all in school and show promise of being good students--prospects perhaps for higher education. However, during the past year, Ana-Maria has been having fainting spells and, although she has not seen a doctor, believes that she may be suffering from high blood pressure. The ten-year-old and the five-year-old have both had rheumatic fever and must be made to get sufficient rest, high protein diet, and have regular physical check-ups. This "medical care" exhausts the family's meager budget. Joao has been going out almost every night--attending some sort of "meetings." His wife is very worried about him, and he refuses to discuss his "meetings" with her. One night, they are awakened from their sleep by a loud command at their door. Before they can open it four men, identifying themselves as DGS, have entered the small apartment. The children scream in fear, and Ana-Maria faints as Joao is led away to Caxias.

This then, was the soil out of which the MFA Revolution grew. The apathy, depression, grief, and pain were the elements sown by a political-economic system which had maintained law and order in Portugal for 50 years.

NOTES

1. Cf. William Minter, Portuguese Africa and the West
(London: Penguin African Library, 1972). This persistent appraisal
is also reflected in almost every published work on Portugal or Portuguese Africa during the decades of the 1960s and 1970s. As Ronald
H. Chilcote points out in his Portuguese Africa (Englewood Cliffs,
N.J.: Spectrum Books, Prentice-Hall, 1967): "In his book, written
in 1930 . . . Cunha Leal attacked the policies of then Colonial Minister Salazar . . . argued that Salazar's designation Portuguese Colonial Empire is unsuitable and pretentious and the idea of forcibly
halting colonial deficits is ridiculous." James Duffy, Portugal in
Africa (Baltimore, Md.: Penguin African Library, 1963), described
the incongruous relationship between the exports of Portuguese Africa
which profited foreign investors primarily and the cost to Portugal of
maintaining its military forces in those places.

2. Harry Makler, "The Portuguese Industrial Elite and its
Corporate Relations: A Study of Compartmentalization in an Authoritarian Regime," paper presented for Yale Mini-Conference on Contemporary Portugal, March 28-29, 1975, p. 5.

3. Ibid.

4. Ibid., p. 6.

5. Douglas Wheeler, "Days of Wine and Carnations: The
Portuguese Revolution of 1974," New Hampshire Council of World
Affairs Bulletin (July, 1974), pp. 1-3.

6. Ibid.

7. Ibid.

8. William Minter, Phillippe Schmitter, and Stanley G.
Payne, A History of Spain and Portugal, Vol. 2 (Madison: University of Wisconsin Press, 1973). All seem to blame the prolonged
African wars as the source of economic drain on Portugal. Minter
makes a further point in explaining that the profits from African resources are primarily lining the pockets of investors in countries
other than Portugal.

9. Minter, op. cit.

10. Ibid.

11. Ibid.

12. Ibid., p. 32.

13. Ibid., pp. 132-33.

14. Ceasar Oliviera, The MFA and Socialist Revolution
(Lisbon, Portugal: Diabaril Editorial, S.A.R.L., 1975).

15. Communication with Fields, interview in December 1974
with Minister for Social Affairs, Dra. M. L. Pintassilga.

16. Information bulletin, Ministry for Social Communications,
March 1975.

17. Housing Survey, published by Ministry for Economics, Portugal, March 1975.

18. OECD Survey, Portugal, 1974, p. 5.

19. Ibid.

20. Ibid.

21. Ibid., p. 16.

22. Phillippe C. Schmitter, "Retrospective and Prospective Thoughts about the Liberation of Portugal," paper presented at Yale University, mini-conference on Portugal, sponsored by the Council on West European Affairs, March 28-29, 1975, pp. 12-13.

23. Ibid.

24. Interview with Minister for Social Communications, May 1975.

25. OECD Report, op. cit.

26. Transcript from Decree Law on Labor, issued by Portuguese Ministry for Overseas Territories, 1899.

27. Basil Davidson, The Liberation of Guinea (Baltimore, Md.: Penguin, 1969).

28. Cited in Minter, op. cit., p. 23.

29. Ibid.

30. Marvin Harris, Portugal's African Wards (New York: American Committee on Africa, 1958).

31. Minter, op. cit., pp. 24-25.

32. Confidential communication to author by MFA Cabinet Minister.

33. Interview with Minister for Social Affairs, op. cit.

34. Ibid.

35. O Seculo, April 25, 1975.

36. Ministry for Social Affairs, Report on Health, 1975.

37. Ibid.

38. Interview with student, Eduarda Fernandes, 1975.

39. Interview with Dr. Alfonso Alburquerque, 1974.

40. Ministry for Social Affairs, op. cit.

4

THE POLITICAL
SOCIALIZATION OF
REVOLUTIONARIES

A week after the April 25, 1975 elections, in Sesimbra, a
small town in Setubal district, a young man shouted and waved his
fist in anger at a building across the narrow street from where he
stood. At his side were two young boys. He shouted at a woman,
apparently located somewhere in the upper story of the large building he faced: "You filthy fascist sow! You beat this child like a
fascist whore! Anyone who beats a helpless child is a filthy fascist
scum! You should be sent to jail for such behavior! You don't be-
long in a socialist country!"[1]

The young man was not a highly educated person, nor had he
studied political philosophy or child-rearing practices, but had in-
tuitively recognized the relationship between an authoritarian state
and corporal punishment inflicted on children. His recognition of
this sophisticated concept in spite of the fact that it contradicts all
he had been taught as a child in a fascist state, casts doubt on the
assumption that youth are the uncritical products of their early political socialization and thus inevitably the perpetuators of the present system. Dawson and Prewitt had suggested that

> A youth growing up in a rural village in one of
> the many transitional countries of the contempo-
> rary world very early learns important lessons
> about politics and authority relationships. The
> young must defer to the old. Leadership in so-
> cial, religious, and political affairs is achieved
> through seniority. Hierarchies are established
> according to traditions which are not to be ques-
> tioned. The youth learns patience and tolerance in
> the face of authority. Now let us assume that this
> boy does well in primary school, passes his ex-

aminations in secondary school, and goes to
the nation's major university in the capital of
his country. In this new setting he is exposed
to different socializing stimuli. He learns that
positions of authority should be achieved by
talent and accomplishment. He finds that egalitarian notions are in vogue . . . he learns that
he can and should do something to alter the traditional order of things. . . . The youth has
been exposed to incongruent socialization agents
and experiences: there has been considerable
discontinuity in his political learning.

Experiences of this kind are frequent in the
new nations of Africa and Asia, in much of Latin
America and Eastern Europe, and to a lesser
extent even in the more highly industrial nations
of the West. . . . In periods of rapid political
and social change such discrepancies (between
culture and a polity) may be both extensive and
long lived.[2]

In examining the MFA revolutionaries, it is useful to remember that they had experienced considerable discontinuity between
political culture and polity.

Three important factors, mentioned briefly in Chapter 1, bear
on this issue. First, there was ongoing and frequently dramatic
political organization and opposition throughout the 50 years of the
Salazar-Caetano regime. Second, education included not only the
formal system of higher education within Portugal, but access to
study and travel abroad, to books and periodicals from other countries, and to interactions with people from all levels of society.
Third, the experiences of the colonial wars had exacerbated the discrepancy between political culture and polity.

If we view the MFA commitment to revolution from a psychological perspective, we can apply the classic model of conversion
phenomenon. According to this model in stage 1, the individual experiences alienation from the larger society; in stage 2, he experiences feelings of isolation from family and close friends; in stage
3, he experiences alienation from self, from personal identity. This
model explains the shame and guilt feelings the MFA members acknowledge, but it fails to explain the particular political turn they
chose as the means for rectifying their alienation.

Members of the MFA were men of varied social backgrounds,
educational levels, political experience, rank, and age. If at first
April 25 was referred to as "The Captain's Revolution,"[3] it was also

apparent on that date that not only were generals and admirals directly involved in organizing and planning the revolution, but the chief of staff of the Joint Military Command, General Costa Gomes, was such an active participant that he was deposed by President Tomas when his sympathies were recognized in March 1974.

The fact that junior officers were heavily represented in the MFA Congress (Assembly) and in front-line positions reflects only that, as in any other hierarchical organization, there were more of them; and that in some cases, senior officers were too conspicuous to be risked in liaison functions.

It was evident to all of them that each man was entering the conspiracy from his own individual level of political experience, and orientation and that in order to weld themselves into a coherent group, the form and structure of that group would be critical for survival as well as being the form for their revolution. There was consensus that means would, in this case, determine ends. And the essence of the revolution was indeed reflected in the democratic, dynamic, and catalytic process which emerged. As an air force colonel said, "We know that we had no experience in democracy, and if we wanted democracy we had to start with ourselves."[4]

In order to identify the uniqueness of this movement and to place it in the context of the political culture in which it emerged, it is useful to examine some concepts about the military and society and about the process of political socialization itself.

BIO-DEMOGRAPHIC CHARACTERISTICS
OF MFA LEADERS

Of the MFA leaders serving in positions on the Council of the Revolution (two of these served formerly in the seven-man Junta of National Salvation) and those holding ministerial level posts in the Portuguese cabinet one year after the revolution, none is on record as having previously been a member of a political movement or opposition party. However, the time they spent in civilian institutions of higher education, in service in the colonies, or in previous administration posts provide clues as to the origin of their revolutionary orientation. At least two of the MFA leaders held positions in the Caetano regime of vital importance to the enactment of events on April 25. Others had senior command positions in proximity to Lisbon and were thereby enabled to move their forces into strategic centers such as transport and broadcasting stations. General Francisco Costa Gomes was Chief of the General Staff until he and General Spinola were removed from office on March 12 preceding the revolution.

   Table 4.1 describes the typical backgrounds of the MFA leadership. It is based on the lives of MFA cabinet ministers and members of the Revolutionary Council (insofar as information has been publicly available on the latter). Of the 29 members of the Council, 20 had been senior officers prior to the revolution. Of these, 8 held prerevolutionary ranks of colonel or major (or their service equivalents in the air force and navy), and one had been raised in rank from lieutenant to captain.

TABLE 4.1

Experience of MFA Leaders
(as of April 25, 1975)

Age	Cabinet	Council
Between 20-29	0	4
30-39	3	1
40-49	2	5
50-59	3	6
60 or over	1	1
Rank		
Lieutenant	0	2
Captain	0	6
Major	4	8
Colonel (or equivalent)	3	2
General	2	10
War service		
Goa	1	n.a.
Guinea	4	n.a.
Mozambique	4	n.a.
Angola	8	n.a.
Military or service academy		
Pre-1958	6	14
1958 and after	3	15

n.a.: not available.

Source: Compiled by the author.

   It is clear that the balance of age and rank in the Cabinet and Council implies a movement whose adherents were born and grew up under fascism, and who had also achieved status and some degree of power under that system. Although the representatives elected to the MFA assembly may include a higher proportion of junior officers and younger men whose service academy experience and military role were not unrelated to the machinery of the provisional government in such that the Council and Cabinet personnel are their elected leaders. Perhaps the senior officers in the movement were marginal persons in the senior ranks. However, at the time of the revolution, the MFA included many senior officers, like Spinola, who were mainstream career men and not enthusiastic leaders of their forces in insurrection. The MFA comprised more than 50 percent of the total officer corps.

Because of Portugal's membership in NATO, almost all of the officers had had working experience in England, France, Holland, Germany, or Italy. Many had also been stationed in the United States. Several of the naval officers said that their experience in France, absorbing French political philosophy and observing activist organizations, had served to politicize and radicalize them. Other officers took university degrees in the United States during the period when the antiwar and student movements were questioning the legitimacy of foreign wars, imperialism, and institutional violence.

In fact, the MFA's political socialization bears a striking resemblance to the socialization in the student movements of the 1960s. As one senior air force officer described it:

> We would study and talk about our problems in our small group; then we would put the issue to our delegates, who would discuss them at the central meetings and bring back recommendations. We would study these, discuss them, and give our votes to the delegate, who would transmit the result to the next central meeting, so that each time you knew exactly how many people were in favor of one solution and how many were against it. We had a lot of small meetings, a lot of work at that time.[5]

It is important to note that the MFA took deliberate steps to politically socialize itself. Their experience of political systems and ideologies left them very sensitive to the paucity of political awareness among the Portuguese people. In many social aspects the MFA recognized they were really in the same condition as the peoples of Third World countries.

At the same time, the Portuguese people were quite aware that their government had asserted its hegemony by force, and that it spoke for no one but the people in the government itself. As an MFA senior officer described it:

It was very hard to try to tell the Portuguese
people, whether they came from the rural north,
or the Latifundi in the south, or from the mountains of Guarda, that the military service and
sacrifice required of them was to defend their
country. The government had to try to tell them
that to die in the jungles of Angola, was like dying in Lisbon. . . . It was very difficult for
these people to believe that, because for so many
years they had not received anything from Angola. That's when the armed forces began to
understand that the arms they had to defend the
people were being used to destroy the people.
Angola, Mozambique, and Guinea were places
where people had gone to get rich and it was only
a certain class who got anything from it. In this
war, the awareness of both groups--the people
and the military--was intensified by the contradiction imposed on them for 13 years of colonial
wars.[6]

There remains one knotty aspect of the MFA's political socialization. How is it that the officers, rather than the enlisted men,
formulated the rebellion? When U.S. casualties and civilian alienation increased as a result of the escalation of war in Southeast Asia,
it was the enlisted men who in scattered instances refused to fight
and, in some cases, killed their junior officers. Likewise, during
the campaign in Korea, the U.S. prisoners of war who refused re-
patriation were men in the low ranks[7] rather than officers. Certainly in the African wars, the officers were never as exposed or
vulnerable as were the men in the ranks. Why did the revolution
not start with the draftees?

Part of the reason is that draftees in Portugal often left the
country rather than go into the army. In addition, large numbers of
men in service deserted: some estimates range as high as 15,000.
There were also instances in which units refused to fight. In Guinea,
without announcing an insurrection, Portuguese units had ceased
fighting months before the revolution was proclaimed. In Mozambique there had been a similar situation.

But the crucial differences in political awareness and political
efficacy between the officers and the enlisted men were attributable
to differences in education. Most of the men in the ranks had the
equivalent of an elementary school education or less. They were
unaccustomed to taking political action, and especially to insubordination to a hierarchical authority. Of course, because Portugal

enforced universal military service and maintained its draftees in service for four years--longer than any other European army--there was also a high proportion of highly educated young men in the military. The university graduates and young professionals were inducted into the officer corps. The career officers who became the MFA were among the most highly educated of all. Thus, while the distinction of class origins no longer played a key role in distinguishing officers from rank and file, there was a definite distinction by educational level. Progress in the educational system through the universities had provided officers with the "discontinuity" experience requisite for reorientation toward traditional authority systems. Students at institutions of higher education, by nature of their location in the major cities and nonuniversity housing, were continually confronted by the kinds of situations described by Dawson and Prewitt in their hypothetical case. [8]

It was not in the process of military training that the officers became antifascists, but in their condition as students when they experienced that which is common for students. One of the experiences shared by university students in Lisbon during a five- or six-year period of the 1960s was a student cooperative bookstore, through which students could order books and periodicals from any country. Facility in other languages helped them to read Marx and Engels in French, or James Connolly in English, and Marcuse and Böll in German. As a consequence, one may find among the MFA officers an amazing breadth of knowledge and memorized passages from works which only now are being published in the Portuguese language; and only since the revolution have they been imported into Portugal legally in any language. Yet, during the years of its existence, the student book co-op functioned above ground. As one officer said, "Because if you are not allowed to do something--if you are cut off from it--we, especially as Portuguese, will try to do it."[9]

The generation of activists, both civilian and military, would seem to be predominantly between 30 and 50. This is substantiated by the ages and experiences of civilian cabinet ministers and leftist party leaders, who are also in that generation. Of these, the eldest is Alvaro Cunhal who, like President Gomes, is 61. They were therefore too young to have personally experienced the democratic era of Portuguese politics between 1910 and 1926, and they were for the most part too old to be part of the international student rebellion of the 1960s. Among Irish revolutionary Republicans, there is a familial or clan socialization process by which membership in a particular family, and pride in that identity, almost mandates the revolutionary aspirations of each new generation. [10] But with the exception of Dr. Mario Soares, whose father played a leading role in the earlier democratic state, few of the present leadership came from families with a tradition of revolution or leftist ideology.

The experience of Portuguese youth with fascism was marginal and increasingly negative. One MFA officer, about 50 years old, described it this way:

> I believe that fascism in Portugal did never have
> the capability to mobilize people. I remember not
> many years ago that even Salazar did not have his
> party, that after so many years he did not have the
> capability of having a party. He could not even with
> all his force or might, organize a party. So I think
> that people become gradually more and more aware
> that what we had here was a political system of re-
> pression which was put to the service of very few
> people and everybody else was just a victim and
> compelled to work for that small group. In the be-
> ginning you could go to a small village or a small
> town north or south; you'd find young people and
> older people in fascist organizations, but even those
> became demoralized and apathetic. I remember
> when I was in high school; the first years of high
> school, there was the organization of Portuguese
> Youth, which was a kind of Nazi organization--uni-
> forms and all that. In my first 2 years of high
> school that organization was still leading and by my
> third and fourth year it had disappeared by inertia.
> Nobody had any enthusiasm--no people, no idealism
> in that, you see. It was just a way of living and a
> way of exploiting, allowing people to exploit people. [11]

But 50 years is extreme longevity for a fascist government. Few others have lasted so long. This in itself suggests that new generations were being socialized into the system in an orderly progression and that apathy or disaffection were the only alternatives. Although the political police system had extended manpower and operations considerably in each new decade, this in itself was not necessarily a response to the growth of active subversion or revolutionary development. In fact, the political police quelled even minor threats to the regime by incarcerating or executing recognized leaders of antigovernment groups, and these actions seemed to have had a different effect. In explaining this phenomenon, an MFA officer cited a Spanish study comparing the Spanish and Portuguese political personality:

> This compares the Portuguese to the Spanish and
> it says that Spanish are very exuberant and Portu-

guese are very quiet and calm. It says that Spanish are like the bull, always fighting. It compares
the Portuguese with the goat because it is quiet,
it accepts everything up to a moment and at that
moment he goes and destroys everything. Then
he is calm again. I think that this is very clever
because it has happened a lot of times with us.
Even with censorship, without freedom of press
everybody knew what was going on. Everybody
knew that the big politicians, some of them, got
a lot of money because of the public foundations,
public work and things like that. Even people at
the beginning, youth who believed in fascism
gradually lost their faith. [12]

One of the most serious problems both for the revolutionaries
and for the Portuguese people now and in the years ahead, is their
relative lack of indigenous political and behavioral models for the
leftist humanist society suggested in the MFA program. While there
are models for successful revolution in Portuguese history, and even
models for democratization, there have been few alternate social
role models. Fifty years of fascism engendered a "social self"[13] in
response to the expectations of a paternalistic, authoritarian, and
pyramidal society. Socialization itself was a function of the social
control mechanisms which the society adopted in order to perpetuate
its values, and the institutional forms assured the dissemination and
enforcement of the norms. The military institution, for example, is
predicated on the system of society recognized as the nation-state.
The nation-state itself is viewed as in jeopardy from those outside of
it, and therefore must be defended by its military institution. Thus,
their very existence within the context of the nation-society, is predicated on (1) external malevolent forces and (2) the value of or serving (conserving) the extant nation-society. The only function then
of the military is a conservative function. [14]

Ordinarily the self-selection and normative behavior of officer
candidates assures that those who reach high ranks will have incorporated the ideological and behavioral values of their society into
their individual personas. [15] Portugal is a unique instance where
these generalizations failed to apply. However, it is well to look
also at the organization and movements in the civilian sector of Portuguese life, in order to test whether generally held expectations of
social role behavior and models differed from those that the regime
attempted to disseminate.

The MFA themselves made an analysis of the political culture
of Portuguese society as it was manipulated and shaped to bring the

people's value systems into closer conformity with polity. In November 1974, the MFA Bulletin published their analysis:

> Culture is always conditioned by its period of
> time and represents its humanity insofar as it
> corresponds to the ideas and desires, the neces-
> sities and hopes of an historical situation; in this
> it is also a quest for constant development.
>
> Culture is a dangerous weapon for oppressive
> systems because while it leads to an understand-
> ing of social phenomena it creates the necessity
> to alter them. As science and technology pro-
> gress, societies must follow in development in
> order to adapt themselves to their new relation-
> ship with production. Because of this we have
> lived through 48 years of mystification while the
> development of our country remains one of the
> lowest in Europe. They managed to keep the
> relationship with production in the condition in
> which it had been so that there would be no ne-
> cessity to alter social relationships and privi-
> leges.
>
> To this end, they cultivated the myth of the
> "good peasant" for whom the appropriate role
> was "to know how to read and write and to be
> happy. . . ." Culture was restricted to the
> elites of privileged positions and disconnected
> from the problems of reality. Literature and
> art were mystified in order to hide reality.
> The social conditions, real phenomena and con-
> flicts of our time have been transposed to fantasy
> outside of time. They sought alienation rather
> than understanding. The regime installed in 1926
> closed schools and reduced the length of time for
> study. Any improvement of the cultural level of
> the population would fatally involve changes and
> this is not what they aspired toward.
>
> But it is impossible to indefinitely maintain a
> country in mystification and because of that, the
> 25th of April happened as the victory of a whole
> people, who wanted change. . . .
>
> Culture cannot be imposed, culture is born
> out of the people. It is in the everyday battle
> that culture is created. We must devote our-
> selves to taking to the people that which belongs

to the people by setting out on a campaign of
cultural dynamization.[16]

This theme has been repeated in various forms since the revolution and was of considerable concern in the planning for the revolution. There were several cultural variables which were expanded
upon and utilized by the Salazarist regime in order to ensure that the
political socialization of the masses did not evolve in a direction
which would endanger the regime. The institutions of the society
were employed to reinforce this objective.

First, Salazar's 1944 Concordat with the Vatican assured that
Catholicism, the dominant religious affiliation of the Portuguese
population would not only institutionally support his regime, but
would, through its own anti-Marxist ideology, provide still another
deterrent to the spread of leftist revolt.

Second, the Latifundi--large irrigated plantations which provided the major cereal crops--were not made economical by utilization of agricultural technology. The absentee owners were able to
enjoy the continued profits of their estates while the sharecropping
farmers, living under the happy peasant myth, were totally pauperized. Similarly, in the north, where landholdings were small and
the terrain more difficult, neither irrigation nor technology nor
agricultural cooperatives were initiated. Again, the myth of the
happy peasant was supplied as the cultural history.

Third, local government was monopolized and corrupted to
function as another institutional control agent preventing change.

Fourth, education was maintained as a private enterprise
privilege. State schools as well as church schools maintained total
responsibility for the curricular and extracurricular lives of the
students. They provided traditional role models and politically safe
instruction. Because of limitations on the number of schools, geographic accessibility, programs, and residence facilities, even
secondary level education became the prerogative of the most moti-
vated and politically acceptable. Administration of all educational
institutions was hierarchical, nonparticipatory, and authoritarian.
Student revolts against the irrelevance of the curriculum and teaching,
which broke out at Coimbra University in 1959, were quelled by force,
as was customary.

Tables 4.2, 4.3, and 4.4 provide some index of the proportion
of the population for whom education was accessible. Even the basic
compulsory seven years of attendance was not enforceable given the
distribution of facilities. For those who did matriculate through
these grades, their education for citizenship consisted of obedience
training, that is, stressing adherence to traditional authorities,
loyalty to the state, and filial duty.

TABLE 4.2

Educational Establishments
(scholastic year 1972-73)

Branch of Education	Number of Establishments
Primary	16,404
Preparatory cycle	1,140
High school (liceu)	461
Professional, technical	190
Other secondary schooling	100
Normal school	138
Median technical	12
Higher education	60

Source: Ministry for Education and Culture, data compiled and released March 1975.

TABLE 4.3

Teaching Personnel

Branch of Education	Scholastic Year	Number of Teachers
Primary	1972-73	31,312
Preparatory cycle	1972-73	12,919
	1973-74	16,596
High school (liceu)	1972-73	9,138
	1973-74	10,172
Professional, technical	1972-73	8,764
	1973-74	9,540
Normal school	1972-73	997
Median technical	1972-73	620
	1973-74	560
Other secondary schooling	1972-73	1,480
	1973-74	1,534
Higher education	1972-73	3,433

Source: Data referring to scholastic year 1973-74 derived from the Preliminary Inquiry concerning teachers and students of the basic, preparatory, and secondary education programs. The inquiry was carried out at the beginning of that school year by the Ministry for Education and Culture, March 1975.

TABLE 4.4

Students Matriculated

Branch of Education	Scholastic Year	Number of Students Matriculated
Primary	1972-73	976,734
	1973-74	934,164
Preparatory cycle	1972-73	202,752
	1973-74	234,092
High school (liceu)	1972-73	178,547
	1973-74	159,328
Technical professional	1972-73	140,195
	1973-74	136,485
Normal school	1972-73	7,470
Median technical	1972-73	11,362
	1973-74	10,443
Other secondary schooling	1972-73	11,727
	1973-74	14,021
Higher education	1972-73	53,999

Source: Data referring to the scholastic year 1973-74 are derived from the Preliminary Inquiry concerning teachers and students
of the basic, preparatory, and secondary education programs. The
inquiry was carried out at the beginning of that school year. Information provided by the Ministry of Education and Culture, March
1975.

THE SOCIALIST HERITAGE

Despite vigorous attempts to obscure from the people's mem-
ories the heritage of political role models which would be antithetical
to the survival of the fascist regime, this heritage survived. On
January 10, 1975, the history of the existence of a socialist party in
Portugal was 100 years old. The old Socialist Party had existed
from 1875 until 1933, and even earlier, in 1856, there was a
communard-proletariat class movement, which had sympathizers
among the progressive intellectual circles in Lisbon and from among
the working classes, typographers, and tobacco workers. In the
1870s several organizations developed in Lisbon which were affiliated with international workers' democratic socialist or Marxist
groups. In 1872 the first organized labor strikes occurred in Lisbon,
among workers in typography, metallurgy, and tobacco. By 1875,

when the Socialist Party was officially founded, labor organizing and class consciousness had been actively in process for two decades.[17]

From 1887 on, the anarchist and anarcho-communist political organizations were gaining adherents, and by 1909, at the first Union Congress, the revolutionary syndicalists had emerged as the dominant force and the Socialist Party was dying.

The General Confederation of Workers emerged in 1909-19 and gradually abandoned revolutionary syndicalism for anarcho-syndicalism.

The philosophic differences among the leftists of late nineteenth and early twentieth century Europe have important parallels in the present. However, at that earlier period, syndicalism--the organizing of the working class through common struggle--was a modus operandi. As the political ideologies defined and shaped themselves, there were apparent differences between the communist-syndicalists; the anarcho-syndicalists, and finally, the revolutionary syndicalists. In contemporary terms, such positions may be reflected in the Portuguese Communist Party, the MRPP or CP-ML, and PRP or AOC, respectively. The Revolutionary Anarchists, then as now, were a relatively small group of intellectuals and idealists who captured the imagination and loyalty of some working-class syndicalists.[18]

Perhaps one of the major appeals of the anarchist movements in the Iberian peninsula generally, and in Portugal specifically, is their decentralization objective. While Portugal has never had the equivalents to the Basque or Catalonian Separatist movements, much of the social, political, and economic organization of Portugal has been regional or even more effective in local districts. The disparities between life in Guarda and Lisbon, or between Alenteja and Coimbra, are evidenced in almost every dimension.

In May 1975, scrawled on a wall in a village near Setubal was the slogan "Anarchy is life, life is Anarchy." Was this a timely re-emergence of political memory?

On May 28, 1926, the parties opposing the Salazar coup were the Socialist Party, the Democratic Left, and the Communist Party. All the other parties, including the Republican and Democratic parties, supported the coup and confirmed that they would allow themselves to be replaced by an authoritarian regime.

In 1927, the leftist political organizations were made illegal, although the Socialist Party was allowed to continue until 1933, when they held their last legal conference in Coimbra. It has been suggested by the prominent scholar, Cesar Oliviera, that the reason the Socialist Party was allowed to continue was that Salazar wanted to use it as a bridge to the working class, since it had their respect, and he knew that as a party it was weak, vacillating, and without a base of organization.[19]

The last gasp of the Republican regime had been in the government of the leftist faction of that party, the Democratic Left (ED),
which had begun to institute agrarian reforms in 1925. This initiative
brought out a strong coalition of capitalist forces to depose the regime. At the same time, labor, the Communist Party, the Labor
Confederation (CGS), and the other factions of the left, expressed
themselves in a major demonstration which could have, according to
Olivera, resulted in the development of a popular front of the left.
Instead, the Republican Party, in deference to the right, put down
the cabinet, and acquiesced into what finally became the destruction
both of itself and of political alternatives. On July 3, 1926 General
Costa da Gomes entered Lisbon in triumph, formed a triumvirate,
was deposed by his military colleagues and replaced by General
Carmona in July 1926.

After the destruction of the Socialist Party, the only part of
the left which persisted as an organized force and resistance movement was the Communist Party.

In 1945, a group--some of whom had been expelled or had resigned from the Communist Party--began to organize another opposition force, the Movimento de Unidade Democratica--Movement of
United Democrats (MUD). As a consciousness-raising and basically
urban middle class, nonideological, liberal movement they were
primarily centered in Lisbon. They had been given impetus by
Salazar's promise of free elections. Some of the main figures re-
emerged in the contemporary Socialist Party and in some of the
other leftist movement and political parties after April 25.

The anarcho-syndicalists had been totally destroyed by imprisonment and murder in 1934. Over 300 of them were jailed, and
many, never heard from again, were presumed dead.[20]

From 1939 on, the Communist Party had gained sufficient
strength to organize unified popular front opposition by initiating
clandestine labor unions, student groups, and movements.

In 1958, the MUD backed the candidacy of General Humberto
Delgado for president, while the Communist Party gave its support
to the candidacy of Orlindo Vicente. One of the paradoxes of this
election campaign was that masses of people turned out in behalf of
Delgado, who cautioned against disruption or "taking to the streets,"
while Vicente and the Communist Party, who were determined on
moving the masses into the streets, had very little mass following
and, in the end, joined in the campaign for Delgado's candidacy.
Mario Soares, leader of the present Socialist Party, worked closely
with Delgado in this campaign.

The period of 1958-62 marked the most intensive period of
organizing and consciousness-raising activity by the antifascist opposition. It culminated in 1962 with massive demonstrations,

strikes, and an eight-hour battle of agricultural workers in two
provinces, Alenteja and Euvora.

According to Oliviera, the events of 1962 marked an important
turning point in the strategy and tactics of political opposition. The
events of that year had aroused many segments of the population,
and the strikes and demonstrations were met by massive repression.
Many were killed and hundreds jailed. Many others went into exile
or underground to begin long-range planning. The Movement of
Revolutionary Action (MAR) arose at that point as a separate leftist
movement apart from the Social Democrats and the Communist
Party. Their aim was to form a front of leftist action, a kind of
popular liberation movement.

By 1969, the younger generation, those who had been student
strikers in 1962, had evolved into two major movements in conflict
with each other on theoretical grounds and both in conflict with the
Communist Party. Both groups were Marxist-Leninist action movements, their major difference was in regard to scope with one de-
siring broad-front Socialist Party politics and the other calling for
developing a new and native Portuguese interpretation of a Marxist
perspective. These were university-based movements and as such
had a strong commitment to formulating a sound theoretical basis
for revolution. It was clear to them after living through the events
of 1962, and studying the earlier attempts to depose the fascist regime through parliamentary or legalistic means, that such activity
could only ensure defeat and greater repression. They recognized
that they had to move outside of the existing system in order to
overturn it.[21]

In addition to these major revolutionary movements, the 1960s
also produced movements for social change based on Catholic humanist principles. Although there was scant support for even minor changes among the clergy and hierarchy, these movements
served to extend the general revolutionary ethos into yet another
sphere.

Movements as such were not necessarily in contradiction to
the enforced one-party system. They operated as pressure groups,
or as interest groups within or transcending the officially recognized organizations. Their expressed purpose as pressure and
consciousness-raising groups made them somewhat safe.

Meanwhile, in the dominant socioeconomic bloc, the combined industrialists and Latifundists, a major rupture occurred.
The gremio system under the Caetano regime lost the necessary political support for extending and supporting its interests (see Chapter 3). Thus, the basis of support which had initially propelled the
regime to power, the interests which had sustained it in power despite all kinds of opposition, found that the machinery of government

had become less relevant to their continued prosperity and progress.
At the same time the political maturation of the Portuguese people
at large had been affected through the process of the contradiction
of the authoritarian state with their basic cultural belief in human
nature as positive.

For the revolutionaries in the armed forces, the contradictions
between their aspirations for personal identity (as defenders of their
people and nation) and the reality they faced daily over a prolonged
time, the forms of political organization and action with which they
came in contact both at home and in the African wars, the political
history of their own country and the developments in other countries,
and finally their pride in their nationality all determined their course.
They set out to politically socialize themselves and emerged as
catalysts in the political socialization of their countrymen.

NOTES

1. Overheard by the author in Sesimbra, May 2, 1975.
2. Richard E. Dawson and Kenneth Prewitt, Political Socialization (Boston: Little, Brown, 1969), pp. 84-86.
3. Phillippe Schmitter, in the paper already cited in Chapter
2, maintains that those who entered the military academies after
1958 formed the dissident party because of their frustrated mobility
aspirations. This theme is also reflected in the paper by D.
Wheeler, "Days of Wine and Carnations: The Portuguese Revolution of 1974," New Hampshire Council on World Affairs Bulletin.
The misconception has also been perpetuated in the popular media.
Part of the misconception may have been fostered by the expression
"captains' revolution" which was directly translated from the Portuguese, but ignoring the multiple meanings of "Capitao." For example, in naval rankings "Capitao-tenante" means Lieutenant Com-
mander--a rank considerably higher than the U.S. "Captain."
Furthermore, because promotions were being delayed, many of the
individuals at Capitao ranks were older than would be expected.
4. Direct quotes from interviews with MFA men.
5. Ibid.
6. Ibid.
7. Adam Yarmolinsky, The Military Establishment: Its
Impacts on American Society (New York: Harper & Row, 1971).
8. Dawson and Prewitt, op. cit.
9. Interviews with MFA, December 1972.
10. Rona M. Fields, A Society on the Run: A Psychology of
Northern Ireland (London: Penguin Ltd., 1973). In the chapter
entitled "Patriot Children," the background of young members of

junior paramilitary organizations in Northern Ireland indicates
these familiar political-revolutionary orientations. This is also
mentioned in Morris Fraser's Children in Conflict (London: Secker
& Warburg, 1973).

11. Interviews with MFA, December 1974.

12. Ibid.

13. Dawson and Prewitt, op. cit. The concept of the "social
self" emanating from such social theorists as Cooley and Mead, emphasizes how group relationships affect behavior and attitudes.

14. Samuel P. Huntington, The Soldier and the State (Cambridge: Harvard University Press, 1957). The concept is also discussed at length in Morris Janowitz, The Professional Soldier; A
Social and Political Portrait (New York: The Free Press Paperback,
1960; London: Macmillan, 1971).

15. Dawson and Prewitt, op. cit.

16. Movimento-Boletim Informativo das Forcas Armadas,
November 12, 1974, trans. by Milea Froes and R. M. Fields.

17. Cesar Oliviera MFA E Revolucao Socialista (Lisbon:
Diabril Editora, SARL, 1975).

18. Ibid.

19. Ibid.

20. Ibid.

21. Ibid.

From its inception, the MFA had of necessity included all
career officers who disagreed with the way their country was being
governed. One year after the revolution the MFA was still characterized by wide diversity in political opinions and ideological commitments. But during that year, there was considerable narrowing of
the differences, both through attrition and through the socializing influence members had on each other.

In the course of the first year the MFA revolutionized itself.
Some of its original leaders left hurriedly in March 1975 for France
and Brazil, after two attempted coups. Through the MFA Democratization and Dynamization Programs, membership came to include
noncommissioned officers and several civilians in consultative capacities. It is important to recognize that these membership shifts did
not result in civil war, nor did the organization itself split into warring factions. Furthermore, there were no executions or vendettas
after the September 28, 1974 or March 11, 1975 attempted coups
even after the armed counterrevolutionary actions on March 11.

Some revolutions mark their birth from the start of armed conflict. Others take the date of organizing their armed forces, and
still others the date of the new government's accession to power. The
MFA considers April 25, 1974 the starting date of its revolution, and
although on that date MFA members became the provisional government, that position had not been their revolutionary objective but
served rather as the necessary springboard for the revolution. They
describe the events of April 25 as a coup (a change of government by
force), but the revolution itself, they say, commenced on September
28, 1974. On that date, their one-time leader, General Antonio
Spinola, was forced to resign from the Presidency because of his
close relationship with those forces that advocated changing the

leadership without changing the sociopolitical or economic structure of Portugal.

On April 25, 1974, the MFA included personalities as diverse as General Antonio Spinola and then Colonel Otelo Saraiva de Carvalho. One year later, the charismatic Carvalho was ubiquitous and Spinola, the herald of the revolution, was writing his memoirs in Brazil. These two figures emerged as the polar stars of the intense drama which the MFA calls "Freedom Year One in Portugal."[1]

Their conflict as individuals was inevitable, since each represented to the other a potential threat to the revolution. Both were army men, Spinola from the generation for which pride and honor were the essential attributes of a career officer, Carvalho from a younger generation more concerned with social justice and sensitized to analyzing actions in terms of their political implications. Each man was cognizant of the disaster befalling his country, each was aware of the personal risks of revolution and willing to take those risks, each recognized the necessity for implementing a new social and political order. Spinola had articulated his vision of a new Portugal in a book which challenged every dimension of the established fascist regime. Carvalho, more given to speaking and acting than to writing, had managed to maneuver the metropolitan-based military forces around Lisbon into a disciplined army in position for the bloodless coup of April 25, 1974.

Even while Carvalho and Spinola worked together to overthrow the Caetano regime, each had a different vision of the sociopolitical scheme which should supplant it. They came from very different backgrounds. Spinola at one point had resigned his commission to take a top management job in the United Manufacturing Company (CUF), one of the major industrial companies in Portugal. Carvalho had no aspirations for a business career, preferring his military role in combination with political action. Their roles in the provisional government suited their experiences and expertise. It was not surprising that Carvalho would be security chief and Spinola, a very prominent figure who was already a symbol of controversy and antiestablishment sentiment, chosen as nominal leader of the MFA and new chief of state.

Spinola, whose ideal of the future of Portuguese society was articulated in Portugal and the Future,[2] contributed to the formulation of the MFA program and, months after he resigned the presidency, argued that he had always adhered to that program. The program itself (see Appendix 5.A) was relatively straightforward and unambiguous. The three guiding principles--democratization, decolonization, and development, all in a socialist context--while agreed upon by all parties to the movement, meant different things to different individuals. To Spinola, for instance, "decolonization" meant forming a commonwealth kind of government in which the African

participants would have local autonomy but look for economic and international policies to Lisbon. The pluralistic concept of political
party participation meant to Spinola a coalition of centrist parties,
incorporating the economics of private enterprise with an extension
of the public domain into service functions--social security and unemployment benefits, health care, extension of public education
facilities, and governmental cooperation at all levels with private
enterprise.

Whether one believes that this economic philosophy reflects a
naive idealism or a commitment to a viable social-democratic ideology, it suggests the possibility of maintaining democratic justice
within a free enterprise system--workers would share in the decision
making within corporations that would remain under private ownership. Spinola opposed nationalization of industry as "state capitalism" and thus no more democratic than the monopoly capitalism
prevalent in advanced industrial societies. He also advocated immediate local elections as the process through which to guarantee
maximal participation by the people in choosing their own political
destiny, and warned against the extension of the military force in
political life. [3]

Spinola considered his governance of Guinea as a model for
stimulating and evolving a self-determining, self-governing state.
Yet, during his five years as military administrator there, the fighting escalated, PAIGC succeeded in gaining territory, and by May
1973 the Portuguese military and civil authority was all but entirely
eroded.

Through all of his experience, Spinola retained a vivid fear of
what he thought of as the disruptive potential of the Communist Party,
and he viewed the masses of his people as the prospective prey of
this usurper of freedom. In fact, he had less fear of the revolution
being overtaken by the forces of reaction than he had of it being subverted by the forces of Marxism. His political thinking was shaped
by his belief in the myth of a monolithic communist conspiracy. [4]
His relative conservatism within the MFA is also suggested by the
fact that he feared moving too rapidly. He took the world economic
crisis and Portugal's particularly weakened economic condition to
be warning indicators against trying to move rapidly into political
socialism.

The initial government formed by Spinola included Professor
Palma Carlos (as Prime Minister), a man who had governmental responsibility under the previous regime; the Junta of National Salvation, consisting of seven generals and admirals believed to be "democratic"; and the Council of State, which included the seven men of the
junta, seven MFA officers, and seven civilians, some of whose positions in the previous regime had given them political legitimacy.

The first cabinet itself, all civilians, was an impossible coalition of contradictions. Its membership ranged from Alvaro Cunhal, long-time leader of the Portuguese Communist Party, to an economics minister whose idea of revolution was to initiate an American economic system immediately.

Spinola, like the others, had had little experience with democratic government, and his interpretation of the MFA program called for a "holding action" kind of provisional government which would quickly get a constitution in order while the people elected new representatives. Spinola had served under Franco in Spain and had spent part of World War II as an observer with the German army. His political sympathies were National Socialist, with a strong central government and elite cadres directing the machinery and a Gaullist kind of presidency. [5]

By July 10, this first cabinet had fallen apart and the behind-the-scenes revolutionary struggle commenced. This was the first real test of the political acumen and strength of the MFA. The issues being tested were decolonization and self-determination for the African territories, direct action by the government in social and economic affairs as against waiting for the new constitution and government, and the coherence of the cabinet itself. Spinola was quickly seen to be out of step with the MFA Assembly. So too were the "centrist" parties which had been in the crucial economics and finance positions on July 13. A new prime minister, the MFA candidate Vasco Dos Santos Goncalves, brought together a cabinet more responsive to the program plans of the MFA (see Appendix 5. D). This cabinet included seven MFA leaders with ministers selected from the PPD (Popular Democrats), the PSP (Portuguese Socialist Party), PCP (Portuguese Communist Party), and several nonparty independents.

The process of cabinet decision making was designed to minimize party differences and maximize action. Each minister was charged with organizing the cabinet for his or her own ministry, appraising conditions, and formulating action programs. Cabinet meetings, like those of the MFA Executive, were to proceed by consensus. But consensus with their president and the junta remained a serious problem. The ministers were ready to set a new track record for getting a socialist system under way, and the junta and Spinola were saying, in a sense, "We have to start the industrial revolution and reach advanced capitalism before we can think about socialism." Spinola said:

> We will only be a truly democratic country when
> we activate the institutions through which the
> citizen can concretely intervene. These institu-

tions must comprise three essential fields: community life, economic activities, and political
participation. . . . At the economic level there
will have to be efficient and representative interest associations. [6]

Between July 17, when Goncalves and the new cabinet took office, and September 28, the date of the second crisis, President
Spinola became afraid of the legalized Communist Party and their
participation in the government. He himself had named Cunhal to
the cabinet, but the presence of Cunhal, the militant activism of not
only the PCP, but the myriad political parties which sprang up to
the left of it, the increased agitation to reach a settlement in Angola,
and the depth of the economic problems facing the country seem to
have overwhelmed him.

In pursuit of economic stability, Spinola and his closest associates set out to reassure and gain the support of the major monied
families. Many of them had already begun sending their fortunes
out of Portugal after the aborted Caldas Barracks rising in March,
which had preceded the coup. By April 26, $120 million had already
left the country, and despite the freeze placed on withdrawals, the
process continued. [7] Portuguese, French, and English banks outside
of Portugal were encouraging Portuguese emigrants to keep their
money out of Portugal. Factories and small businesses began to lay
off workers rather than meet the new minimum wage requirements,
and foreign-owned businesses had strikes which were alleged to have
been masterminded by management in order to force the government
to provide guarantees against new labor demands. [8]

To make matters even worse, foreign orders for Portuguese
goods were cancelled, and Portugal's place in the vital Index to Investment in the United Kingdom was downgraded from Class A to
Class C. [9]

The MFA Coordinating Council developed several mechanisms
for heading off and dealing with perceived threats. One group was
formed into the Fifth Division, Armed Forces Movement Educational
Group (EMGFA), to function as the information and communications
arm of the MFA. This structure followed an organizational program
which had been created by the MFA in Guinea in June and which had
proved successful as a forum and as a vehicle for recruiting and ac-
tivating the MFA there. On September 9, the first issue of the
Movimento 25 de Abril: Boletim Informativo Das Forcas Armadas
(The April 25 Movement: Information Bulletin of the Armed Forces)
was published under the auspices of this new communications group.

The biweekly Bulletin carried program and policy statements,
news on the progress of the revolution, notices of legislative actions

taken by the coordinating council and by the MFA assembly, statements on economic and social conditions, explanations of program
innovations, and interpretations of international events. It grew
from four to eight pages within a few months and was made available
to newsstands and by subscription. What was intended to be a kind
of house organ and possibly a means of explaining to the general
population the rationale and purposes of MFA actions soon became a
widely circulated, popular periodical, which regularly included a
new "Pop Art" style poster. The communications group was also
responsible for MFA radio programs.

The second important organization formed during this period
was a special contingent charged with maintaining internal security.
Leadership of this group was given to now Brigadier Carvalho, who
was charged with specific responsibility for regional military action.
Carvalho became one of the most colorful and controversial figures
in the MFA. Unlike the majority of his colleagues, who seemed to
prefer collective anonymity rather than personality status, Carvalho
became a symbol of MFA progressivism. His instinctive sense for
drama and absolute candor have made him a favorite target for reporters.

It was Carvalho in an interview published January 4, 1975, who
accused Spinola of negotiating with U.S. President Richard Nixon for
American aid to subdue the liberation forces in Mozambique and
Angola. It was Carvalho who accused the CIA of instigating the coup
attempted on March 11, 1975. And it was Carvalho in May 1975,
who, during a serious interparty crisis, told the press that perhaps
the MFA would just abolish the political parties.[10] But Carvalho always made it clear when he was speaking for himself. It was because of his position and charisma that his statements were often
misinterpreted by the press, especially the foreign press, as official MFA statements.

An incident that occurred on April 25, 1975, the day of the
elections for the Constituent Assembly, illustrates Carvalho's in-
stinct for publicity. An international press corps of nearly 1,000
reporters was gathered at the Gulbenkian Foundation in Lisbon,
where press headquarters had been arranged. Just before the elections President Costa Gomes, Prime Minister Goncalves, and many
of the ministers of state and members of the Revolutionary Council
had addressed the press. During a relatively quiet period, while
many of the journalists were expecting word of violent outbreaks and
illegal practices at the polls, there was a sudden loud noise outside.
Reporters rushed to the door and saw a huge crowd gathered at the
gates, Military Commando Security Forces (COPCON) soldiers with
their weapons at the ready, and a military helicopter whirring to a
stop on the lawn. While photographers took photos and reporters

ran to the teletypes, Carvalho emerged from the helicopter and proceeded with his guards into the building, laconically remarking, "No
press conference now" while he engaged in a half hour's conversation
with an MFA colleague, the crowd swelled and the journalists waited.
Then the chief of COPCON exited as he had arrived, with no statement. Several days later, when Carvalho did give a press conference, the auditorium was jammed. He was asked more questions
than any of the ministers of state who had held press conferences
that week.

But prior to September 28, Carvalho was accorded relatively
little importance in the popular press. His role in the events of
late September marked a major turning point in the whole revolution--
both for the MFA and for the people of Portugal.

President Spinola, at the urging of some of his close associates,
had called for a demonstration of solidarity. The chronology of
events as reported in the Bulletin for October 3 was as follows:

Previous Days:
The Prime Minister and the CEMGFA informed
    the President of the Republic of the objectives
    that might be behind a demonstration that
    seemed aimed at taking advantage of the
    sentiments of the Portuguese People.
They advised the President to consider the
    demonstration inopportune.

Thursday, September 26:
In Campo Pequeno there was a bull fight spon-
    sored by the Liga dos Combatentes (League
    of Fighters). The President of the Republic
    was applauded and the Prime Minister and
    the MFA were hissed. At the end of the
    fight there were incidents between reac-
    tionary groups and the population that was
    on the outside.

Friday:
Elements of the Coordinating Commission of the
    Program (CCP) informed the President of the
    Republic of the existence of the conspiracy be-
    hind the demonstration. One of the objectives
    of the demonstration was to substitute an-
    other figure for him not identified with the
    MFA and its Program.

At the end of the afternoon, the unions made appeals through the radio stations to convene
the associations to their respective headquarters.

In Belem, a meeting of the Board [Council] of
Ministers with the President of the Republic
took place. When the meeting was finished
the President of the Republic met in Belem
with the Prime Minister, CEMGFA, Minister
of Defense, and the Commanders of the COPCON,
GNR and PSP; they stayed there until the early
hours of Saturday.

Superior orders were given for occupation of the
radio stations by the GNR and PSP. They were
closed except for the EN [National Station],
the newspapers were closed.

Saturday:

Around 2:30 A.M., the Minister for Social Communication read on the EN a communication of
the provisional government about the demonstration and it was repeated every half hour.

Many foreign radio stations gave notice that there
was a coup in Portugal and that General Spinola
would assume full powers.

During the night of September 27 to 28, an operation began to watch suspect individuals who might
be implicated in a counterrevolutionary plot.

At 7 A.M., approximately, Brigadier Saraiva de
Carvalho arrived at COPCON headquarters accompanied by the Minister of Defense. Around
9:15 A.M. the first communication of the MFA
was read. A communication from the President
of the Republic was given in which he stated that
the demonstration was not to convene. After-
wards, a communication from the MFA cancel-
ing the demonstration was read.

The Prime Minister went to Belem where he
stayed for a few moments. During the day
detentions of suspect individuals continued.

At the end of the afternoon, COPCON substituted
for the GNR and PSP in the radio stations,
which meanwhile began to go on the air.

Sunday:

At 9 A. M. of September 29, the CCP was called
to Belem, where they met with the JSN.

The CCP met with the Junta of National Salvation
and the President proposed disbanding it,
which was not accepted. The CCP presented
a document which states that the MFA withdraws the mandate of the Generals Jaime Silverio Marques, Manoel Diogo Neto, and Galvao
de Melo. Into the room came the news that
armed groups of people were assaulting and
occupying installations of the GNR, in some
places on the south bank of the Tejo.

The meeting was immediately suspended by the
President, who convened the Council of State,
whose members had been already notified the
day before of the meeting for 10 o'clock. The
President of the Republic informed the Council that he proposed to declare a state of
siege. It was verified that the news received
was inaccurate. The consensus of the Council was not in favor of a declaration of state
of siege.

Right after the meeting of the Council of State,
the meeting of the CCP continued with the
JSN. Generals Jaime Silverio Marques and
Galvao de Melo did not attend it. General
Diogo Neto left in the middle of the meeting.

In this meeting it was agreed that the three generals would be dismissed from the JSN and a
proposal for institutionalization of the MFA
was proposed for later consideration by the
President of the Republic and CEMGFA.

This meeting passed in a climate of understanding
and frankness.

After many communications with the MFA, Brigadier Otelo Saraiva de Carvalho on TV read a
communication in which he asked the vigilante
groups guarding the roads to dissolve themselves, for they would be substituted by
forces of COPCON.

It was announced that the President will speak on
TV on September 30 at 11 o'clock. Around
midnight the Prime Minister talked to the
Nation.

Monday:
>Around 11 A. M. , before the Council of State, General Antonio de Spinola resigned the position of President of the Republic. His speech of resignment was transmitted directly by the radio and TV stations.
>
>The Junta de Salvacao Nacional after a telephone call with Admiral Rosa Coutinho, elected as new President of the Republic, General Costa Gomes.
>
>Civil and military elements of the Council declared that they did not agree with the analysis of the situation in Pörtugal that was announced to the country by General Spinola.
>
>Before the members of the Council of State the new President of the Republic, General Francisco Costa Gomes, took the oath.[11]

The effects of the September crisis were reflected in the broadcast speeches given by the new president and the prime minister he reappointed. These speeches also reflect the MFA's new degree of sophistication about the democratic process. Prime Minister Goncalves said:

>We have just lived through the first attack of the reaction against the movement of the 25 of April, in ways that are already classic, and are adopted by reactionaries in all parts of the world. These ways consist of taking advantage of the lack of political preparation of persons who have at heart motives of national interest and of the population, particularly by using activity reused by "slogans,"
>. . . [However] the possibility for the Portuguese people to make a choice about the social economic status in which they want to live is now more probable than ever, because the elections of March will certainly be reached with this governmental cast. . . .[12]

Goncalves spoke of the susceptibility of the Portuguese people to the rhetoric of the previous regime. He recognized that the Salazar-Caetano regime had inspired, for many of them, a fear of socialism and anxiety about progress. He continued: "They agitate the same bug-bears that fascism agitated for 48 years--and it is not amazing if they obtain some success for the ideologies, the mentalities forged,

formed along 48 years, are not modified from one day to another
. . . ."[13] The Prime Minister commented on the cooperation between the military, especially COPCON, and the nonviolent vigilance
committees which were formed by members of PSP and PCP to
screen vehicles entering Lisbon. He then informed the listeners
that the MFA would initiate special efforts to disseminate information to all the people of Portugal:

> We made a revolution, of which the consequences
> are still in process of development. . . . This
> crisis strengthened the conditions of development
> of the democracy in Portugal and permitted our
> positions to come to light. We will take the MFA
> and the FA to all points of the country for the
> people to get to know our objectives. . . .[14]

The new president, General Francisco Costa Gomes, communicated his program in a radio broadcast at 8 P.M. on September
30. He announced that there would be no deviation from the decolonization program of the MFA. He made a special point of stating
that the provisional government would not be bound in any way to
preconceived rigid schemes, but rather, it would adhere to great
principles "to orient the evolution of events to the constant change
of the adjusted political structure."[15]

President Costa Gomes made a plea for unity amongst the Portuguese people and reminded them that they had already enacted a
revolution "simultaneously so deep and so little marked by blood."[16]
He concluded his message with reassurance:

> No Portuguese who loves the people to which he
> belongs ignores today that the work, the order
> and the unity are the essential marks that guar-
> antee the democratic liberties and the respect
> by the fundamental rights of Man. . . .
>   In the general plan is to be able to inter-
> pret into Constitutional Laws the essential points
> of Program of the MFA.
>   I leave you with assurance that the FA, mili-
> tary and militarized, are quickly integrating them-
> selves in the new spirit and are becoming more
> able to guarantee to the Provisional Government
> and to the People, the climate of order and free-
> dom for which we long in order to dedicate our-
> selves to the work with certainty that we are going
> to build a better future, more just more demo-
> cratic.[17]

In the evening of the same day the prime minister gave a press conference at which he said:

> We are, in fact, going through a difficult period.
> It is not without punishment that a country lives
> for 50 years under a fascist regime. At the end
> of 5 months we have problems inherited from the
> former regime that was in flagrant crises, crises
> that were hidden through an iron censorship of in-
> formation and from the exercise of repression of
> all kinds.
>
> Today we have, in fact, problems to solve
> in various sectors of the national life, we have
> the means to solve them.
>
> We do not live in anarchy as was said today.
>
> Will there be a greater proof of civilization
> and of order than what we have gone through in
> these last days in Portugal. We have changed
> the President of the Republic and, today, we did
> not establish [martial law]; life continues nor-
> mally for all persons.
>
> The people walk on the streets and show
> themselves without cordons of security. These
> "controls" that were built up on roads in order
> to hinder the reactionary coup that was planned
> were exercised without violence, but with per-
> suasion and collaboration of the very persons who
> were inspected, with the exception of those that,
> in fact, brought hidden weapons and were not inter-
> ested in showing them. Therefore, we do not live,
> by any means, in anarchy, but on the contrary, this
> country is a country of order.
>
> We have no information that would allow us
> to affirm [Spinola's participation] and we have no
> doubts as to the behavior of Gen. Spinola. The
> Honorable General Spinola was the victim of a
> campaign set up to pretend [intended] to use his
> name but which had goals precisely against him,
> and against Portuguese democracy.
>
> As to the three generals of the JSN I must
> say that a democracy cannot be made without
> democrats, but these gentlemen were not in-
> volved in any coup. [18]

The MFA stepped up its efforts to effectively perform the task
it had set itself--to be the catalyst for the political socialization of

the masses. Immediately after the thwarted coup attempt, the MFA
launched two of its major campaigns: the Cultural Dynamization program and the program for the Democratization of the Armed Forces.
Both campaigns incorporated a little Marx, a little Mao, and elements of Gandhi, Garibaldi, Michael Davitt, and the Peace Corps.
They were basic grass-roots efforts. The more dramatic and far-
reaching campaign began at the ministerial level with an appraisal
of the resources and needs--economic and social--of the country and
its people. This campaign was to culminate in the nationalization of
banks, insurance companies, and large businesses--steel, for instance, and transportation. At the same time the campaign laid the
groundwork for a national social security system, national health
service, minimum wages, a single trade union organization, a press
law, and a judicial system. From this point on, the government
leadership and the MFA won the nickname "the sleepless ones,"
since their meetings would often last all day and into the night.

     In the summer of 1974, university students had organized into
work teams to teach rural peasants to read and write. However,
after they went into the mountains of the north with their knapsacks
and books and settled with the villagers, they quickly realized that
the malnourished, superstitious, and introverted rural poor had
other priorities than literacy. The students then tried to set up cooperatives and appraise communal needs, but soon found themselves
in conflict with the old local priests, the landlords, and the petite
bourgeoisie of the small towns.

     To the rural poor, the students were communists and there-
fore anti-Christian. In fact, the students had been drawn largely
from the various leftist movements, and very few were members of
the Communist Party. The government provided them travel money
and a subsistence allowance. They lived among the peasants and as
nearly as possible survived on the same nutrition. Although the experience demonstrated to them that there were levels of basic needs
which would have to be met before the people would have the strength
and will to learn reading and writing, the students did remain enthusiastic about taking responsibility for working in the countryside.
Many of them suggested that it be made a regular part of their educational requirements.

     The MFA's program for Cultural Dynamization sprang from
idealistic roots close to the sources of the students' project. Grouped
in fives and tens, members of the MFA (as the year proceeded this
included enlisted rank and file as well as officers) went into the countryside to talk with the people and explain the MFA program, the
voting process, and the meaning of their new freedom. On a practical
level, these groups aided farmers and artisans, arranged for supplies
and development facilities, helped people repair houses and farm

equipment, and provided transport to the polls. The ideological
basis for this program was articulated in an editorial in the November 12 issue of the Bulletin:

> The fascists always tried to maintain the Portuguese people in ignorance in order to maintain
> their exploitation of them.
>
> They did not provide for them the necessary
> schools, nor associations for their advancement,
> nor opportunities through which they could know
> and analyze their problems and search for their
> own solutions. For the fascists, it goes without
> saying that cultural affairs were a special gift.
> We, on the contrary, admit that there are diffi-
> culties to enjoying the gifts of the spirit when
> there is no money.
>
> The fascists extolled the virtues of the good,
> tranquil, docile Portuguese people . . . a profound-
> ly reasonable race. . . . And as the fascists pro-
> gressed through long decades they destroyed the
> intellectual life of the Portuguese people through
> censorship, prejudice, tortures and assassina-
> tions.
>
> On April 25 the future commenced. And in
> spite of attempts by the fascists to estrange the
> people, the armed forces have affirmed their con-
> fidence in the program of the MFA as have the
> Portuguese people, whose efforts and knowledge
> and dignity will bring democracy to our country.
>
> On October 25, the Fifth Division of EMGFA
> was appointed to take responsibility for a Program
> of Cultural Dynamization and Political Clarification.
>
> The Program of Cultural Dynamization has
> these objectives: 1. To coordinate and immediate-
> ly support all of the cultural associations of the
> country, and in whatever possible way, spread a
> cultural network throughout the territory, to pro-
> vide a future basis for the cultural life of the Por-
> tuguese people. 2. To actuate politicalization,
> through the effective presence of military groups
> in the population to allow the acceleration of
> reasoned thinking about the situation and the na-
> tion, and to accommodate the situation to facili-
> tate understanding through discussions of the
> program of the MFA.[19]

In the same issue of the Bulletin, the democratization of the armed
forces was outlined. The democratization program was already in
effect in the officer ranks, since promotions and representation had
already been organized along democratic lines. For instance, the
subordinates and superiors of an officer being considered for promotion made recommendations and, along with his peers, were responsible for granting or denying the promotion. The new plan was intended to extend this system into the noncommissioned officer ranks.
Democratization was intended to produce military personnel capable
of questioning orders. The MFA recognized the need for military
discipline as essential for effective operation, and also the need to
end the blind obedience often characteristic of the military.

The idea of democratization had been widely misunderstood.
Some observers saw the democratization decrees as an attempt to
restrict rebellion from the ranks by incorporating a larger proportion of the military into the MFA and broadening the base of support
in order to prevent any antiregime action. To others (more than
those in the armed forces themselves) this was a threat to the traditional process and discipline and could only result in chaos. The
purpose and process were therefore outlined in the Bulletin as much
to quell the misrepresentations as to clarify exactly what was intended. (See Appendix 5.B.)

Even while it was occupied with defining itself and the revolution in Portugal, the MFA was initiating and enacting the decolonization process. This proceeded with alacrity after the resignation of
Spinola and the concomitant surge of renewed confidence in the MFA
on the part of the people. In some instances simultaneous talks were
carried through with several liberation movements. While accords
were signed in Algiers to assure the independence of Guinea-Bissau,
negotiations for the independence of Mozambique had begun in Lusaka.
Within less than a week, the Provisional Government took control in
Mozambique and Portugal and had announced de facto recognition of
the Republic of Guinea-Bissau. (See Appendix 5.C.)

Talks with the leaders of insurgent groups in Guinea-Bissau
and Mozambique had been relatively smooth. In the case of Angola,
however, where Spinola had allegedly requested help from the United
States during his talks with President Richard Nixon in June 1974,
no effective decolonization plan existed prior to President Costa
Gomes' appointment. This knottier problem had been a partial basis
of the discord between Spinola and the other MFA leadership. Spinola
had met with President Mobutu of Zaire in regard to Angola's independence. However, Mobutu's leverage among the liberation armies
of Angola was only in relation to the FNLA through their leader Holden
Roberto. For many of the MFA Council members, the key organizations for an Angolan settlement were the MPLA and UNITA.

By November, the Portuguese provisional government was meeting with the leaders of Sao Tome and Principe independence movements arranging the process of their decolonization.

Having begun with idealism, the MFA developed its ideology as it proceeded, existentially. This is perhaps one of the most difficult aspects for those outside of the movement to understand. The appearance of contradiction between their determination to stay in NATO and their determination to remain independent of the major power blocs is typical of these seeming contradictions. The contradiction between their insistence on a pluralistic political society and their decision announced in February 1975 to form a monolithic organization of labor unions has also precipitated confusion in those who would classify the regime according to an existing ideological framework. These are not irreconcilable contradictions but rather they result from attempting to define the MFA program in accordance with other models. Repeatedly, in its press conferences and in its media reports, the MFA has asserted a nonideological approach and the development of a "Portuguese Solution" rather than emulation of any existing model. The members' concern with popular culture, both in the sense of "the culture of the masses" and "providing access to culture for the people" typifies their quest for a specifically Portuguese egalitarian society.

The outside observer must realize that many of the alternatives chosen have special validity in terms of the political history of Portugal, its contemporary literacy and economic status, and the nature and objectives of the present political parties and forces. From its inception, the provisional government has been a precarious balance of the MFA and the ambitions of the political parties both in and out of the government.

The evolving ideology of the Movement is expressed in the editorials of the <u>Bulletin</u>. Thus, the relationship of the MFA to the political parties and to the masses, as it evolved out of the events of September 28, was mirrored in the following editorial:

> Whatever is the motivation offered by all those who try to interpret the 25th of April, what is right is that, in an example almost unique in the world, the Portuguese Armed Forces accomplished in the memorable date a military coup of progressive and popular essence. And despite all the efforts by those who desired a 25th of April of conservative appearance, the 28th of September came to show how the majority commitment of the Portuguese military was centered in rigorous defense of the democratic ideal and progressivist in its revolution.

Such sympathy between the Armed Forces and
the people cannot be restricted to moments of
crisis, when the democratic conquests of a people
are in danger. It must be developed and deepened
in everyday life, by the active bonding of the military to their people, by their permanent identification with the desires and problems of this people.
That implies a new understanding of the role of the
Armed Forces in the totality of the Nation.

The Armed Forces are the people in arms,
are the armed arm of the Nation, the vanguard
(not the only one of course) that, in certain moments, the people use in defense of the territorial
integrity of the nation, in the defense of liberty of
people against the threats of servitude, in the defense of this interest of the people against all and
any exploitation. [20]

The editorial continued to explain the relationship between the
military and civilian populations as conceived in the MFA model of
a "liberation Army":

To set free a people is not just to make a military
coup. It means to ensure until the end the realization of a body of reforms that, going into the core
of the problems, in reality sets free the people
from misery, oppression, exploitation. No group
[body] of revolutionary reforms (in the measure
that it is necessary to subvert the order based on
the injustice and inequality in order to raise an
order in an inverse sense) can be accomplished
without the Armed Forces being deeply tuned in
with the people, with the poor and the humble
with the exploited of their country. No real revolution is accomplishable without Armed Forces of
democratic and progressive ideology allied to the
working people.

We understand that we are not only the
guardians of a DEMOCRACY IN ABSTRACT, but
rather of a DEMOCRACY IN CONCRETE. That
we understand that it is not by watching the effort
of collective reconstruction of a country, that we
will accomplish the objectives of the 25th of April--
but rather PARTICIPATING with the people in an
effort, in a collective labor. That we understand,

finally, that this not-expecting to do alone a fight
that belongs to everybody, does not mean that we
judge ourselves--even if invoking the popular in-
terest--as only a governing vanguard, because
this would be substituting the democratic and progressive sense of our revolution for a paternalism
leading in a short time to autocracy.[21]

The MFA saw itself not as a substitute for political parties,
nor as a political party themselves, but rather as partners with them
in reconstruction and democratization, "in the battle of the dignifica-
tion of the oppressed and humiliated of this country."

Like other groups entitled "liberation armies" or "people's
armies," the MFA saw itself as the vehicle for mobilizing the human
and material resources of an underdeveloped country. They viewed
their Cultural Dynamization program as an example of their function as catalysts:

The example of the project of Cultural Dynamization needs to be taken as a starting point. The
dynamizing action of the Armed Forces has to be
developed rapidly. The military have to use their
immense prestige and their power in order to impose reforms where they have not appeared, in
order to correct injustices where they persist, in
order to act in the midst of the people (in synchrony
with the government structures, whenever that it
is possible). The military have to go near the
people, get to know their problems, hear their
complaints and desires--in sum: learn to act with
the people. The Armed Forces have to stimulate
(and to participate in) defined programs of action
in the fields of health, inhabitation, agriculture,
civil engineering, transportation, etc.--in a complementary actuation to the civil structures and,
whenever necessary, mobilizing and correcting
these very structures. And, in the development
of this action, to lead the combat against bureaucracy and corruption.
With the civic body, the Armed Forces of
our country have to accompany all the battles of
their people for social justice, democracy and
freedom. (They have to be not) a classic and
apolitical army, but a civic institution, brothers
(with their people in all their fights, by their side

everywhere) where misery, injustice, oppression,
exploitation exist, where persist the reasons that
made of the 25th of April one of the most glorious
dates in the history of the Portuguese Armed
Forces. [22] [Emphasis mine.]

By October 1974, the MFA was ready to move ahead rapidly,
and as they viewed it, revolutionarily, to combat the problems of
decolonization, cultural dynamization, and even an overhaul of the
economic structure of Portugal:

In the session of the 18th of last October the
Board (Council) of Ministers decided to create a
group to work with toward presenting a plan of
economical-social action.
        We believe that this Plan must assume the
character of exception, foresee measures of
short term and begin the bases for indispensable
reforms at the structural level. It must try to
face inflation, unemployment, the deficit of the
commercial and payment balances, the cost of
production in some sectors, etc., but must do it
beginning from the principle that to the collectiv-
ity, through the State, must be reserved progressively a greater role in the economic activity, must
be by direct "control" of the Departments through
the collective participation of the workers, true
creators of national wealth. This aspect assumes
special prominence in the agricultural sector
where old fashioned forms of exploitation continue
to exist in the zones of latifundium and exploita-
tions with low income where the property is very
much divided.
        We suppose that the characteristics, be it
of elaboration, be it of execution and "control" of
this Plan, require that they take place outside of
the bureaucratic-traditional mechanisms of the
Ministries, especially the Ministry of Economics,
needing to be passed above all by the Prime Minister or a Minister without portfolio, being served
by the structure of Technical Secretariate, today
integrated in the Secretary of State of the Economic Planning.
        Will this Plan be the star element of an
economic policy more committed to the defense

of the levels of population more disfavored? Will
it constitute an important element in the consolidation of the democratic process in our Country?

In sum, will this Plan translate the concerns of social justice that have always informed
the M. F. A. and lead them to meet the deeper aspirations of the Portuguese People?

The People awaits. The M. F. A. trusts and
is attentive. [23]

In January, the Minister for Social Affairs, Maria de Lourdes
Pintassilgo (the first woman cabinet minister in Portuguese history),
stated for the government, "We are placing social priorities first.
The economic priorities will naturally follow . . . the major priority
right now is reorganizing the social conditions of the agricultural
sector. . . ." But meanwhile, in December, the government had
nationalized 51 percent of nine key industries including the steel,
gas, and electric industries. They then moved for public financing
of low-income urban housing, initiated a national health care and social security program, and increased welfare and pension benefits.

Nationalizing industry and energy resources created little opposition within Portugal. Worker management was quickly initiated
and worker-shared ownership of enterprises within a couple of
months became a common circumstance. Nonetheless, the issues of
organized labor, strikes, layoffs, minimum wages, and unemploy-
ment--especially as draftees and colonists returned to the labor
force--all contributed to growing concern.

The MFA recognized from the history of the first Portuguese
republic and the more recent case of Chile (a case which loomed
large in Portuguese nightmares) that labor strikes could not only re-
tard their progress, but initiate violence and leave an opening for
reactionary reestablishment. This concern was not diminished by
the fact that within the first month of the revolution, there was a
series of wildcat strikes that had to be quelled by decree laws. The
problems with the unions were not too different from the problem of
local government authorities. Both had been long dominated by individuals associated with the fascist regime. In both cases, immediate
reorganization following the April 25 revolution had resulted in replacement of the leadership by the well organized cadres of the Portuguese Communist Party. No elections had been held and no machinery for reorganization had been developed. In fact, there was
no reason to suppose that the constituencies of either the local government authorities or the unions were sufficiently politically educated to be able to effect such machinery.

The more militant extreme leftist movements and parties were actively engaged in usurping through minority action the direction of the unions. The common tactic was to call a workers' meeting and distribute agitators around the meeting hall armed with prearranged speeches and other delaying tactics. The meeting might start at 8 P.M. with 500 workers present, but the haggling that would ensue would deliberately drive the issues further and further away from the employment situations and into the abstract of ideologies. The majority of workers would become bored, leave the meeting, and by 2 A.M. only those few remained who had initiated the issue. Then a vote would be taken, and the rest of the workers would be notified of the decision.[24] Since no machinery for arbitration had been established by this point, these wildcat strikes would proceed without any possible resolution.

This tactic was utilized by the extreme right as well, albeit with rhetorical differences. Furthermore, the nightly meetings of unions and associations had begun by July to be theaters for ideological dispute rather than vehicles for work or professional considerations. In such cases, the object was often to elect officers of a particular political party and find ways of eliminating the expressions of other parties. These procedures were not inconsistent with the participants' experience of fascist political behavior. The difference was merely one of rhetoric.

By mid-January, the provisional government realized that not only did they need to devise arbitration machinery, but some kind of central coordination of union activities would also have to be devised. This issue brought about the first serious division between the political parties included in the coalition cabinet and some of the other political parties and the MFA. The 20-member executive of the MFA had drafted a law that would combine all of the unions into a monolithic Congress of Labor, which would then act as the arbitration body and the intermediary for labor and government.

This is not a system unknown in democratic countries. Ireland and the United Kingdom have had congresses of trade unions. However, the unions had exercised democratic prerogatives for electing leaders and representatives in those two countries. In the case of Portugal, such elections had not transpired and, to worsen matters, the unions had become the battleground for political party organizing. Nonetheless, at the end of January 1975, the provisional government established the Intersindical and on April 30 named it as the official arbitration agency. The political disputes and the disputes between the MFA and the political parties which grew out of this decision are described at length in Chapter 6.

The beginning of February saw another crisis. That month also marked the beginning of heavy electoral campaigning for the Constitutional Assembly elections scheduled for March. Political demonstrations and meetings were fervent and frequent. The MFA was committed to support freedom of speech, assembly, and the press, and determined that there would be no violence or political imprisonment. But this became difficult, especially in the face of NATO naval maneuvers off the Portuguese coast and some unfounded rumors that the Soviet Union was seeking berthing rights at the resort of Figueroa da Foz, 150 miles north of Lisbon. While angry leftists rallied and protested the NATO exercises, the MFA leaders investigated the rumor and insisted that there was no basis to it. Major Antunes was dispatched to Washington, where he reaffirmed Portugal's commitment to NATO and the MFA recognition of the strategic importance of that commitment. Between the anger over the creation of Intersindical and the agitation on the issue of the NATO maneuvers, commando patrols were called out to control street demonstrations and permits were refused for rallies. On February 8, the Junta for National Salvation (JSN) announced that the elections need not take place in March, but would be before April 25.

The intention of having elections in March seemed less realistic as the month of February progressed. It also seemed to the MFA that their original plan for returning to "barracks" once a civilian government had been elected was unrealistic. At numerous meetings that month, the problem of interparty rivalries and fascist orientations within political organizations was a topic of concern. It was furthermore apparent that reactionary forces, led by prominent figures from the industrial monopolies, were once again forming around General Spinola.

The elections were scheduled for April 12, with the campaign officially designated to open on March 20. Within the MFA, elections were being held to advisory committees, the Assembly, and the Coordinating Committee. Various rumors suggested that the rightist forces were mobilizing for these elections and would attempt to replace Goncalves and Carvalho in the Coordinating Committee. And although the leaders had carefully avoided criticism of General Spinola or suggestion that he had played a direct role in the counter-revolutionary event of September 28, it seemed increasingly that his resignation from the presidency was becoming a focal point for dissidents.

On February 21, in addition to establishing the Intersindical, the MFA announced that with the political parties it would develop a format for its own continuance in the government for three to five years under the new constitution. This expedient was necessary, Goncalves pointed out, because of the unresolved issues of agrarian reform, and economic danger, and because of the necessity for the MFA to guarantee the aspirations of the working class.

During the first week in March the PPD and rightist Christian Democrats held angry and violent rallies against this pronouncement. On March 8 in Setubal, an industrial city about 50 miles south of Lisbon, far leftists, trying to stop a rally of the PPD at which this pact was being hotly protested, broke through a police cordon and entered the meeting hall. When the police attempted to remove them, fighting broke out and the police fired into the crowd. One young man was killed and 19 others injured. The protesters then besieged the police station, which was being guarded by a military unit. When foreign correspondents emerged from the police station they were attacked by the mob and one British journalist, Christopher Reed, was hospitalized.

The tempo of demonstrations and counterdemonstrations increased after this incident, and on March 11, the second attempt at a violent overthrow of the provisional government transpired. While the MFA was blaming the political parties for alienating the masses from the revolutionary objectives, and leftist elements were increasingly pushing the worker management of banks and insurance companies, General Spinola, in a speech at a gathering of military college alumni, announced that "the fight will continue." Dr. Alvaro Cunhal denounced the PPD as "reactionary." Meanwhile, dissidents among the MFA and businessmen speculated that the popularity of the leftists in the MFA was sufficiently diffuse that a coup attempt initiated from within the armed forces might attract wide support and succeed. The fear of the apparent escalation of Communist Party influence in the government and the bid for continuity of MFA leadership in the new government both contributed to the feeling that the time was ripe.

The events of March 11 suggest the same kind of misestimation as characterized the Bay of Pigs action against the Castro regime in Cuba 12 years earlier. In both cases it was assumed that there would be popular support for an anticommunist action and that would supplement the relatively small armed force.

Whatever was the level of Spinola's involvement in planning the March 11 coup may never be known. However, his years of successful military experience would have made him extremely skeptical about the strategy of initiating armed insurrection with only a small force. This must have appeared especially risky if he realized that the paratroop regiment spearheading the plan was ordered out ostensibly to put down an insurrection of the leftist First Artillery Regiment. There had been some articulation of disaffection with the Goncalves government by leaders of PSP and PPD, and certainly, the nationalization program had not set well with CDS. The Secretary General of CDS was one of the conspirators in the coup, Air Force Major Sanches Osario who had been Minister for Social

Communication in the second cabinet. Most of the officers involved in planning the March 11 fiasco had been involved at various levels in planning the successful MFA April 25 coup. From that experience it should have been obvious that the necessary factors for success were absent from the March 11 strategy.

The paratrooper attack on RAL #1 (Light Artillery Regiment) resulted in some injuries among the artillerymen but the latter assumed an offensive stance and the paratroopers were soon surrounded by angry civilians on one side and their intended victims on the other. Within two hours of the attack on RAL #1, civilian activists, COPCON and EMGFA, had mobilized to counter the offensive. When the radio emissions center at Porto Alto was assaulted and communication interrupted at 1 P.M., it was restored within minutes.

In the afternoon following the attack, bank workers went on strike and financial institutions did not reopen until they were nationalized, five days later.

Brig. Otelo Carvalho was interpreted by journalists as suggesting that the United States was involved in planning the coup.[25] The popular reaction to the attempt had not required any such statement by Carvalho to have immediately focused on U.S. and CIA involvement. There had already been an outcry about the new U.S. ambassador, Frank Carlucci, who had served in Zaire where he allegedly functioned as the CIA director. In addition, of course, there had been many parallels drawn between the Portuguese revolution, the Cuban revolution, and the "lesson of Chile."

The bombing attack on the artillery regiment left one dead and 18 wounded. General Spinola and 18 of his closest aides and their families left Portugal before the day was over to seek first refuge in Spain and then, finally, exile in Brazil. Later Spinola claimed that he had been advised to flee the country because the Communists had gotten up an assassination list and were planning a "Great Easter Massacre" of those who opposed their hegemony. He also claimed that he had no prior knowledge of the attempted coup and had retired to the air base for his personal safety.[26]

The aftermath of the second attempted coup was almost predictable. Where the MFA had previously been loath to take political prisoners or to limit in any way the process of a pluralistic party system, they now felt compelled to take strong and immediate actions. After an all-night meeting of the 200-member Assembly, the Junta for National Salvation and the Council of State were totally abolished in favor of a Revolutionary Council; the intention of the MFA to remain indefinitely in the government was reaffirmed. The MFA said that elections would take place on April 12, and proceedings were established to arrest and imprison those suspected of complicity in the plot.

The period of tension lasted for several days. The president
and prime minister expected further attempts at overturning the government, and the evidence was strong that the Social Democratic
Center Party and the Christian Democrats had been involved in planning the coup. Twenty business and financial figures, and 33 military officers were imprisoned within 24 hours of the attempted coup.
By March 17, 102 persons--56 officers and 46 civilians--had been
arrested. (See Appendixes 5.D, 5.E, and 5.F for descriptions of
the government before and after March 11, 1974.)

Besides the banking and financial reorganization, the High
Council of the Revolution also announced intended changes in land
ownership. The latifundi were to be broken up into smaller plots of
land; the nonirrigated sectors (primarily in the north) would receive
financial assistance to make improvements, and in all areas, agricultural cooperatives would be developed to assist the small farmers
in making the best use of equipment, resources, and facilities.

On March 12 the cabinet resigned and the prime minister faced
the task of putting together a cabinet which would be agreeable to the
Revolutionary Council and to the political parties. One new development in the cabinet was the inclusion of members of MDP, a political
party which was formerly a mass democratic movement, but which
became, after its development as a party, reflective of a political
ideology to the left of the Communist Party. Their inclusion in the
government was protested by PPD and PSP. Each of the parties was
given two cabinet posts, while seven posts were distributed to MFA
officers.

In formalizing their actions, the MFA, in a plenary session
lasting two days and including 170 delegates, put forth a proclamation:

> 1. The military revolt carried out demo-
> cratically by the Armed Forces on the 25th of
> April and the prolonged, legitimate struggle of
> the Portuguese people against fascism, and the
> struggle of the colonial people for liberation is
> the revolutionary process of Portugal and is a
> unique process. As these forces together, re-
> sisted the industrial alliance and its components:
> the revolutionary vanguard of the armed forces,
> the MFA and the Portuguese people organized
> within progressive political parties and other
> mass organizations.
>
> 2. As the Portuguese revolution develops
> it acquires its lasting form. Through the poli-
> tics of progressivism the economics of large
> monopolies and the alienation of the latifundi

> have been the principal sustenance of fascism,
> colonialism and imperialism. Therefore, after
> the 11th of March these interests will instead be
> put to the service of the Portuguese people. . . .
> To strengthen and consolidate the alliance be-
> tween the people and the MFA, the Portuguese
> people have now the strongest reasons to proceed
> with advancement of the revolutionary process. . . .

The proclamation concluded:

> . . . in order to advance and consolidate the
> democratic process and the revolution's course,
> in order to end colonialism and neo-colonialism;
> in order to totally liberate the Portuguese work-
> ers from chains of capitalistic monopolies; for a
> society that ends exploitation of person by person,
> for the future well-being of the Portuguese people,
> for SOCIALISM. [27]

Clearly, the ideology of the MFA is formed after its actions. In
fact, they have often reiterated Che Guevara's maxim "Ideology
evolves from action."
    Meanwhile, interparty fighting did not stop with the thwarted
coup. Although the MFA had made it clear that they would remain
in the government and, with the consent of the political parties,
formulate an outline for the constitution, on March 22, PPD supporters besieged the headquarters of the Communist Party in Porto,
where their electoral strength was strong. (PPD was retaliating for
the earlier instance of a PPD rally disrupted by extreme leftists
which resulted in ten persons injured.) Members of the PCP fired
warning shots at the demonstrators from within their headquarters.
    Three political parties were barred from entering candidates
in the forthcoming elections because they had "interfered with the
democratic process":[28] the Christian Democrats (who then merged
with the Center Democrats) on the right and the Movement for Reorganization of the Proletarian Party (MRPP) and the Commission
for Agrarian and Factory Workers (AOC) on the extreme left. (Chapter 6 contains a more complete analysis of the ideologies and tactics.)
On April 4, the political parties signed a pact with the MFA agreeing
to the outlined constitution, the commitment to retain the existing
cabinet until the legislative elections, and adherence to the veto power
of the Revolutionary Council.
    Another source of ongoing conflict with the MFA surfaced again
on April 13, when the military and the Church took opposite positions

in advising the people on voting. Officers had been advising people
who could not decide between the political parties to cast a blank vote.
The Portuguese bishops announced that nobody should cast a blank
ballot. The bishops' statement said that it was not necessary to ex-
haustively analyze party programs, but to remember that Catholics
are forbidden to vote for parties which "by their ideologies, objectives and historical trend are incompatible with a Christian concep-
tion of man and his life in society."[29] By this directive, they reminded their parishioners that Marxist parties and politics were anti-
Christian. The election results from the northern provinces, which
voted heavily for CDS and PPD, where the influence of the Church
was strongest, reflected the Church influence throughout the electoral campaign.

The suggestion of the blank ballot has been one of the most
widely confused issues arising from the campaign and the MFA relationship with it. According to members of the Revolutionary Council, the blank ballot option was intended to provide a means for exer-
cising personal political responsibility without jeopardizing the integrity of the voter. Because of the many traumatic events preceding the elections--the interparty violence, the attempted coup, the
continual barrage of party propaganda from media and meetings--
and because this was the first experience for the majority of the population in an open electoral contest, the MFA had put forth this option.
There was, in addition, the fact that the 12 parties were not included
in all of the districts' ballots. The blank vote could well reflect the
absence of the party choice. Some members of the MFA themselves
later admitted having personally cast a blank ballot because of their
own ambivalence about the various leftist parties. However, this alternative was interpreted by U.S. and British media people as an attempt to thwart the efforts of the center parties. *

On election eve, the President spoke to the people of Portugal
and voiced his confidence that their expression of democracy and
political pluralism at the polls would be as conscientious and considered as had been their efforts through the past year at making democracy and liberty a reality in Portugal. And that night, nearly all
night, the people of Lisbon spontaneously turned out on the main
thoroughfares, celebrating their own freedom. Portuguese flags
were everywhere in evidence, young people climbed the fountain in
the Rossio and dived into it, an armored car was heaped with flowers
thrown by the celebrants, and everywhere people were singing
"Avante Comerade" or the MFA song "Grandola"--the playing of

---

*See Chapter 7, pp. 177-82.

which on the radio at 12:20 A. M. the year before had signaled the start of the revolution.

The results of the election were widely interpreted by the Portuguese press as a victory of the alliance between the MFA and the people. The results gave the Socialist Party the largest share of the votes, and reflected a coalition of leftist parties not too different from those already included in the coalition cabinet.

Official statements by the MFA and by the provisional government, both before and immediately following the election, reflected their confidence in the voters, pride in the large voter turnout, and the peaceful process of this "first exercise in democratic process." They considered it a "learning experience" and a preparation for the election of the president and legislative assembly which would take place later in the year.

NOTES

1. Portugal: Freedom Year One (Lisbon: Ministry for Social Communications, 1975) (pamphlet).

2. Antonio de Spinola, Portugal and the Future (Lisbon: Arcadia Press, 1974).

3. From statements by General Antonio Spinola, in Expresso, interview published on January 4, 1975.

4. Ibid., and interviews with General Spinola reported in the New York Times, March 16, 1975; wire service report of interview with Spinola in exile in Brazil, Boston Globe, March 24, 1975.

5. In a rather remarkable political cartoon, which was reprinted in the Sunday Times (London) on June 30, 1974, Fons van Woerkom depicted General Spinola maturing into Portugal's DeGaulle. The caption said, "Will General Spinola mature into Portugal's DeGaulle... or will the contending forces in his army be too much for him?"

6. Expresso interview, op. cit.

7. Jane Kramer, "Letter from Lisbon," New Yorker, September 28, 1974.

8. Ibid.

9. As described in a press conference by Major Costa Martins, Minister for Labor, Lisbon, April 29, 1975.

10. Reported in New York Times, March 13, 1975. Carvalho was later questioned on these charges during a press conference in Lisbon on April 28, 1975. He elaborated further on his thesis that Ambassador Carlucci was considered "by the Portuguese people" to be suspect for his role in Zaire. Carvalho insisted that his statements to the effect that Carlucci's security could not be assured resulted from his own professional appraisal of the mood of the people.

11. Movimento das Forcas Armadas Boletim, October 3, 1974.
12. Ibid.
13. Ibid.
14. Ibid.
15. Ibid.
16. Ibid.
17. Ibid.
18. Ibid.
19. Movimento das Forcas Armadas Boletim, November 12, 1974.
20. Movimento das Forcas Armadas Boletim, December 24, 1974.
21. Ibid.
22. Movimento das Forcas Armadas Boletim, March 25, 1975.
23. Movimento das Forcas Armadas Boletim, April 8, 1975.
24. New York Times, March 13, 1975.
25. AP Wire Service (Rio de Janeiro), interview with General Spinola, datelined March 24, 1975.
26. Movimento das Forcas Armadas Boletim, April 8, 1975.
27. New York Times, March 19, 1975, "The Parties Banned from Political Process"; this was a direct sequel to the incidents of March 8, 1974 when far leftist groups disrupted a PPD rally in Setubal. Shortly after the incident, and in conjunction with the attacks on foreign journalists, Commander Jorge Jesuino, Minister for Social Communications, gave a press conference and castigated those who had enacted the violence, apologized to the foreign press, and announced that disruption of the normal democratic process would result in the suspension of some groups from the ballot.
28. Interview with Brigadier General Carvalho.
29. From a statement issued by the Hierarchy in Portugal, April 16, 1975.

APPENDIX 5.A

Actions of the Provisional Government in its First Year

Dismantling the Fascist Regime

Those military and civil servants of the State who had been dismissed, retired or placed in the reserve for political motives were readmitted to their positions.

The managing bodies of the People's Centres were purged of fascist elements and replaced by democratically elected administrative committees. A start was made on weeding out the paramilitary and military forces and the civil service.

Political prisoners were freed and extensive amnesties and free pardons granted.

The National Committee of Enquiry was set up to investigate the acts of violence committed against individuals and the cases of corruption occurring between 28 May 1926 and 25 April 1974.

Enquiries and financial investigations begun into embezzlement and irregularities committed in governmental organs and departments under the fascist regime.

A start has been made on the reform of the judicial system and the legal departments. The access of women to careers as judges and barristers facilitated.

The Higher Judicial Council, the highest organ of the law profession, replaced by a new Council, not now dependent like its predecessor on the government.

The Portuguese Government and the Holy See have made preliminary contacts for a revision of the Concordat, signed in 1940 with Salazar's government, with a view to solving, among others, the question of the impossibility of divorce in Catholic marriages, which contradicted the concept of the equality of citizens in the face of the law.

Abolition of the censorship and prior examination system of all the media.

The new press law has been drafted.

The government has published laws regulating the right to strike, to associate, to meet and to manifest opinions.

It has approved laws on parties and political associations.

It has dismantled the corporative system, and has abolished both corporative and employers' associations.

Trade unions are now free without any state interference.

Cultural Development Program

With the support of the government, the MFA has started a campaign to publicize its Programme and to accelerate cultural development. The government has set up regional Social and Cultural Development Committees dependent on the interministerial Committee for Social and Cultural Development.

The government is supporting an experimental literacy and pro-hygiene campaign being carried out by students. It is legislating for the democratic management of state schools and universities.

Elections

It has publicized the Electoral Law, to regulate the conditions of election of the Constituent Assembly.

For the first time the right to vote is granted to citizens of 18 and upwards.

25 April 1975. For the first time in 48 years Portugal will hold free elections to fulfill the Programme of the Movement of the Armed Forces, as has already been announced to the nation by the President of the Republic.

Economic and Financial Measures

Support and encouragement for the creation of agricultural co-operatives.

Institution of the Agricultural Reorganization Institute, laying down the conditions ruling the leasing of uncultivated or underculti-vated lands.

Outline of an autonomous programme for the agricultural, stock-raising and forestry development of Tras-os-Montes province, esti-mated to cost 350 million escudos.

Programming of major investment in the Alentejo and the Azores to increase agricultural and stock production.

Ban on afforestation of land suitable for farming.

Abolition of the industrial conditioning system which, under the fascist regime, brought about gross favoritism and privileges.

Setting up of the Institute for Aid to Small and Medium-sized Undertakings.

Further repression of fraud, antieconomic activities, infringe-ments of public health legislation, so as to prevent excessive profits, speculative price rises and the offering for sale of substandard goods. A call for watchfulness on the part of the people as the most effective way to put such legislation into practice.

Increased interest rates for time deposits to attract savings and to place at the disposal of state and private banks and credit institu-tions finance to encourage and develop investment.

Nationalization of the issue banks: Bank of Portugal, Bank of Angola, and the National Overseas Bank.

Creation of the Coordinating Committee for Public Credit In-stitutions and the Advisory Committee on Credit, to organize and discipline the operations of credit institutions.

Issue of bonds for a redeemable domestic loan under the title Treasury Bonds for National Reconstruction, to finance state invest-ments.

A start on fiscal reform, to correct certain aspects of the former system, to make the burden of taxation more equitable and to simplify procedure.

Due to the economic and financial state in which the country was found to be after the revolution, the government undertakes to effect through the administration a policy of austerity, to reduce, or hold at its present level, expenditure, limiting it to what is strictly necessary.

With a view to finding a solution for the serious economic and social problems of the country, as a result of structures unable to respond to the real needs of the Portuguese people, the government has put forward an Economic and Social Development Plan to cover three years.

The government has approved the General Budget for 1975, which includes the following measures of importance: (a) reduction of 40 percent in military expenditure over the previous year; (b) increase of 7,500 million escudos in investments; (c) allocation of over 5,000 million to housing; (d) allotment of over 3,000 million to health, a rise of about 40 percent over the previous year; (e) allotment of over 10,000 million to education, a rise of over 50 percent on the previous figure.

Social Measures

Institution of the minimum national wage of 3,300 escudos per month. Although it is still considered to be too low, the fact is that it has benefited about half industrial and service workers, and about 68 percent of civil servants.

The social welfare system has ceased to be a capitalistic body engaged in investing in shares and financing undertakings. It will henceforth apply social welfare payments to the social security schemes and to administration.

Grant of the holiday-with-pay and extra month's pay at Christmas system to civil servants and local authority workers.

Increase of over 100 percent in retirement and disablement pensions to a minimum of 1,650 escudos per month.

Grant of a Christmas bonus to disablement, old age and widow's pension holders.

Family allowances set at 240 escudos for each child per month, a rise of 50 percent.

Incentivation of, and support for, the creation of low-cost housing cooperatives.

Reduction in, or exemption from, property transfer tax on houses bought for owner-residence.

Limitation of permission to demolish urban buildings, conditioning of size of rentals and ban on eviction because of subletting, in certain areas of the country.

State financing of economic-rental housing building. The Housing Development Fund has an allotment of 1,200 million escudos.

Research into the basis of a National Health Service.

Foreign Relations

Portugal has been readmitted to UNESCO, from which it had been expelled.

It has gained the support of the UN due to the new policy of decolonization.

Portugal had broken off diplomatic relations with several countries, she has already restored them, or established new relations with the following countries: Bulgaria, Czechoslovakia, Congo (Brazzaville), Ivory Coast, Ghana, Guinea-Bissau, Hungary, Indonesia, Yugoslavia, Liberia, Morocco, Poland, East Germany, Senegal, Tunisia, Indian Union, USSR. In some cases agreements of commercial, cultural, or technical cooperation nature have already been signed.

Decolonization

Decolonization was one of the priorities of the MFA in organizing the liberating operations of 25 April. Putting into practice the ideology in the name of which the Armed Forces have been acting has led to: the end of the colonial wars; recognition of the right of peoples under colonial administration to self-determination and independence.

Major steps in this irreversible process have been:

Recognition of the Republic of Guinea-Bissau as an independent state, and the commencement of collaboration with it at all levels.

The Lusaka Agreement with Mozambique Liberation Front (FRELIMO), setting up in Mozambique a transitional government and a mixed military commission to work until 25 June 1975, when independence will be proclaimed.

Signature in Algiers of the Agreement between Portugal and the Liberation Movement of Sao Tome and Principe Islands (MLSTP), for the setting up of a transitional government. The islands will be declared independent on 12 July 1975 by an assembly elected by the people.

An agreement was signed in Lisbon between Portugal and the African Party for the Independence of Guinea and Cape Verde (PAIGC), setting up a transitional government until the declaration of the independence of Cape Verde on 5 July 1975, to be proclaimed by an assembly elected by the people of the islands through direct, universal suffrage.

Signature of the Algarve Agreement between Portugal and the Angolan Liberation Movements--National Angolan Liberation Front (FNLA), People's Movement for the Liberation of Angola (MPLA), and National Union for the Total Independence of Angola (UNITA), for the constitution of a transitional government and a national defence committee to work until the declaration of the independence of Angola on 11 November 1975.

In Timor a plebiscite is to be held to decide the political future of the colony.

There are no difficulties as regards the future relations of Macau with Portugal because the former has never agitated for independence or for integration with the People's Republic of China, and also because Portugal is ready at any time to hold talks with the Republic of China.

APPENDIX 5.B

Democratization of Armed Forces

There is a need to clarify exactly what we must understand by democratization of the armed forces, or by democratic armed forces. There is a lot of confusion in this respect that it is necessary to clarify.

Being the military power (in a society where the political power has emerged democratically), one of the components of the political power, we must guarantee at any cost that the military structure reaches the maximum of its efficiency in the development of its missions that are for attainment of national objectives as defined by the political power, without the possibility of overpowering it.

The restrictive condition imposed on the Armed Forces of a democratic society--nonpossibility for overpowering the political power that emanates from the people--would put aside by itself, if other factors did not exist, the democratization of the Armed Forces in the sense that its commanders in various echelons are selected by election of the bases. A practice of this kind could lead to a situation of confrontation between the Armed Forces and the legitimate power, this one designated by the whole nation from the basis that the latter ones constitute a part. To admit the democratization of the military institutions in the sense of their being structured by the electoral way would be to admit that, from the game of the votes inside the Armed Forces (in an environment relatively reduced to the nation and its interests) the phenomenon of the Caudilhismo (leaderism, chiefism, headism) be institutionalized and, with it, we return to the time when the legions imposed the emperors on the nation that was obliged to submit itself to them. Then, at the cost of something pretending to be democratic, we would finish off democracy.

It is, therefore, definitely the wrong idea to have electoral campaigns in the military environment. As a matter of fact there is not one army in the world where this, not even slightly, happens.

Such a solution would be dangerous to the democracy, in fact it could lead to situations when the chiefs would not have the necessary knowledge of the performance of their functions, since many facets of choice could weigh in the electoral "campaign."

The process recently adopted of reclassifications of the personnel by the ways (routes) of the boards of Arms/Classes/Specialties, is not by any means the way to this false democratization of the Armed Forces. It really was a solution that enlarges the elements leveled by similar technical knowledge to the performance of determined functions of the participation in the classification of its components. It was a measure of great proportions that is interesting to maintain and improve with bases in the institutionalization of a system of well developed individual information.

Is the designation of certain parties to the JSN from the elections by the Board of Services not a sign of this false democratization. It is filling of political places demanded by an exceptional period during which the Armed Forces will have as its task the objective of establishing democracy in Portugal.

In democratic Armed Forces the leader of each echelon is the first responsible for defense of the conquests of democracy. In this sense, the military chief will try to obtain the maximum possible efficiency of the group he commands. For such he must make use of the democratic processes of command, and must leave aside the type of autocratic command.

In the democratic command the leader:
- makes the group intervene;
- the lines of action arise more as a result of the group than as a unique (single) action from above to below;
- permits the more active participation of the subordinates, increasing their sense of freedom and of responsibility.

It is a whole process of alteration of chief-group, that will lead necessarily to the taking of the best decisions by the chief.

Therefore, there is need of making an effort in the sense of introducing in the Armed Forces the democratic processes of administration, generators of more egalitarian and dynamic solutions. The democratic command in itself is a dynamic command.

To mix up the adoption of democratic ways of governing with inversion of hierarchy or with the "false democratization" to which we have already referred, is pure threat to the democracy we intend to build.

Some Practical Aspects

In the present stage of the national life, Armed Forces have an important mission--the unrelenting defense of the Program of the

MFA, which is the same as to say, to ensure the advancement of the democratic process that began on the morning of April 25th.

Many will ask if the democratization will not have to begin by the very Air Force.

As to this point, it is necessary that we take into consideration the word Democracy applied to the AF if we understand it as the establishment of a climate of mutual and conscience respect, of definitions of the responsibilities of each one, finishing with the anachronism of the situations, with favoritism and the abuse of authority, then, democratization is a priority in the AF....

The AF have to keep themselves ready for any intervention against forces that want to sabotage the democratic process and retreat to the dictatorial situation that oppressed us, just as it happened in the 28th of September.

This intervention can only come to happen if the AF are structured, joined, and cemented by a conscientious discipline, where the hierarchy of the competences substitutes the former hierarchy. . . .

In order to be effectively guarantor of a renewed Portugal, emerged from the chaos of 48 years of dictatorial "order," the AF have to maintain themselves united and firm (steady) ready to face any attempt of deviation to the program, providing to the Portuguese People the construction of a new country.

As very concrete examples of democratization in the AF, and in the specific case of the Navy we have the Dispatch (official communication) of the Chief of Staff of the Navy #84/74 of 1/4/74, that rules the Service of the Well-being in that Section (see Bulletin #3, page 2).

In this regulation one can find some innovations that, by being initiated in the Portuguese AF, much will contribute to the awakening of a renewed spirit.

This democratization does not come to shake the hierarchy and the discipline, rather it reinforces and rationalizes it, if we keep under attention the self characteristics of each section of the AF.

Either officers, sergeants and soldiers can and must collaborate in common initiatives of interest for all without damaging the discipline.

We can cite for instance meetings of enlightenment about the objectives of the Government and of the MFA: administration of snack bars and cooperatives of the unit; promotion of meetings of cultural character, organization of libraries and collaboration in sports activities.

Another process of collaboration, as the dispatch 8/4/74 of the CEMA emphasizes, is the consultive character of the CBE in what concerns discipline, being a precious help of the commands. Another mobilizing initiative is the publication of unity newspapers and wall newspapers.

   With all that we desire that the different classes of the AF
look at each other not as opponents, but rather as complements of a
common task that, today more than ever, transcends all of us--the
construction of a New Country.

   Source: Bulletin of the Movement of the 25th of April, November 12, 1974.

APPENDIX 5.C

Calendar of Decolonization

Guinea-Bissau

May 6, 1974 - The Executive Committee of the Popular Front set the
     conditions for negotiation with the new Portuguese regime.
May 16, 1974 - The Minister for Foreign Affairs, Mario Soares,
     met with the Secretary General of PAIGC, Aristides Pereirra
     in Dakar.
May 24-31 - Mario Soares and Commander Pedro Pires of PAIGC
     carried the negotiations on in London.
June 13-14 - The negotiations were completed in Algiers.
July 27 - The President of the Republic, General Spinola, announced
     the intention to grant independence.
August 26 - The accord through which the conflict was ended was
     signed in Algiers.
September 10 - Portugal announced de facto recognition of the Re-
     public of Guinea-Bissau.

Mozambique

May 12-13, 1974 - General Costa Gomes got in contact with FRELIMO.
May 20 - The Minister for Internal Administration visited Lourenzo
     Marques.
June 5-6 - Preliminary conversations took place with FRELIMO in
     Lusaka.
September 5-7 - Negotiations in Lusaka were completed for indepen-
     dence.
September 7 - The agreements were signed.
September 15 - The Provisional Government took control.

Angola

June 14, 1974 - The UNITA (Savimbi's group) stopped fighting.

September 14 - A meeting took place between General Spinola and President Mobutu at Isle de Sol, Cape Verde.

October 15 - Conversations took place between the Portuguese delegation and FNLA in Kinshasa, Zaire.

October 15 - FNLA ceased fire.

October 21 - The cease fire with MPLA became official.

January 4-6, 1975 - The liberation movements met together to discuss joint action in Mombasa, Kenya.

January 10-15 - Agreement was signed between the Portuguese and FNLA, MPLA, and UNITA at Penina for the process of Angolan independence.

S. Tome and Principe

November 23-26, 1974 - A meeting took place in Algiers between the Portuguese delegation and MLSTP for arranging the process of decolonization.

January 10, 1975 - Arrangements were agreed upon with MLSTP for the independence of S. Tome and Principe.

Cape Verde

September 30, 1974 - Arrangements were made for a transition government.

Source: Translated from Portugal: Information (in French) Ministry of Mass Communication, 1975.

APPENDIX 5.D

July 13, 1974 - March 11, 1975 Cabinet

Prime Minister: Colonel Vasco dos Santos Goncalves (MFA)
Ministers Without Portfolio:
　　Major Victor Manuel Rodrigues Alves (MFA)
　　Major Ernesto Augusto Melo Antunes (MFA)
　　Dr. Alvaro Cunhal (PCP)
　　Dr. Joaquin Magalhaes Mota (PPD)
Ministers of:
　　Interterritorial Coordination: Dr. Antonio de Almeida Santos (IND)
　　Foreign Affairs: Dr. Mario Soares (PSP)
　　Labor: Captain Jose Inacio da Costa Martins (MFA)
　　Finances: Dr. Jose da Silva Lopes (IND)

Social Communications: Major Jose Eduardo Sanches Osorio
   (MFA); Feb. 1975 Cmdr. Jorge Correia Jesuino (MFA)
Social Affairs: Engineer Maria de Lurdes Pintassilgo (IND)
Environmental Affairs: Engineer Jose Augusto Fernandes (MFA)
Economics: Dr. Emillio Rui Peixoto Vilar (IND)
Education and Culture: Dr. Vitorino Magalhaes Godinho (PPD)
Defense: Lt. Colonel Mario Firmino Miguel (MFA)
Justice: Dr. Franisco Salgado Zenha (PSP)
Internal Administration: Lt. Colonel Manoel de Costa Bras
   (MFA)

APPENDIX 5. E

March 16 - April 25, 1975 Cabinet

President: General Francisco da Costa Gomes
Prime Minister: General Vasco dos Santos Goncalves (MFA)
Ministers Without Portfolio:
   Dr. Alvaro Cunhal (PCP)
   Dr. Magalmaes Mota (PPD)
   Dr. Mario Soares (PSP)
   Dr. Francisco Perreira de Moura (MDP)
Ministers of:
   Interterritorial Coordination
   Foreign Affairs: Major Ernesto Augusto De Melo Antunes (MFA)
   Labor: Major Jose Ignacio da Costa Martins (MFA)
   Finances: Eng. Jose Joaquim Fragoso
   Social Mass Communication: Commander Jorge Correia Jesuno
      (MFA)
   Social Affairs: Dr. Jorge de Carvalho SA Borges (PPD)
   Environmental Affairs: Col. Jose Augusto Fernandes (MFA)
   Economics: Dr. Mario Murteira (MPD)
   Education and Culture: Col. Jose Emilio da Silva (MFA)
   Defense: Commander Silvano Ribiero (MFA)
   Justice: Dr. Francisco Zenha (PSP)
   Internal Administration: Major Antonio Carlos Arnao Metelo
      (MFA)
   Agriculture and Fisheries: Eng. Fernando Olivero (MFA)
   External Commerce: Dr. Jose da Silva Lopes Baptista (MFA)
   Transport and Communication: Alvaro Veiga de Oliviera
      (PCP)

APPENDIX 5. F

Members of the Council of the Revolution
April 25, 1975

General Francisco da Costa Gomes, President and Chief of Staff of the Armed Forces

Brig. General Vasco dos Santos Goncalves, Prime Minister

Vice-Almirante Jose Pinheiro de Azeveda, Chief of Staff of the Army

General Carlos Alberto Idaes Soares Fabiao, Chief of Staff for Training

General Narciso Mendes Dias, Chief of Staff for the Air Force

Vice-Almirante Antonio Alva Rosa Coutindo, Member of Former JSN

General Anibal Jose Coentro de Pinho Freire, Member of Former JSN

General Nuno Manuel Guimaraes Fischer Lopes Pires, Member of Former JSN

Brig. General Otelo Nuno Romao Saraiva de Carvalhi

Lt. Colonel Manual Riberio Franco Charais, Coordinating Commission of MFA

Lt. Commander Carolos de Almada Contreiras, Coordinating Commission of MFA

Major Pilot Jose Bernardo do Canto e Castro, Coordinating Commission of MFA

Major Air Force Engineer Jose Gabriel Coutinho Pereira Pinto, Coordinating Commission of MFA

Captain Vasco Correlia Lourenco, Coordinating Commission of the MFA

Captain Engineer Duarte Nuno de Ataide Saraiva Marques Pinto Soares, Coordinating Commission of the MFA

1st Lt. Jose Manuel Miguel Judas, Coordinating Commission of the MFA

Naval Captain, Construction Engineer Manuel Beirao Martins Guerreiro, Representative of the MFA

Major of Infantry Pedro Julio Pazarat Correia, Delegate of the MFA

Major Aeronautical Engineer Jose Manuel da Costa Neves, Delegate of the MFA

Captain of Artillery Rodrigo Manuel Lopes de Sousa e Castro, Delegate of the MFA

1st Lt. Naval Medical Corp Ramiro Pedroso Correia, Delegate of the MFA

Captain of Aeronautical Engineering Vitor Manuel Graca Cunha, Delegate of the MFA

Captain of Artillery Manuel Joao Ferreira de Sousa, Delegate of
    the MFA

Captain Engineer Lous Ernesto Albuquerque Ferreira de Macedo,
    Delegate of the MFA

Lt. of Infantry Antonio Alves Marques Junior, Delegate of the MFA
Major Victor Alves
Major Melo Antunes
Major Costa Martins
Vice Admiral Victor Crespo

6

ORGANIZING A
GOVERNMENT

Dr. Alvaro Cunhal, minister without portfolio and head of the Portuguese Communist Party, might never win an election for president of his country, but the very fact that he and his party, proscribed for so long, were campaigning openly and participating in the new government seemed a personal victory for many Portuguese who would never vote for the Communists.

Drs. Cunhal and Soares, along with a host of others, returned from exile to their homeland within a couple of days of the successful overthrow of the Caetano regime. One year later, after the constitutional assembly elections and during the May Day celebration of the new socialist state, they joined battle against each other more distinctly and viciously than they had even during the electoral campaign or the earlier debate over the formation of the Intersindical. The distinctions between socialism and communism have been and will continue to be played out in Portugal with exceptional vehemence. The election results confirmed that prospect. Even though the second largest vote was garnered by the Popular Democrats (PPD), a kind of hybrid Social Democrat and Socialist party, their significance pales before the polarities represented by the Socialist Party and the Communist Party. (See Table 6.1.) PPD could not form a working coalition with the minuscule forces of the Center Democrats (CDS) and not as a Marxist party. The people had clearly placed the majority of their votes into the Marxist box. But which kind of Marxism? And what party could claim to be the "real Marxists"?

In the four parties represented in the cabinet at the time of the elections were many who had been imprisoned and tortured during the previous regime. Others had been dismissed from their jobs or, under the threat of death or imprisonment, forced to flee into exile. Many leaders of the Socialist Party and the Movement for a Demo-

TABLE 6.1

Political Parties in April 25, 1975 Election

Abbreviation	Name	Motto
FEC	Frente Eleitoral Comunista (Marxista-Leninista) (Communist Electoral Front)	"O grito do Povo" ("The cry of the People")
FSP	Frente Socialista Popular (Popular Socialist Front)	
LCI	Liga Communista Internacional (International Communist League)	"Luta Proletario" ("Proletariat Struggle")
MDP/CDE	Movimento Democratico Portugues (Portuguese Democratic Movement)	"Unidate" ("Unity")
MES	Movimento da Esquerda Socialista (Movement of the Left Socialists)	"Esquerda Social-ista" ("Left So-cialist")
PCDS	Partido do Centro Democratico Social (Party of Center Social Democrats)	"Democracia 74" ("Democracy in 74")
PCP	Partido Comunista Portugues (Portuguese Communist Party)	"Avante" ("Forward")
PPD	Partido Popular Democratico (Popular Democratic Party)	"Povo Livre" ("Free People")
PPM	Partido Popular Monarquico (Popular Monarchist Party)	
PSP	Partido Socialista Portugues (Portuguese Socialist Party)	"Portugal Social-ista" ("A Social-ist Portugal")
PUP	Partido de Unidate Popular (Party of Popular Unity)	"A Verdade" ("The Truth")
UDP	Uniao Democratica Popular (Popular United Democrats)	"Voz do Povo" ("Voice of the People")
		"Cause Operaria" ("The Cause of the Worker")
		"Folha Comunista" ("Leaf of Com-munism")
		"Ribatejo na Luta" ("The banks of the Tegas in Strug-gle")

Source: Compiled by the author.

cratic Portugal (MDP), a party to the left of the Communist Party, had also been members of the underground Communist Party, breaking with it either after the 1939 Hitler-Stalin pact, or when the PCP failed to oppose the Soviet invasion of Czechoslovakia in 1968.

The irony is that the program of the Portuguese Communist Party, which should have been most antagonistic to the pluralistic MFA program, instead has proven compatible to it. Some observers have suggested that this is because the PCP, acting on the Moscow line, is trying to preserve "detente" by not attempting to impose a monolithic Communist Party on a West European NATO state. Others have described the MFA as Communist Party allies, followers, or dupes.

The truth is that the MFA leaders have deliberately kept themselves apart from any party affiliations or ideological commitments. The few who deviated from this pattern were those who had affiliated with the rightist groups after September 28 and were then involved in the coup attempt on March 11. The MFA seems almost as embarrassed by the fervent support of the PCP as it is puzzled and wearied by the antagonism of the PSP.

Three parties were suspended for antidemocratic actions in late March, meaning that they had precipitated riots at the rallies of contending parties, created public disturbances at meetings, destroyed party property, or threatened to injure members of other parties. Two of the parties were extreme leftist. The other, the Christian Democrats, disbanded as a party, with its conservative centrist membership moving on to the CDS or PPD.

Table 6.2 shows the final distribution of electoral votes; Map 6.1 shows the location of the major election districts.

Differentiating the party programs and analyzing their campaigns as well as their relationships with the MFA becomes particularly complicated because as the year proceeded new parties formed, others faded, and the existing ones evolved and changed leaders. The other part of the problem is the nature of the MFA itself. As previously mentioned, that movement has also evolved and changed, with many of the original leadership having left Portugal and relatively obscure officers rising to prominence.

Perhaps the most amorphous major political parties at the beginning of the year were the Portuguese Socialist Party (PSP) and the Popular Democratic Party (PPD). In a sense, they have become even more so, as they absorbed the membership of other defunct parties. They are not amorphous in terms of stated party program, but frequent membership changes have created a history of diffuseness and variability.

The milieu in which the political parties have developed is a very unusual one. Military coups, and even revolutions, seldom

TABLE 6.2

Electoral Distribution

District	Electorate	Seats	Percent Voting	Percent Distribution[a]					
				CDS	MDP	PS	PCP	PPD	Other[b]
Aveiro	358,885	14	91.79	11.0	3.8	3.2	3.1	42.8	
Beja	139,357	6	91.77	2.0	5.0	35.0	39.0	5.0	MES 2.5
Braga	367,055	15	93.00	18.0	29.0	27.0	3.7	37.7	
Braganca	109,866	4	90.82	13.5	3.6	24.5	2.7	43.0	
Castelo Branco	167,905	7	90.67	6.4	4.0	41.3	5.7	24.0	FSP 2.3
Coimbra	295,849	12	89.12	4.6	4.5	43.3	5.7	27.0	MES 2.2
Evora	135,144	5	94.26	2.8	7.9	37.8	37.0	6.8	
Faro	227,468	9	90.65	3.3	9.5	46.4	12.3	13.9	
Guarda	137,790	6	91.92	19.5	3.6	28.2	2.9	33.3	
Leiria	264,487	11	89.81	6.8	3.4	33.1	6.4	35.5	
Lisbon	1,371,559	55	91.95	4.8	4.1	46.0	18.9	14.9	
Porto	889,295	36	93.84	8.9	2.6	42.5	6.7	29.4	
Portalegre	107,813	4	94.44	4.0	4.5	52.4	17.5	9.8	FSP 2.4
Santarem	321,957	13	91.67	4.3	4.1	43.0	15.1	18.8	
Setubal	402,339	16	93.27	1.5	6.0	38.1	37.8	5.7	
Viseu	261,218	10	89.22	17.9	4.0	21.0	2.3	44.0	FSP 2.3
Villa Real	156,507	6	89.29	7.0	2.3	2.7	2.9	46.0	FEC 2.3
Vianado Castelo	156,884	6	88.63	14.5	7.0	24.4	3.8	36.0	
Angra do Heroismo	49,812	2	90.89	6.1	1.8	23.0	2.3	62.8	
Horta	25,749	1	89.77	--	3.1	23.0	2.3	67.6	
Ponta Delgada	84,365	3	90.46	3.0	2.7	30.3	1.5	54.8	
Funchal	141,133	6	89.10	10.0	1.3	19.4	1.6	62.5	
Total	6,172,437	247	91.74	12.0	3.0	95.0	25.0	58.0	

[a]Percentages rounded to nearest tenth.

[b]Only included if 2 percent or more.

Number of Deputies: One administrative deputy; one PS deputy.

Source: Ministry for Social Communications, April 26, 1975.

MAP 6.1

Portugal: Election Districts

Island Voting Districts

Açores — Angra do Heroismo
Horta
Ponta Delgada

Madeira

Funchal

have a civilian political component. According to Gabriel Ben-Dor, often the military suddenly withdraws from rule after the coup and then returns after a short period of civilian instability. In other instances, there is a gradual development of simultaneous civilian participation and military withdrawal. Occasionally, the military itself undertakes the political socializing of the civilian sector.[1] Portugal is the only case of a modern revolution where the military attempted (and succeeded) in forming a partnership with a civilian coalition to whom it left the process of politicizing the electorate. It is not unusual for a military regime to first achieve governmental stability and then invite civilian participation, nor is it unusual for a military coup to operate simply to change a civilian regime. But the concept of a revolutionary army which incorporates within itself, or is in conjunction with, a particular political movement or party is a relatively frequent one.

In his survey of civilianizing military regimes, Ben-Dor makes the following observations:

> Gradual and partial civilization of Arab military regimes . . . is most certainly in evidence. One of the most significant questions of Middle East politics is the possibility of civilianizing Arab military regimes. Armies have intervened to protect their own interests, yet, when they have done so, at what point will they feel that these interests are assured to the extent that with-drawal from direct rule is possible and desir-able ? . . . They may have moved in with the limited aim of removing a certain regime. . . . Such removal may open so many wounds . . . and may create so much enmity and so many threats that the officers may consider withdrawal much too dangerous, and in fact, impossible. They may have been motivated by goals of reform and "modernization" . . . can we imagine any army claiming that "modernization" having been "ac-complished," it is time to return to the barracks ?
> Elsewhere, in the world we find numerous other examples (Ghana, Burma, Argentina and so on) of abrupt withdrawals by armies, then short period of civilian rule, followed by the reentry of the military to a dominant role in po-litical life. . . . The abruptness of sudden with-drawal is probably caused by factors which are temporary and transitory.[2]

The MFA from its inception assumed a collaboration between the military and civilian politicians. In setting a date for their withdrawal from government within the very context of the MFA program, there was a clear assumption that the political parties would be ready to function quickly and that the major effort by the MFA would be to protect the new freedom from the forces of reaction.

The scheme appears extraordinarily idealistic, more than slightly naive, and entirely without precedent. In earlier Portuguese history, military-civilian partnerships had existed in government, and the nearest antecedent, Dalgado's campaign, suggested the probability of accord. The unknown variable had always been the effects of 48 years of fascist political life.

In Nigeria, we find a military regime rhetorically committed to sharing power with a civilian political system and, in fact, to turning the machinery of government entirely over, eventually, to the civilian sector. But what happened during the 1960-66 period when the Nigerian military and civilians shared authority? An attitude survey of Nigerian civilians involved in government with the military reflects some of the problems both groups face when they try to work together:

> We have seen that politicians played important
> roles under a military regime, that they did so
> while maintaining hostility to the very idea of a
> military regime . . . for the most part they
> perceived the armed forces' unwillingness or
> inability to return rule to them. Politicians had
> complicated rather than simplified views of
> military performance and of their own relation-
> ships to military personnel and the military re-
> gime. They focussed on the role of civil ser-
> vants. Those in the cabinet were less skeptical
> about military withdrawal from rule because
> they were most conscious of friction within the
> armed forces. They clearly perceived limited
> to effective military rule in Nigeria but they
> also recognized the military's ability to con-
> tinue to rule . . . the former president of Ni-
> geria, Dr. Namde Azikiwe . . . argued that
> without the wisdom and experience of civilians,
> the military establishment could not rule demo-
> cratically and that the civil rule depended on the
> military establishment in any form of govern-
> ment . . . the press was almost unanimously
> against Azikiwe's proposals.[3]

In 1974, eight years after the political party system in Nigeria
had been banned, civilians were again dismissed from the government.

> But the need for civilians has not diminished; mil-
> itary elites have not yet developed their own net-
> works for handling political cleavages and demands
> throughout Nigeria. If they try to develop such net-
> works, they will operate in a system where civilian
> elites are still very active and have been legitimated
> by the military itself. . . . The military could dis-
> engage politicians from open politics and dismiss
> them from formal governmental roles. . . . They
> are cut off from the grass roots again, and they
> risk mobilizing wider segments of the civilian
> population into active opposition. [4]

Another example of military-civilian collaboration in government is the Chinese model. While the role of the military in politics
has not officially been defined as such, Janowitz suggests that the
relationship between the government and the military in China is a
"reactive militarism" syndrome, in which civilian politicians recruit
the military to help solve social problems that would be intractable
without army assistance:

> Revolutionary regimes are prone to reactive mili-
> tarism, because their commitment to change gives
> rise to social enemies whom the military is bound
> to keep in check. The general policy cycle in
> China may therefore have a tendency to involve
> the army increasingly in politics at all levels. [5]

There are evidently those within the MFA who would prefer a
PLA approach to the issue of involving civilians in the political apparatus. There are others, especially since the May 1975 feuding
between the Socialist and Communist parties, who would argue to
delegitimize all existing political parties and develop a new party
themselves. However, the MFA has persisted in developing a pluralistic political system and incorporating civilians into the government increasingly as they represent (or are selected by) their political party apparatus. Their Cultural Dynamization Programs allow
them to serve as catalysts getting the citizenry to take part in political decision making. But outside of advocating pluralism and socialism, they remain scrupulously apart from party politics. Among
a people who have lived so long under the rule of a single political

party and who have sworn allegiance to military figures as heads of
state, it is obviously very difficult to disseminate the idea that the
MFA itself is neither a political party nor the advocate of a party.
Individuals send in contributions of money to the MFA much as they
would, in other democracies, contribute to funding political party
programs. These contributions are carefully recorded in the Bulletin. Since February 1975, these donations have been listed as contributions toward the MFA Cultural Program for the workers or as
contributions for the Cultural Dynamization program. [6]

THE POLITICAL PARTIES

The Portuguese Communist Party, in a publication of the Ministry for Mass Communication, March 1975, described itself as
follows:

> For the consolidation of liberty, construction of
> democracy and to assure our national indepen-
> dence; this is the program of the PCP. To attain
> these basic objectives: we advocate destroying
> the fascist regime and installing a democratic
> regime; liquidating the monopolies and promoting
> the general economic development; agricultural
> reform by distributing the land to the workers;
> raising the level of life of the working class by
> democratizing access to culture; to liberate Por-
> tugal from imperialism by granting the indepen-
> dence of the Portuguese colonies; to pursue a
> political policy of peace and friendship with all
> peoples.
> The PCP considers that its objectives corre-
> spond with the interests of the proletariat and
> other antimonopolistic classes who also seek the
> national interest.
> After the 25 of April, once again the program
> of the PCP was re-examined and additional plans
> were made. As of this time, the PCP considers as
> important problems: the re-establishment of the
> democratic state . . . the pursuit of decolonization
> . . . rehabilitation of that which was sabotaged by
> the large proprietors and land owners; continuing
> the struggle against the reactionary forces which
> continue to manifest themselves.

The Portuguese communists know from personal
experience the price of liberty. For that reason,
the PCP is committed to the struggle for a democratic Portugal with assurance of all liberties and
integrity, and against activities of partisan politics.
The communists also declare that the real conditions for the construction of a democratic society
cannot be achieved without the PCP nor is the PCP
going to act against the will of the masses.
The position of PCP in the struggle is for a
democratic Portugal, peaceful and independent,
engaged in the struggle for socialism, abolishes
the exploitation of man by man and assures the continual development of the utilization of the means
of production for the material and spiritual welfare
of the workers. [7]

The Portuguese Socialist Party had been organized in exile two
years prior to the revolution. The leadership includes persons who
were well known in Portugal for their years of opposition to the
Salazar-Caetano regime. Some of them had at one time been members of the Communist Party and were either expelled from it or resigned as a result of ideological disputes. Others had worked in the
campaign of General Delgado or the student movement of 1962. This
is how they defined themselves and their program in the same pamphlet.

The PS considers that the process initiated on
April 25, in accord with the primary facts of the
historical condition necessary for transition into
socialism and for the peaceful process of democratic politics.
PS affirms that liberty is revolutionary and that
the Portuguese people are not reactionary. The
essence of the challenge emanating from the April 25
Program of the MFA to the constitutional assembly
will result from the will of the Portuguese people,
in liberty and without subterfuge and restrictions.
At the constituent assembly, PS will defend the
constitutional model of democracy that will reinforce the alliance of the people and the democratic
forces with the MFA.
PS considers that the base of public liberty is
the defense of the interests of the workers and that
the exercise of their liberties is the condition for

participation by citizens in political, economic,
social and cultural life.

In light of the historical experience of the
bourgeois democracies, PS considers that it is
not sufficient to proclaim these liberties. It is
incumbent upon the socialist to actualize themat-
ical, economic and social conditions of the constituency as the uniquely effective possibility of
liberty. PS promises a foreign politic of national
independence of solidarity and cooperation with all
peoples. A politic of progressive disengagement
will be adopted in reference to the political and
military blocs and conducting a policy of non-
alignment. Conscious of the conditions of foreign
politics in relation with the actual condition of the
Portuguese that our first objective is the consolidation of democracy (an indispensable condition
for the commencement of the socialist ways of life)
PS estimates that the process for external alliances
should proceed in a diversified and even manner,
that extraneous quarrels do not consume our great
strength. [8]

The Popular Democratic Party (PPD) is non-Marxist, progressive, and left of center. Their party leaders were deeply involved
in opposition politics, but many were members of Movement for
Democracy (MUD) and various reformist Christian-humanist associations. They have been subjected to repeated violent demonstrations and attacks by extremist left groups who see them as "bourgeois democrats." They are relatively vulnerable, since they are
the major center, only non-Marxist party in the first year government. While the PCP has drawn financial support from the Soviet
Union, and PSP has acknowledged financial support from the European socialist parties, PPD has gotten support from Portuguese
emigrants in the United States and Canada. PPD describes itself as
follows:

The Party of Popular Democrats is a social-
democratic party, whose principal objective is
constructing a socialist society with equality,
solidarity and liberty for all the people. For attaining this objective, PPD proposes a progressive transformation of Portuguese society through
profound reforms in the economics, social and
cultural structures, through extending the self-
determination of the population as expressed by vote.

This will achieve a democratic society in Portugal.

It is our aspiration to construct a democracy through a political condition which assures the economic, social and cultural integrity of the country.

In our concern for democratic politics, PPD proposes to grant citizens fundamental liberties with the vote as the fundamental expression of popular will. We propose to defend the impartiality of the organs of information of the society, to affirm the right of opposition, and to promote a politic of peace and solidarity with other peoples, especially through integration with the European Community.

PPD proposes a profound redistribution of wealth and national revenues, a system of employment, health and social security to recognize the needs of the workers and the employers without recourse to damaging the expectations of the rest of the population; to defend agrarian reform and intervention primarily in the sectors of housing, transportation and environment.

The political program of PPD stresses the necessity of a democratic economy achieved through elaborate, democratic planning, without repercussions to either wages or the fiscal system. In regard to the means of production, PPD are in favor of subordination of the economy to the political goals and of putting the private interests to the benefit of the community. For that reason, the nationalization and the control by the state of monopolies and the major sectors of the economy is necessary. The private sector must accept the initiative of social utility.

In conclusion, PPD proposed a realistic transformation, secure and progressive, for Portuguese society, to actualize our liberty.[9]

Their descriptions of themselves suggest that the three major parties are fairly similar. Each is certainly in the mainstream of European politics. Social Democrat, Socialist, and Communist parties are to be found throughout western Europe except for Spain. (Spain does not accept the legitimacy of any but the National Party.) Clearly the PPD is in favor of maintaining ties with the Western

allies (EEC, NATO) and in maintaining a private (albeit controlled)
enterprise system. Neither the Communist nor the Socialist Party
seems to want separation from NATO or isolation from the EEC.
In fact, in their campaign literature, the Socialist Party strongly
urged adoption of all the necessary steps to full membership in the
EEC.

All three parties, moreover, support the MFA program. If
the Socialist Party specifically articulates its support, the Communist Party program is almost plagiarized out of the MFA literature.
In fact, at their October 1974 congress, the PCP eliminated from
their statement of objectives the phrase "dictatorship of the proletariat" because, as they explained, the Portuguese people had had
enough of dictatorships. All three parties stress working in a
pluralistic democracy.

There were four smaller parties. The Social Democratic
Christian Party (PCSD) or (PT), also called the Workers Party,
identified itself with the old regime but accepted the essential principles of a socialist politics and decolonization. The Independent
Social Democratic Party (PSDI) considered itself independent of the
historical stereotypes of social democrats. Their favorite issue
was decolonization, which they believed should proceed according to
the decisions of the colonists.

The Christian Democratic Party (PDC) was founded after
April 25. It has remained fairly obscure, having presented a program favoring private enterprise and humanistic values. Neither
the PSDI nor the PDC ran candidates for the constitutional assembly.
Members of these parties and of the PCSD had, by the time of the
elections, gravitated toward other center and center-right parties.

The party which seems to have consolidated centrist sentiment
is the Center Social Democratic Party (CDS). CDS obtained 7.6
percent of the popular vote in the constitutional assembly elections,
and has 12 representatives to that assembly. However, it did not
secure representatives in cabinet posts--although it had been heavily
represented in the cabinet prior to September 28, 1974. Because of
the demonstrations against them and the threatened violence to their
party's candidates, CDS made relatively few public policy statements
during the campaign.

The CDS is a social democratic party more akin to the Italian
Christian Democratic party than to the Scandinavian one. CDS stands
to the right of PPD on issues of private enterprise, centralization,
and close alliance with Western Europe and the United States. CDS
political figures have expressed solidarity with the Brazilian government and are in favor of agrarian reform based on government
grants to farmers and price supports. Many CDS leaders held minor
offices in the previous regime and are therefore associated in the

public mind with that dictatorship. They have strong support from the rural north and central areas, primarily from people who are church oriented and entrepreneurial. They had agreed to the MFA pact with the political parties in early March and so accepted the de-colonization program. Earlier, as a party and as individuals, they had advocated slower decolonization and the formation of a kind of commonwealth arrangement with the colonies. There is ample evi-dence that their support in terms of funds and sympathy comes from Portuguese in the United States, but they did not appear on the ballot in the United States, so the 4,000 absentee votes were almost entirely for PPD.

Also to the right of the parties in the cabinet is the Popular Party of the Monarchy (PPM). This party, which would restore a constitutional monarchy with a social democratic economic system, grew out of support for Princess Maria Pia de Saxe-Coburg, the Duchess of Braganza, daughter of King Carlos and Queen Manuelista, claimant to the throne. The princess had returned to Portugal from exile in 1965, and because of her support of the Social Democrat Directory and the National Liberation Front, was exiled again. She returned to stay in Portugal after April 25. PPM drew a slightly better percentage than some of the extreme leftist parties. This in itself, and the fact that this vote again came from the subsistence farming areas, indicates the persistence of a diffuse affection for one or another brand of social democrat politics.

Parties to the left of the PCP, many of them outgrowths of the various movements of opposition, were considerably active in the campaign. Two of these movement-parties were almost entirely student groups. The largest of these is the combined Portuguese Democratic Movement/Democratic Electoral Commission (MDP/CDE), which merged in October 1974. Their campaign slogan was "Unity" and in fact they attempted to bridge the distance between PS and PCP politicians. PS and PPD view them as another Communist group, and a tool for PCP to obtain inordinate representation. MDP, which had been a broad leftist opposition movement before the revo-lution, attempted for a while after April 25 to remain a movement with general leftist support. When the MFA included this party in the cabinet after the aborted March 11 coup, speculation was rampant that the MFA was trying to force a greater proportion of PDP power than could be legitimately warranted. This was underscored by the fact that the other extreme left parties were embroiled in bitter ar-gument with the PCP, which they called "false leftists." Among the far-left groups, only the MDP/CDE escaped being classified as "infantile leftists" by the PCP. Perhaps the major difference be-tween MDP/CDE and PCP is that PCP looks to Moscow and MDP/CDE adopts a more classically Marxist interpretation. At any rate, this

is a fine point rather than a broad difference. MDP members tend
to be younger and come more often from the ranks of the professional and student classes.

Movement of Leftist Socialists (MES) is a Christian-Marxist
organization of dissidents who opposed the prior regime. As a political party, this group also suffered from the draining of some of
its membership into the PSP, FSP, and PPD after the revolution.
It supports unity with the MFA and an "acceleration of the struggle
of anti-capitalism and the transformation of existing institutions."

The Popular Socialist Front (FSP) broke away from the PS in
early 1975 toward a more militant antifascist stance. This is one
of the groups which advocates the formation of armed antifascist
cadres among the masses. Another party with a similar but less
effective electoral support is the League for Revolutionary Action
(LUAR). They advocate an armed struggle against fascism and
capitalism and oppose large political parties.

Perhaps the most ubiquitous, if not the largest, of the extreme
leftist groups is the Movement for the Reorganization of the Party
of the Proletariat (MRPP), a Maoist group comprised almost entirely of students and professionals. They actively oppose both the
MFA and the PCP and consider them, along with the other political
parties and movements, to have betrayed the working class by functioning in a coalition with "capitalists" and taking a "gradualist,
non-revolutionary stance."[10] Their actions have included disrupting
other parties' meetings and rallies, and unlicensed mass demonstrations. During May, June, and July, MRPP organized demonstrations for immediate decolonization and formed a coalition with
Alliance of Workers and Peasants (AOC) and Union for a Popular
Democracy (UDP) along the lines of a Marxist-Leninist-Maoist popular front. MRPP members have the dubious distinction of having
been the first leftists placed under arrest by the MFA. They were
also refused admission to China when a delegation flew to Peking in
March 1975. They have consistently led anti-American demonstrations and were responsible for the illegal arrest and detention of
two U.S. marines in Lisbon. Both the MRPP and the Portuguese
Communist Party-Marxist-Leninist (PCP-ML) label the PCP "revisionist," and advocate a violent struggle in order to achieve the
overthrow of the capitalist classes. These two groups have fostered
several other militant leftist parties. One of these, the Alliance of
Workers and Peasants (AOC), growing out of the PCP-ML, has made
inroads on union organization and initiated violent wildcat strikes.

A Trotskyite organization, International Communist League
(LCI), has assumed some importance in the northern districts, in
particular in Porto. Militant anarchists and anarcho syndicalists
have formed the Movement for Portuguese Liberation (MLP), not

to be confused with the Portuguese Liberation Movement, which is a paramilitary organization believed to be based in Spain with the objective of overthrowing the provisional government and restoring a fascist state. Union for a Popular Democracy (UDP), another Marxist-Leninist group, won one seat in the constitutional assembly.

The Trotskyite group, the League of International Communists (LCI), has consistently criticized the participation of leftists in the constituent assembly and favors formation of local councils. LCI did run candidates for the assembly, nonetheless, and received the smallest percentage vote (.19 percent).

The MFA as a whole considers the political philosophy of the social democratic parties and the Maoist parties incompatible with their view of Portuguese socialism. On the other hand, members have indicated that it should be possible for the PS and PCP to form a working coalition as socialists--at least, this is what they would like to have.

Perhaps, had the MFA initiated the revolution with totalitarian military rule, these two warring parties might have found common cause to push for civilianization and democratization. However, given their histories and the recent failures of socialist-Communist coalitions in France and Italy, it is highly unlikely that they would have established any bond of trust or mutual regard.

The leadership of these two groups is composed of experienced and competent politicians and political scientists. Throughout years in exile, the leaders of both PS and PCP took an active role in international economic and political affairs. Perhaps Soares' experience of French politics enhanced his sensitivities and anxieties about working in coalition with a Communist party. Certainly Cunhal's experience in Czechoslovakia reinforced his commitment to Soviet-style Communism, and did little to convince him that a Maoist popular democracy approach to socialism was appropriate to a European country.

Interparty antagonisms have been rife from the very inception of the revolution. PCP literature challenges the legitimacy and even the personalities of those in the Maoist, Trotskyite, and Marxist-Leninist groups. There are allusions to counterrevolution by rightist reactionaries and to the bourgeois appeal of social democracy, but the PCP is particularly aware of the danger to the revolution presented by the extreme or, as they put it, "pseudo-radicals" of the left.

PPD propaganda is directed at the danger of totalitarian rule. PPD supporters in the United States staged a massive demonstration in Washington, D.C. in March 1975 where 10,000 people protested "totalitarianism of any kind in Portugal." This was taken by PPD as a direct response to their position after the anti-PPD violence in Setubal--which PPD attributed to a subsidiary of PCP.

The Portuguese Socialist Party appears to view PCP as the major threat to a pluralistic socialism. Much of PS's large electoral support is working-class support, and the fact that workers are often members of labor unions headed almost entirely by Communists fans PS-PCP enmity. While PS accepts common cause with PPD in opposing PCP, the socialists are not comfortable with that kind of alliance either.

One of the major strengths of the Socialist Party is its close relationship to the various European socialist parties. Besides offering direct financial aid, most of the other European counterparts are party to coalition governments through which they can have relevance to the faltering economy of Portugal by directing economic aid and trade policies. Many of these countries are members of the EEC, and Portugal views entry to the EEC as an economic priority. On the other hand, the Communist Party certainly has parallel connections with the Soviet bloc--if Portugal really wanted to commit itself to that economic and political sphere, which is, however, unlikely.

The predominance of PPD and PS in the government after September 1975 assured Portugal's eventual acceptance in the European community, and through the EEC and an $85,000,000 grant from the United States, some prospect of economic equilibrium.

DIRECT MFA INTERACTION

The troubled relationships among the MFA and the political parties make little sense if examined in terms of agreement over political ideology. They do make sense in the context of the novelty of parliamentarianism after 50 years of dictatorial government. Many party members, with no experience of pluralism, have in the name of a libertarian ideology behaved like fascists toward other political groups. The extreme left has demanded armed vigilante corps; some groups have violently interfered with rallies and meetings, and even attacked the offices of rivals. At the May Day 1975 celebration rally, PCP members and PSP members seated in adjacent sections of the stadium shouted epithets at each other rather than joining in communal festivity. All of this indicates that democracy and pluralism in Portugal's first year of freedom have been more often rhetorical than actual.

The MFA has taken a hand in quelling the disturbances and violent outbreaks among party enthusiasts. Sometimes they have been criticized by the parties for not having acted quickly or forcefully enough: It was criticized particularly in the case of the Setubal actions against the PPD meeting of March 8 and again, at the May

Day rally in Lisbon when Dr. Soares was denied a seat on the speaker's platform, and when it failed to settle immediately the issue of
the typographers' union strike at Republica newspaper in mid-May
1975. In each case, the MFA has been reluctant to use force in
what was perceived as a political arena.

Taking these crises chronologically, let us try to analyze (1)
how the situation appeared to the political parties involved, (2) how
it appeared to the MFA, and (3) the outcome of MFA action in terms
of political party reaction.

The first clash between the civilian politicians and the MFA
climaxed on July 10, when the first provisional government cabinet
resigned. The parties in that cabinet--the Christian Democrats,
the Social Democrats, the Popular Democrats, the Socialist Party,
and the Communist Party--were a coalition of irreconcilables, and
the combination produced a do-nothing policy. As Jane Kramer
astutely described it:

> There was a provisional government of civilians
> which included a Communist Labor Minister of
> Soviet persuasion, a Socialist Foreign Minister
> who modelled himself on Francois Mitterand, a
> Capitalist Economics Minister with American
> ideas about money, and a weak Prime Minister
> who adored the president (Spinola). And there
> was finally the Movement, which did not want to
> enter any of the arguments and consequently did
> not know what to do about Spinola when he went
> off barnstorming the country, talking as if Portu-
> gal was his. . . . After a month of lavish and un-
> comfortable praise of the program, Spinola and
> his junta simply began to disregard it. . . . They
> tried to censor television; the captains had to put
> their own men into the studio to stop them; they
> turned against the press, this time with a decree
> permitting the suspension of newspapers and jour-
> nals for "ideological aggression"; when they shut
> down a small Maoist paper, the captains deferred
> to them, but when they shut down Lisbon's three
> best daily newspapers for reporting an anti-war
> demonstration, the captains had to force them to
> lift the suspensions. . . .
>
> By July, it was clear to the captains that their
> reluctance to assume power had benefitted no one
> in Portugal except Spinola and his partisans. . . .
> Spinola had his friend, a lawyer named Adelino da

Palma Carlos, formally present the Council of
State with a number of proposals that would give
them direct control over the country's policies.
Palma Carlos would ask for the right to name--
and by implication--dismiss the Ministers,
claiming, with some justification, that it was difficult to work with a Cabinet whose Socialists and
Communists felt free to challenge decisions publicly that they helped make privately. . . . [The
Council and the Junta rejected the proposals and]
Spinola characteristically abandoned the bitter
Palma Carlos--who resigned, taking with him
four Ministers, among them two from the moderate PPD, which until that moment expected to have
the General as its Presidential candidate--and
began to maneuver one of his own most ardent
Army, partisans. . . .[11]

Kramer's account provides an excellent insight into why the
MFA's original intention of governance by civilian politicians was an
idea ahead of its time. The political parties, as well as the people
themselves, had time neither to understand the MFA program, nor
to formulate positions in relation to it. Nor had there been time for
anyone in the government, including the MFA, to appraise the real
conditions of the economy or the society they were attempting to govern. At the time of the dissolution of the cabinet, the rightist and
center parties began to interpret the MFA position as inspired by the
Communist Party. The Socialist and Communist Parties, on the
other hand, saw the MFA position as a legitimate one and did not
protest their lost ministries nor their new coalition with independents
and MFA ministers.

PS and PCP were forewarned about the intended September 28
coup.[12] They demonstrated their support of the MFA by communicating the information and calling up their membership to stand
vigilante duty, guard the roads into Lisbon, and search for concealed
weapons. Neither of these parties or PPD were implicated in the
attempted coup, although the rightist parties, which called for the
demonstrations supporting Spinola, were clearly implicated.

Meanwhile, throughout the summer, wildcat strikes had been
occurring. Although there were no union or municipal elections,
activist members of PCP and MDP/CDE (until February 1975 still a
movement),according to PS and PPD sources, were working their
way into positions in union leadership and municipal offices. PCP,
in full cooperation with the MFA had repeatedly ordered its unions
back to work. In so doing they lost constituencies,as AOC and some

of the other more extreme leftist groups increased the fervor of
their opposition to coalition.

Spinola and his supporters were eager to have elections as
quickly as possible in order that an organized center-right following,
coupled with the general's charisma and the inexperience of the majority of the voters, would quickly halt the leftist momentum of the
provisional government. PS, PCP, MDP/CDE, and MES argued
that the electorate was politically naive and unaware of its options.
The MFA leadership agreed with them, but elections had already
been scheduled for March 1975.

In December, the labor organizations recommended that the
unions be joined together into a single body. This was clearly intended to prevent further wildcat strikes and also to strengthen the
controls established by the new leftist leadership of the unions. By
January 28, 1975, the cabinet was deadlocked debating legislation to
create such a monolithic labor union. The legislation, originally
proposed by the Communist Party and supported by the MFA Coordinating Committee, aroused the anger of the PPD and PS, two of
the three parties in the coalition cabinet. They threatened to resign
from the cabinet if the legislation was approved. Cunhal who said
that "No isolated force could construct democracy in Portugal,"
feared the destruction of the coalition if the matter was forced. The
Church issued a statement to the effect that while it would not side
with any party, the workers had the fundamental right of choosing
their own unions. But Intersindical was formed anyway and granted
sole privileges for arbitration of labor disputes.

The conflicts among the political parties and between the parties and the MFA mushroomed out of that controversy.

On April 30, the High Council of the Revolution (the body which
superseded the old Junta of National Salvation and Council of State
combined) announced that Intersindical (the monolithic labor union)
would henceforth have arbitration jurisdiction over all labor disputes
and contracts. The next day, at a May Day rally sponsored by Intersindical and the four parties in the government (PPD, PS, PCP, and
MDP) the animosities, which had been growing since December,
erupted publicly. The Intersindical, which had been created by the
January legislation, was headed primarily by Communist Party af-
filiates. On the speakers' platform were the president, the prime
minister, leaders of the Intersindical, and Cunhal. Soares entered
the stadium with the banner bearers of his party, and they sat in a
bloc next to the PCP. What began as a spirited shouting of party
slogans quickly became a volley of angry epithets between the two
groups. Union members and leaders with PS sympathies flocked to
the grandstand occupied by Soares demanding his presence on the
speakers' platform. After 15 minutes of exhortation, Dr. Soares

agreed to seek entrance to the speakers' platform. With 100 of his
followers he was denied admission, and within ten minutes Socialist
banners were massed in the arena and, amid presidential and ministerial pleas for unity, the Socialist Party marched out of the stadium.

Within two weeks of that time, after numerous party rallies
and statements by PS and PPD had condemned Intersindical, the
Communist Party, and the Revolutionary Council, the typographers'
union struck Republica, a major daily Lisbon newspaper.

Nine months earlier, in August 1974, Republica had been one
of the three major daily newspapers suspended from operations by
Spinola's Ad Hoc Press Committee. Editor Raul Rega, a leader of
the Portuguese Socialist Party, had been Minister for Information in
the Spinola Cabinet, but the newspaper had been accused of "betray-
ing the true aspirations of our people for total and unconditional independence," and had already been fined in August 1974 for failing
to publish the complete text of a speech by Spinola.

In response to the typographers' lockout of the newspaper's
editorial staff, the army moved the typographers out of the building
in armored vehicles on May 21. During the two-week crisis that
followed, the Communist Party was charged with violating freedom
of expression, the Socialist Party threatened to resign from the
cabinet (in fact, Soares and Francisco Zenha, the ministers for
justice, did not attend cabinet meetings for more than a week) and
called for support from EEC countries, claiming that the fragile hold
on democracy in Portugal was threatened by a Communist takeover.
The MFA minister for communications, while assigning the case for
adjudication in the courts, also stated that the strikers were in violation of the new press law, and that the editorial staff had the right
to carry its views in the newspaper. However, with no printers to
print the paper, Republica lacked the means for communicating its
views. In the process of the dispute, Soares also called for immediate secret elections in the unions as well as local elections.

On January 28, the legislation creating the Intersindical was
established. The government had banned street demonstrations,
but MRPP, LCI, and other far-leftist groups began demonstrating in
Lisbon against the NATO naval maneuvers which began January 30.
At the same time, rumors were circulated to the press that the Soviet Union had asked for bases for its fishing fleet in Portugal. The
combination of events, coming in the wake of the PS-PCP feud, presented new dimensions for political interaction.

The leftist groups had used street demonstrations and wall
slogans as their principal vehicles; the illegal MRPP demonstration
marked a turning point in their tactics. While they had been consistently pushing the MFA into taking repressive fascistic type actions like political arrests and bans on demonstrations, they now

commenced a campaign of disrupting the meetings and rallies of
other political parties--sometimes violently. In this tactic they
were joined by the Agricultural and Operators Commission (AOC).

Since many of the more politically sophisticated had already
become wary of possible foreign intervention (as in Chile), it was not
long before suspicions were voiced that MRPP and AOC were being
used by the CIA to cause disruptions to polarize the people and bring
on a rightist counterrevolution.

On February 8, the provisional government announced that the
elections for the constitutional assembly would be held not later than
April 25, but would definitely not be held in March. At the same
time, the illegal demonstrations moved to the U.S. Embassy in Lisbon. Two weeks later, the MFA announced to the political parties
that it would seek a major role in the constitutional governments by
creating a Council of State which would have veto powers and the
right to introduce legislation. They had also named April 12 as the
date for the elections.

PPD and PS objected strongly to the proposal, claiming that
such veto powers would deny the purposes of a pluralistic democracy,
since the elected officials would be subject to approval by a nonelected
body. The MFA leadership, which considered itself an elected body
(indeed it was elected by its own membership), was increasingly
alarmed at the prospect of interparty rivalries leaving the way open
for counterrevolution. PPD, on the other hand, saw the illegal and
increasingly violent "antireactionary" demonstrations as a prelude
to a prospective Communist coup or a Communist dictatorship of the
MFA. When rioting broke out against its Setubal meeting on March 8,
PPD laid the blame directly on the Communist Party "and its satel-
lites" and complained of the slowness and inaction of the MFA investigations.

The Christian Democrats had experienced a similar episode on
February 28. Major Sanches Ossario, a close ally of General
Spinola and a CDS leader turned down an army offer to drive him
safely from a Lisbon organizing meeting which had been invaded by
a mob of 2,000 extreme leftists, hurling rocks and shouting epithets
at the 4,000 assembled CDS members. About 15 people were injured
by the stones and 500 troops in armored vehicles and mounted police-
men quelled the demonstration.

While the participants in these violent episodes and in the illegal demonstrations comprised a very small minority of the leftists,
they found considerable sympathy in their March 12 anti-CIA demonstrations. Frank Carlucci, then newly appointed U.S. Ambassador
to Portugal, took up residence there late in 1974. His prior position
in Zaire gave rise to rumors of his being a CIA agent or ally. There
was never an anti-American attitude as such, but there was consider-

able hostility toward suspected CIA personnel. Consequently, the demonstrations at the embassy in February and the attacks on four foreign journalists in early March in Setubal, while condemned by the government, were treated sympathetically in the Portuguese press.

Despite these problems, on March 5, 1975, the council of ministers announced its satisfaction with the technical arrangements developed for the forthcoming April 12 elections. They thanked Eng. Fernandes, the minister for mass equipment and environment, and dismissed the ministry for territorial affairs, since there were no longer any overseas provinces.

The rightist attempt at counterrevolution on March 11 brought a harsh reality to the fears of the MFA and the leftist parties that the center and right could reverse the MFA coup. Major Ossario's Christian Democrats were directly linked with the events of that day, as were individuals in leadership positions with the Independent Social Democrats and the Center Democrats. The MFA, in its investigatory account of the background to the attempted coup, placed partial blame on the PS and PPD, as well as the liberal weekly newspaper Expresso (operated by a leader of PPD) for having stirred up dissension.[13] Indeed, the vociferous allegations by PS and PPD leaders of MFA collusion with the Communist Party, and statements which challenged the MFA decision on unions and the election dates, had probably led the rightist elements to believe that there would be strong popular support for their coup.

The actions of AOC, MRPP, and the Christian Socialist Party resulted in their suspension from the election ballot. The bank workers' strike, the nationalization of the banks and insurance companies, and the agrarian reform decrees which followed shortly afterward were all facilitated by the reorganization of the government that followed upon the unsuccessful coup. (Figures 6.1 and 6.2 illustrate the successive stages in organization of the provisional government.) Many of the civilians representing political parties who were called in to form the new cabinet had already served in cabinet positions. Even one of the MDP/CDE ministers had served in the first cabinet. The radical departure was to eliminate the Junta and the Council of State and replace it with the Revolutionary Council. This was a departure as well from the previous regime's organizational system, which, although it included a Council of State and the Corporate Body, had seldom taken recommendations from them or hesitated in vetoing their decisions. Now the MFA established the High Council of the Revolution, including high ranking officers who, as members of the JSN had demonstrated their support for the MFA program, members of the MFA Coordinating Committee, and representatives elected by the MFA Assembly. Two cabinet ministers (labor and foreign affairs) were also drafted onto the Revolutionary Council, which finally consisted of 28 men.

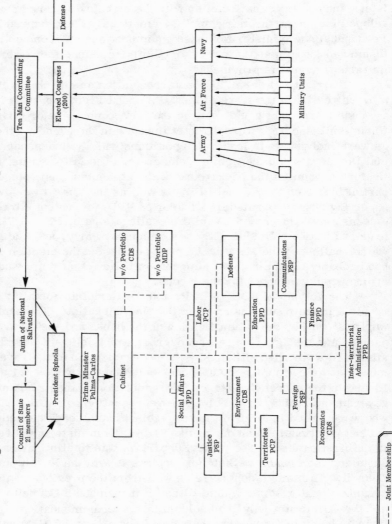

FIGURE 6.1

Portuguese Provisional Government Organization, April 25–July 10, 1974

FIGURE 6.2

Portuguese Provisional Government Organization, March 17, 1975

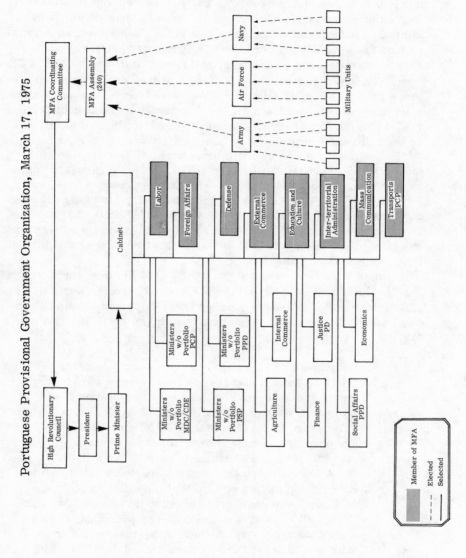

The old cabinet resigned on March 17 and on March 25 a new cabinet was sworn in. In the previous cabinet, there had been some independents, such as Eng. Maria de Lourdes Pintassilgo, Minister for Social Affairs, who had prior experience in government and had taken part in movement work, but had not formed any relationships with existing parties. Notably absent from the new cabinet were any ministers independent of political parties. The 15-member cabinet included seven MFA officers, two PCP representatives, two PPD representatives, two PS leaders, and two affiliated with MDP/CDE.

The major parties were advised that they could accept or reject a pact with the MFA by which they would agree to maintain the same cabinet composition until constitutional elections could be carried out in the fall of 1975, agree to the maintenance of the High Council of the Revolution for a three-to-five year period, and abide by the outline for a new constitution. Despite considerable reluctance, PS, PPD, CDS, PCP, MDP/CDE, and FSP signed the pact on April 4. The six extreme left-wing parties refused to sign.

President Costa Gomes said that he recognized the pact as a controversial action but felt that it was justified on the basis of the turbulence of the months since the provisional government was first established. (See Appendix G for the Agreement and Constitutional requirements.)

In an interview reported on April 14, 1975 a leading figure in the Revolutionary Council and the MFA and a former member of the JSN Admiral Rosa Coutinho, alleged that there remained still another possibility for citizen participation in political life with the MFA:

> But while emphasizing vote "confusion" Admiral
> Coutinho indicated that the armed forces were
> themselves uncertain of the kind of socialism they
> wanted. "We have no definite ideology," he said.
> "There are many different ideas of socialism. We
> are open to any kind of experiment by the people
> that will lead to a Portuguese-type of socialism." . . .
> A few days ago the admiral created a stir by pub-
> licly posing the suggestion that the military needed a
> civilian counterpart on which it could count--the exist-
> ing political parties being too much preoccupied with
> their own interests. He said today that he had in
> mind a coalition of leftist parties, but denied that he
> was talking about a single-party system. Other
> parties, he said, could continue to exist.
> Many voters, the admiral said, cannot decide
> what party to vote for, and have told the armed

forces they wished to vote for them; this, he said,
is impossible because the armed forces are not a
party.

But, he went on, a coalition that backed the
armed forces only could become a "civilian armed
forces movement" and might be ready for legislative elections, possibly in six months.

He singled out the Socialist leader, Mr. Soares,
a former Foreign Minister and now a Minister Without Portfolio, as a man who leaned too far toward
the Social Democrats; the Socialist leaders in general, the admiral said, "are not in the same boat
with us."

Admiral Coutinho said that the Socialist leaders,
through a campaign they began in January against
the Communists and the military, had helped to
create the political climate that led to an attempted
rightist military coup on March 11, . . . [The report should be issued before the election and] would
not implicate the Socialists in the plot itself. [14]

On the evening of April 9, there was another assault on a PPD
meeting, this time in Beja. Beja, like Setubal, is part of the southern agrarian belt which, because of its opposition activism and history of political martyrdom, was affiliated early with the Communist
Party. Many of the people in these districts consider every other
party reactionary.

At this time the MFA was expressing dissatisfaction with the
political parties for focusing on partisan issues rather than acting
to "keep the revolution moving." In contrast with the other parties,
PCP continued to focus on the tasks and priorities announced by the
MFA.

There were organizational reasons as well as evident policy
bases for the different approaches taken by PPD, PS, MDP, and PCP.
The latter two parties knew well in advance that their elector potential was limited. Cunhal had forecast as early as January that PCP
could expect about 12 percent of the vote. MDP/CDE had become a
party too late and had lost too many of its strongest leaders to expect
to make much of an electoral showing. PS and PPD were using all
their energies to appeal to the masses and to distinguish themselves
as new political entities. They pushed especially hard because, despite the fact that PS was receiving financial aid from other socialist
parties in Europe (and announced the amounts and donors publicly),
despite the fact that PPD was receiving private funds from its own
affluent membership and from Portuguese in the Western Hemisphere,

they lacked the full-time experienced staff that had long been a part
of PCP, and that became more numerous and evident as the campaign progressed.

There is no question that the predominance of PCP members
among the union leadership contributed greatly to disseminating information, encouraging attendance at meetings and rallies, soliciting
volunteers, and generally lending prestige to their campaign. Furthermore, the attacks on the other parties, including threats to
assembly candidates and party leaders constituted still another di-
version for limited energies and resources. In efforts to protect
themselves against interparty violence, PPD maintained a full-time
guard system at their various headquarters. PS did so as well.
CDS finally gave up on holding public meetings altogether. But when
violent attacks against political parties ensued in June 1975 the headquarters buildings destroyed were those of PCP and MDP/CDC.

Since there was no interparty debate permitted on the media,
and since none transpired at public meetings, there was no way for
the electorate to compare parties and programs except by visiting
campaign headquarters, attending meetings of all parties, and doing
some pretty intensive reading. The campaign literature, as we have
seen, was somewhat vague and not really amenable to comparison
shopping. Clearly, CDS favored a capitalist economy and democratic politics. But what about the accusations that some of their
leaders were conspirators in the attempted coups? Certainly, PPD
favored free enterprise with state control over essential sectors and
a democratic politic. But what about their often anti-Communist
acts? The Socialist party clearly favored state control of the economy with aid to small business and agrarian reform, but why did
they keep arguing with the MFA, who also proposed this?

These kinds of questions and doubts, coupled with chaotic attacks and repeated threats by extremist groups and their own inexperience of open elections, led some people to suggest voting for the
MFA itself. In response, MFA leaders suggested to the electorate
another option--the blank ballot.

The government was trying to encourage everyone to vote.
There were rumors that penalties would be invoked on people who
did not go to the polls. But instead of compelling people to make a
choice when they felt unprepared to do so, it was suggested that they
register to vote, go to the polls, and cast an unmarked ballot. At the
same time, illustrated literature utilizing a very limited vocabulary
was distributed to explain the voting procedure.

This option of the blank ballot gave rise to widespread misun-
derstanding in the world press on the intentions and objectives of the
MFA in the elections. In fact, only 6 percent of the electorate chose
this option.

The MFA also described the elections as a "pedagogic exercise." They viewed this first experience of open elections as a learning experience for the Portuguese people. They expressed the opinion that the "traumatic events of the campaign" had interfered with the political education of the people.

Since the outcome of the election was largely favorable to the Socialist Party, which got 38 percent of the vote, these suspicions about the capability of the people to make electoral choices was interpreted by the Socialist Party and others as a direct attack on the PS choice.

PARTY REACTIONS TO THE VOTE

The Socialist Party clearly interpreted its large constituency as a mandate for greater decision-making influence in the government. They accepted the choice as an indication that the voters wanted socialism, and wanted the PS brand of socialism--a multiparty system with national welfare schemes, a planned economy, and cooperative enterprise.

PPD expressed satisfaction with the outcome. They pointed to their program of realistic social change and cooperation with the European economy and politics, and viewed their combined majority with PS as an affirmation of the noncommunist sympathies of the people.

The Communist Party, expecting only about 12 percent of the vote (they got closer to 13 percent), felt that they had made important inroads in educating the public. Their campaign slogan, "Who's Afraid of the Communists?", had evoked a response that satisfied them. Furthermore, their combined vote with MDP/CDE and FSP suggested that public sympathy for communism was still stronger than its sympathy for the right-center party, CDS.

By the opening date of the constitutional assembly, June 2, the political parties represented in that assembly had decided that it would be a forum for free debate on national issues as well as the site for shaping a new constitution and a parliament responsive to the public vote for socialism and liberty.

NOTES

1. Gabriel Ben-Dor, "Civilianization of Military Regimes in the Arab World," Armed Forces and Society 1, no. 3 (Spring 1975).
   2. Ibid., pp. 318-19.

3. Henry Bienen, "Transition from Military Rule: The Case of Western State Nigeria," Armed Forces and Society 1, no. 3 (Spring 1975): 340.

4. Ibid., pp. 340-41.

5. Lynn T. White, III, "The Liberation Army and the Chinese People," Armed Forces and Society 1, no. 3 (Spring 1975): 379.

6. Movimento--Boletim das Forcas Armadas, April 8, 1975, p. 6.

7. Portugal: Information, Ministry for Social Communications, March 1975. (Trans. from the French by R. Fields.)

8. Ibid.

9. Ibid.

10. Imperialistas: Forca de Portugal, published by MRPP (July 1974). See also leaflets and other pamphlets published in succeeding months.

11. Jane Kramer, "Letter from Lisbon," New Yorker, September 23, 1974.

12. Movimento--Boletim das Forcas Armadas, October 8, 1975.

13. Commisao De Inquerito Ao 11 De Marco, report, published in April 1975.

14. New York Times, April 14, 1975.

7

Many scholars and journalists who were familiar with the dictatorships of the Iberian Peninsula expressed surprise about the revolution of April 25, 1974.[1] Portugal had, they said, been liberalizing. The Portuguese economy was better than ever. A leftist revolution seemed remote: the dominant institutions of Portugal had not even been pricked by manifestations of radical or dissonant elements. The clergy remained allied with the government, the professional classes were growing and prospering, and the organization of an opposition party for the elections of 1969 was accomplished with far less bitterness than had been the case in 1958 or 1962.[2]

The only pre-1974 opposition which Schmitter recognized was the attempt in December 1973 of some right-wing, procolonial officers to have Caetano removed as President of the Council. This failed due to the opposition of Admiral Tomas, who, as President of the Republic, had the formal authority to remove the Prime Minister.[3]

The publication of General Spinola's book, Portugal and Its Future,[4] was also taken by outsiders to indicate a liberalizing pattern, with room for legitimate dissent. The book suggested a reorganization of the government, but it gave no indication that the kind of change required would be revolutionary, or even leftist.

Perhaps the association of General Spinola with the events of April 25, 1974 misled outsiders. If the take-over itself could only be understood in terms of the military's disaffection as a result of their humiliation in colonial wars, then the reformist Spinola set the tone of journalistic interpretation by implying the take-over was a military coup rather than a revolution.

Often, too, the Portuguese people had been characterized by social scientists as "phlegmatic, conservative, order-loving and obedient."[5] The prolonged tenure of fascism in Portugal seemed testament to the political apathy of the people, and of course the history of antifascist opposition was relatively unknown outside of Portugal. PIDE/DGS and the censorship board saw to it that this history was not publicized.

In 1973 this situation changed as Portugal's political opposition came to world attention briefly in three separate cases. First, there was the suppression of the book New Portuguese Letters and the arrest and imprisonment of its three feminist authors, which attracted considerable attention in the American and European women's presses. [6] Demonstrations by women in other countries focused this attention not only on the abrogation of human rights, but also on the existence of an activist opposition. The same year, Amnesty International published a book on torture of political prisoners all over the world, which included a section describing the torture of political prisoners in Portugal. [7] Finally, in the summer, Prime Minister Caetano made a state visit to England and was met by demonstrators and pickets wherever he went. [8] Many of the demonstrators had been exiled from Portugal for political reasons, and others were protesting the massacres in Mozambique. This unfriendly reception in the capital of "Portugal's oldest ally" brought attention to the growth of disaffection among the Portuguese people.

Initial press reactions in the English-speaking countries to the April 25th Revolution was to expose the previous regime's torture of prisoners, with headlines such as "Caetano's Secret Chamber of Horrors," [9] and to describe the event as a military coup.

The Portuguese in government since April 25, 1974 have been very interested in what others have said about them and about their revolution. A sizable proportion of the population, even the semi-literate population, is able to speak and understand at least one foreign language. The educated population has been accustomed to reading news and political commentary in other languages, and also read many books in the original language rather than in Portuguese translation, since for so long there were few books of interest to these people which were also passed by the censors. Like other Europeans, many Portuguese have radio sets that can pick up broadcasts from several foreign countries: it is possible in Portugal to hear British, Dutch, German, French, and Spanish broadcasts. Astute political party newspaper editors are well aware of this interest and often include newspaper columns on the foreign presses' reactions to Portugal.

In January 1975, a weekly periodical entitled Information and Analysis made its first appearance at Portuguese newsdealers. The magazine regularly records extracts from the foreign press about events in Portugal. [10] Avante, the official weekly newspaper of the PCP, includes regular quotations from Pravda as well as statements

and greetings from other Soviet countries, including reports of the
"social amenities" of various Soviet bloc countries. Even statements on French radio or television about Portugal are likely to be
reiterated in one or another of the daily newspapers in Lisbon. For
example, on March 6th, when a member of the executive of the
French Communist Party spoke on French radio and television to
denounce the Portuguese Communist Party for undemocratic behavior, the report appeared in A Capital.[11] The PPD newspaper,
Povo Libre,[12] on March 11, carried two-thirds of a page on a press
conference between a party leader and the foreign press. The April
25, 1975 Expresso[13] carried a large article on the PCP-PS conflict
as it was described in three successive issues of the French news
magazine L'Express.

The MFA members are very concerned that political and economic policy toward Portugal may be shaped by the media.

In addition to the vacuum of knowledge about the background of
the revolution and the history of Portuguese politics, foreign journalists have another problem reporting events in Portugal--the language
barrier. One example of mistranslation appears in a piece written
by Richard Eder for the New York Times. In a feature story on
political attitudes in the Portuguese countryside, he described an
MFA poster as saying, "The flower is liberation, the fruit is democracy, the seed will be socialism."[14] The poster, accurately translated, reads:

> Flower--Liberation
> Fruit--Democracy
> Seed--Socialism

Eder's translation implies that socialism will follow liberation and
democracy, while the MFA's intention is that democracy and liberation will emerge out of socialism. The MFA (and the political parties)
do not consider that the Portuguese people are already liberated.

There are problems of double meaning. "Popular democracy"
is a catch phrase for a communist political system, but in Portuguese
it also means democracy as practiced (or participated in) by all the
people. Thus, when government figures speak of popular democracy,
they may be referring either to Soviet communism or the PPD brand.

Few correspondents from the Western European and U.S. media
are permanently stationed in Portugal. Most of the U.S. journalists
covering Portugal are based in Madrid and may be thoroughly familiar
with the Spanish political culture--a very different phenomenon from
the one they are covering in Portugal. There is a very enlightening
example of comparative reporting available to U.S. readers, however.
The Time magazine correspondent is a long time resident of Portugal.

Her coverage on any given week differs vastly from the coverage of
Newsweek which employs a Madrid-based correspondent from the
Washington Post. Some examples of the difference are clearly evi-
denced in their differing interpretations of the events of the May Day
Rally in Lisbon on May 1, 1975.[15]

Since the provisional government wanted to ensure complete
understanding of the events surrounding the elections for the constitutional assembly, they made extraordinary arrangements for both
foreign and domestic journalists to have easy access to press conferences, as well as full translations and explanations of government
positions. For the last week of April 1975, the Ministry for Social
Communication set up press headquarters at the Gulbenkien Foundation in Lisbon. These headquarters included not only typing, telex,
wire, and mail facilities, but living arrangements for those free-
lancers on a tight budget, radio and television studios, an auditorium
for press conferences with headphones for simultaneous translations,
and interpreters for any journalist requesting them. In addition to
press conferences, special requests for particular interviews were
also honored. Information pamphlets on many subjects were provided in at least two languages and often in four languages (Portuguese, Spanish, French, and English). There were 961 foreign
journalists registered at the headquarters on April 24.* Cabinet
ministers and officers of the Ministry for Communications were
present at all hours of the day and night. Election results and news
bulletins were continually broadcast on television and radio.

When President Costa Gomes addressed the press on the eve
of the elections, he said:

> You have all come here expecting that there will
> be violence and chicanery. . . . Instead, what
> you have seen is a free people, participating in
> their first free election in 48 years. . . . There
> is no force and no coercion. . . . The whole
> world should know that the Portuguese people can,
> despite the differences among them, work together
> peacefully to transform their society, without
> bloodshed and with justice. . . .[16]

In the days that followed the elections, MFA cabinet ministers
and members of the Revolutionary Council, in their formal press
conferences and informal discussion with journalists at the Gulbenkien

---

*Figures given out by the Ministry for Social Communications
based on the number of journalists registered at Press Headquarters.

Foundation, continually stressed that they wanted the rest of the world to understand the truth about conditions in Portugal. Over and over they explained the intention of their blank ballot alternative. Over and over, they explained that the MFA were not ideologues but idealists, and that the election results showed the people's choice to be socialism--the MFA choice as well.

Prime Minister Goncalves declared, "It's better to cast a blank ballot than to vote unconsciously." He and Brigadier Carvalho described their MFA function as "defense of the Portuguese people," and Carvalho said: "The armed forces will use force if necessary against any actions that may endanger the democratic electoral process. . . . We do not want a single party system, as some western newspapers have been suggesting. . . . We want a pluralistic society under a socialist form of government. . . ." Goncalves was asked what he saw as the role of the Portuguese people in a counterrevolutionary situation. He replied, "If our mother country is in danger, if the revolutionary victories should be at stake, we will necessarily have to engage the Portuguese people, and not only the soldiers, in the defense of the conquests already attained."[17] This did not mean that the government would accede to the demands of the extreme left groups to arm them. Nor did it mean that there would be further militarization: the period of compulsory military service, in fact, had been cut back to two years, and draftees were being discharged as rapidly as possible. But rather that the MFA and the people together would defend their revolutionary gains.

Meanwhile, the European Council in its meetings discussed the Portuguese elections. Some members of that council attacked the MFA leadership for having outlawed participation of some parties in the elections. The Labor Party representatives from the Netherlands spoke out against such prejudgments, because they assumed incorrectly that the Communist Party had somehow already taken over the Portuguese government. The delegate from the Netherlands was well aware that his political party had supplied funds to the Portuguese Socialist Party. This exchange was carried in at least three of the daily newspapers,[18] and like many of the statements made in the press, it reflected a view of the elections as a "crisis." (The MFA continually stressed that the elections were not a crisis, but rather an exercise in democratic process.)

Alexander Solzhenitsyn, speaking from Paris, called on the West to reexamine its position in relation to Portugal.[19] Just prior to the elections, Information and Analysis said, ". . . the journalists cannot let go of the impression that the campaign is an ideological one like the one at the time of the Spanish Civil War, with extreme positions of defense and attack stated in terms of the defense of democracy for the democracies."[20]

This underlines a second major problem for journalists and scholars in understanding events in Portugal. The tendency to place the situation in a comparative context which may be inappropriate or irrelevant is a problem in reporting or studying any political movement or society. It becomes a serious fault when the situation under examination is both a political movement and a society.

The overall negative image of the provisional government in the Western press has suggested to the Portuguese press and people that those very countries which had been satisfied with the fascist regime became hypercritical after the revolution about Portuguese freedoms.

The front page lead article in the MFA Bulletin for November 26, 1974, reflected this interpretation:

> National Independence, the supreme criteria for the fulfillment of the Armed Forces, is not easily attained as our days speed by. We are a small country, as designated by the great powers, whispering dimly and under respectable and self-righteous direction; a little striving country; when as part of the 25th of April we began to define our future and make the necessary reforms . . . our international relations began to become interested in us . . . some of them began a campaign to discredit us by insinuating what is not true and exaggerating details . . . in carrying this out, the most relevant organs have been the newspapers. . . . However, our country is uniformly presented in the press. . . . The western press has tended to denigrate the Portuguese situation . . . it is a most significant phenomenon that the international press has taken such a great interest in the economic and political actions of the legitimately constituted authorities, while the foreign press considered Salazarism like a minor malady (a beneficient dictatorship). . . .
> During fascism, Portugal was always secondary news for the great western press. They never gave accounts of Salazar's treatment of patriots in Caxias, Peniche or Tarafel by the PIDE torturers and the assassinations of anti-fascists. The great international press like "L'Aurore" and "Die Welt" who were quite disinterested in these things, became very interested in the detention of the ex-legionnaires. . . .

> At the time of Salazar and Caetano, they were
> very disinterested in opposition to fascism or the
> internal affairs of the Portuguese military. . . .
> Now they are eager to record every time the MFA
> acts against the forces of reaction to preserve the
> revolution . . . to these events, the foreign press
> gives a calamitous interpretation. [21]

Although there has never been serious discussion within the
MFA of censoring or limiting access to the foreign press, MFA members have speculated on the possible reasons for this kind of distorted coverage. In their first year in government they continually
refined their information service and attempted to facilitate the work
of foreign journalists. But as of June 1975, the MFA was still claiming that the foreign press was misrepresenting their positions and
actions.

On June 6, 1975 at a press conference in Paris, President
Costa Gomes referred to these distortions:

> Secretary of State Kissinger's view of his country "is
> very distorted and very unjust." He publicly invited
> Mr. Kissinger to "spend a few days in Portugal," and
> then he can judge.
>
> President Costa Gomes and three Cabinet Minis-
> ters, including Foreign Minister Ernesto Melo Antunees,
> addressed a press luncheon at the end of their four-day
> state visit to France, the first foreign country they
> have visited. . . .
>
> Next week they are going to Romania. The politi-
> cal balance of the two trips is evidently intended to
> reflect Lisbon's foreign policy.
>
> The Foreign Minister made a point of "the great
> importance to us of the equilibrium in Europe." He
> said that Portugal "cannot allow her political devel-
> opment to perturb the European balance." Just be-
> fore last week's Atlantic Alliance summit meeting
> in Brussels, President Ford and Mr. Kissinger
> questioned Portugal's role as an ally in view of what
> Mr. Ford called "Communist elements" in her Gov-
> ernment.
>
> The Lisbon leaders did not mention the Communist
> party in their comments here today, but the Foreign
> Minister stressed that Portugal did not want to upset
> the East-West "relation of forces in Europe." De-
> tente, he said, is the first aim of all our countries.

President Costa Gomes spoke to Mr.
Kissinger in response to a question about current
relations with the United States. He said that
they were good and that he saw no point of contention that could weaken them. But he said that
Mr. Kissinger was "very skeptical about the political evolution in Portugal."

On domestic politics, President Costa Gomes
repeated the view of the ruling Armed Forces Movement which ousted the authoritarian rightist regime
in April, 1974, that the people of Portugal were
too uninformed to make a "free political choice."

"The classic electoral system is impracti-
cal and dangerous" during the period of transition
from a dictatorship, he said. "But after three to
five years, we can have an electoral democracy
with its consequences and advantages."

He called information the "mightiest revolutionary weapon, more powerful than possession of
atomic, biological and chemical weapons."[22]

There is a relationship between journalistic accounts and "misrepresentations" about the new Portugal, with the injurious actions
of other governments toward them. For example, in its accounts of
the events of March 11, the MFA Bulletin states, "Foreign journalists had already filed stories about a 'successful and widely supported' coup."[23] Some U.S. journalists suggested that the attempted
coup was possibly a "put-up job" by the MFA to consolidate its control. As late as March 18, after numerous official accounts had been
given documenting the coup plan, and admissions had been circulated
by the Spinola supporters then in Brazil of their part in planning the
coup, Henry Giniger of the New York Times said:

That a military dictatorship now exists was strik-
ingly illustrated last week by the decisions to
nationalize the banking and insurance systems.
The decisions were made by the High Council of
the Revolution, a group of 24 officers formed
principally from existing military bodies after
what was termed a right-wing military uprising
was smashed last Tuesday [emphasis added].[24]

Or the description by the same reporter of the new Cabinet:

Lisbon, March 25--The fourth and most left-wing
Government of the 11 month old Portuguese

revolution was formed here today after <u>centrist forces largely lost their battle</u> to halt what they fear is a movement to a military-led Communist state [emphasis added].[25]

The editorial comment, which appeared in the same newspaper on March 19, reflected that the implications of their reporter's statements had been assimilated into policy:

> The mystery is why the Portuguese Communists and their military allies, <u>who have just tightened their grip</u> expose their unpopular Soviet connection in the very week when campaigning opens for the elections to a constituent assembly.
>
> Confirmation of the informal Soviet request by the Information Ministry in Lisbon indicates that the Communists are no longer worried, as they were only recently, about making a poor showing in the elections. It suggests that they now feel confident of their ability to manipulate the election machinery or to intimidate opposing political parties <u>now that they have exploited a purported rightist coup in order to seize the real levers of power in the country.</u>
>
> The Communist-backed military radicals of the "Revolutionary Council" seem to hold virtually dictatorial powers, as shown by their nationalization of banks and insurance companies almost overnight without appearing to consult any other authority, military or civilian. The banning of two extreme left groups and the center-right Christian Democratic party from the forthcoming election has been accompanied by warnings from the Communists to their restive coalition partners, the Socialists, and the centrist Popular Democrats. The latter already have encountered left-wing street violence and now are getting Communist hints that they may be <u>implicated in the alleged</u> rightist coup [emphasis added].[26]

The editorial ignores the fact that the parties were banned earlier because of their violent attacks on other parties. It also maintains, despite the admissions of parties to the coup attempt, that the rightist plot was a deliberate fiction employed by Communists to gain control. This suggests a parallel with the Nazis' tactic

of setting fire to the Reichstag and blaming it on the Communists.
Only this editorial writer contends that in Portugal in 1975 the shoe
was on the other foot!

Portuguese newspapers connected the coup attempt with their
anti-CIA campaigning, suggesting that the presence of U.S. Ambassador Frank Carlucci, whose previous appointment in Zaire was a CIA
post, proved there was a link-up. They pointed to U.S. media reports of "popular support for Spinola" as an indication of the CIA
miscalculation which had led to the Bay of Pigs fiasco in Cuba. So
strongly held was this view that after the coup failed, the U.S. Embassy was beseiged by demonstrators, and Security Chief Carvalho
suggested that the U.S. diplomatic mission be withdrawn because he
could not guarantee its safety.[27] An article which appeared in the
New York Times following the coup attempt summarized much of the
kind of misinformation that had been cited as "proof" of "CIA miscalculation":

Lisbon, March 12--Former President Antonio de
Spinola, who fled to Spain yesterday after the attack
against Portugal's left-wing leadership had gradually been re-emerging from relative eclipse as the
standard-bearer of moderate military and civilian
forces.

Support for what General Spinola represented
had been growing among centrists and conserva-
tives in the armed forces. They had watched with
alarm the disorder in the country's political and
economic life. Members of the Communist party
and other leftists who had helped ease General
Spinola out of the presidency last September appeared to have become nervous, in turn, about
the gravitation toward him--all the more so because the movement had reportedly been joined by
important elements of the Socialist party.

Amid reports that the Socialist party had
been in contact with General Spinola and was looking for him for leadership, Alvaro Cunhal, head
of the Portuguese Communist party, extended an
olive branch to the Socialists, proposing talks to
establish leftist unity now and after the elections,
scheduled for April 12, to head off a possible
rightist coup.

General Spinola left the presidency after
leftists prevented an anti-Communist demonstration in his favor. He resigned with a spectacular

warning against anarchy and the danger of leftist
dictatorship, and retired to semiseclusion on his
brother's farm near Lisbon. He maintained
political and military contacts but made almost
no public statements or appearances.

But if largely out of sight, he had not been
out of mind. At a recent meeting of the Assembly
of the Armed Forces Movement, grouping some
200 officers in a kind of sovereign body, a leftist
officer criticized the general and when one of his
supporters rose to defend him, he was said to have
been applauded by a majority of those present.

Among those defeated in these votes were believed to be Premier Vasco dos Santos Goncalves
and Brig. Gen. Otelo de Carvalho, head of the
Lisbon military district and operational commander
of the military security forces in Portugal.

In barracks throughout the country, officers
have been reported to be looking to General
Spinola for leadership and trying to eliminate
the power of the radical officers, particularly
in the Coordinating Commission.

However, the ordinarily impulsive former
president had been biding his time, although in
the last issue of the weekly Expresso, a leading
Lisbon publication, he is quoted as saying at a
recent lunch of alumni of the military college
that "the fight is continuing."

A major event for the moderates in the
armed forces would be the removal of Premier
Goncalves after the April elections--assuming
the further violence or other incidents do not
prevent the elections. [28]

In late February, an article by Roy Cline (former CIA director)
in the New York Times suggested that it might be a bad tactic to im-
pede CIA covert operations at a time when Portugal was endangering
the NATO alliance by its affinity for Communist politics. [29]

While Pravda, as well as the Soviet government itself, officially
congratulated the provisional government for its successful foil of the
coup attempt, [30] the U.S. press, the President, and the State Department all indicated their hostility toward the behavior of the Portuguese government:

The United States has warned the military leadership in Portugal that the leftward turn there is in-
imical to American and Atlantic alliance interests.

The message, delivered yesterday to President Francisco da Costa Gomes, conveyed essentially the same admonition made public today by
Secretary of State Kissinger at his news conference, United States officials said:

"We are disquieted by an evolution in which
there is a danger that the democratic process may
become a sham, and in which parties are getting
into a dominant position whose interests we would
not have thought were necessarily friendly to the
United States."

"What seems to be happening now in Portugal," Mr. Kissinger declared, "is that the Armed
Forces Movement, which is substantially dominated by officers of leftist tendencies, has now
appointed a new Cabinet in which Communists and
parties closely associated with the Communists
have many of the chief portfolios."

Mr. Kissinger said that a leftward trend
"will of course raise questions for the United
States in relationship to its NATO policy and to
its policy toward Portugal." He added that
Washington was "in close contact" with the other
13 members of the North Atlantic Treaty Organization about Portugal.

A United States official said these concerns
had been raised by Ambassador Frank Carlucci
largely in the form of questions to President
Costa Gomes. "I wouldn't call it a demarche,"
he said. "A demarche is when you ask another
country to do something."

But three top-level American officials said
the Administration and several NATO allies were
considering moves to impose a king of quarantine
on Portugal within the alliance.

"We'll have to deny access to the classified
documents that circulate in the alliance and dis-
invite them to NATO meetings," one said.

Asked what he thought should be done, Defense Secretary James R. Schlesinger replied:
"It will have to take some symbolic form--making
them outcasts without casting them out."[31]

This warning, coupled with the earlier unsympathetic U.S. press and government attitudes, by March 26 evoked a Portuguese response:

> Premier Vasco dos Santos Goncalves today announced a program of "total austerity" as well as further moves toward socialism through the nationalization of basic industries.
>
> He made the announcement at the swearing in of Portugal's most left-wing Government since the revolution last April.
>
> The new Cabinet shows a big increase in Communist influences as well as what the Premier termed, "a new impulse of the revolutionary process."
>
> He called the 21-member Cabinet of civilians and military officers a group of "militants" and combatants in the struggle for progress and well-being.
>
> Despite a leftward trend that has caused alarm in Washington and other Western capitals, the American ambassador Frank Carlucci, in his first public speech here, stressed continuing American confidence in and help for Portugal.[32]

This circumstance gave further ammunition to the Portuguese press attack on Ambassador Carlucci:

> But his effort to dispel the notion that the United States was intriguing against the Portuguese revolution was set back when a few hours after his speech, a Capital, a leading afternoon newspaper, appeared with an accusation splashed across its front page that the Central Intelligence Agency was behind a recently announced effort by Portuguese right-wingers to overthrow the Government. Mr. Carlucci was singled out as a prominent figure in "agitation, sabotage, and overthrow of governments."
>
> The newspaper claimed that it had documentary evidence that the CIA has organized a so-called Portuguese Liberation Army. The attack was one of the biggest of a series against the United States and Mr. Carlucci since his arrival here in January. The Ambassador said they were

part of "an internationally organized campaign"
and cautioned his audience at the American Club
not to believe everything they read. [33]

The "big increase in Communist influence" is not evident in
the number of PCP Ministries--each of the four parties having been
given two ministries! But that is not explained in this article.

Within a week of this exchange, the most popular joke in Lisbon
concerned a telephone conversation between CIA Director Colby and
Secretary of State Kissinger, in which Kissinger, in a heavily in-
flected German accent, upbraids Colby for bungling a political assassination. "Colby," shouts the Secretary, "I said Cunhal, not
Faisal!" The joke was still being told at the time of the constitutional assembly elections.

Neither the attempted coup of March 11 nor the interparty hos-
tilities had really produced a high level of violence in Portugal. The
total casualties were two deaths and several dozen injuries--not even
as high a level as has been the case after soccer matches in Mexico
City or football matches in Liverpool or Glasgow. Yet the U.S. and
British presses continued to emphasize the violent potentials:

> Its economy is in ruins, its politics in turmoil
> and its government perpetually on the brink of
> disaster. To many of its neighbors, Portugal is
> the new "sick man of Europe"--a country all too
> likely to catch the Communist disease and spread
> it elsewhere in the West. "For good or bad," re-
> marked former French Premier Pierre Mendes-
> France after a recent visit to Lisbon, "whatever
> happens in Portugal will set a precedent for Spain,
> Italy and Greece and will (have a) profound effect
> in France." Last week, in the wake of an abortive
> coup, Portugal swerved in precisely the direction
> Mendes-France had feared. After a brief eleven-
> month fling at democracy, the Portuguese had
> apparently replaced a right-wing form of dicta-
> torship with one of the left.
>
> Considering the proclivity for violence that
> all sides in Portugal have shown over the past
> month, it seems likely only the army can keep
> order. The trouble is, the military is also deep-
> ly divided over politics as the military elections
> and the coup attempt showed. Unless it can set
> its own house in order, Portugal may well be
> headed for more turmoil--or even a civil war
> [emphasis added]. [34]

During the month of April, the world press focused on two
major issues in regard to Portugal: the relationship between political parties in their campaign for seats in the constitutional assembly,
and the behavior and function of the MFA in relation to democratic
process. Opinions and impressions were as follows:

Pravda of Moscow, the central organ of the Soviet
Communist Party, reaffirmed on the 20th of April,
through their Lisbon correspondents that the Soviet
Union had no intentions of interfering in the affairs
of the Portuguese or influencing the political parties, and therefore objected to the "inventions of
the bourgeois propaganda that the USSR is preoccu-
pied with the existing situation in Portugal."

Tass, the news agency, in an article referring to the objectives of the Western news campaign, asserts that it is a "digging up of fossils"
and constitutes "a shocking lie with allegations
that" Portugal is becoming a totalitarian society.

Tass also asserted that "the progressive
changes of the Portuguese" inside the context of
international political reality proves that "the
forces of socialism, that democracy and national
independence are more powerful than the war of
the oppressors."

From Komsomolskaya Pravda, the organ of
the Central Commission of the Young Soviet Communists is (the statement that) "the forces of reaction" get assistance to achieve their objectives
from "ignorance" and are threatening to "tyrannize
the communist militancy."

They identify the propagandists (who do this)
as being "the old chiefs of the fascist regime, the
fanatics and monsters of the Salazar regime . . .
the police informers and the activists of the Portuguese Legion."

They do not recognize the impossibility of
going back to the old times of fascism and Police
(state) . . . these traitors to their country make
intrigues and sabotage the efforts of the Armed
Forces Movement to bring an end to ignorance.

In regard to the Portuguese position on NATO,
the organ of the Young Communists affirms that
"the Provisional Government and the Movement of
the Armed Forces think that the problem of Portugal's participation in NATO should be totally

examined and, perhaps, forming some other alliance to develop international and continental
restorations of cooperation between countries
and regimes that are socially different. [35]

The analysis of Swiss journalistic opinion focuses on the Neue
Zurcher Zeitung, a liberal paper which frequently cites or reviews
the other newspapers and was the first Western newspaper to be sold
in Moscow. The other newspaper cited is the Geneva Journal, which
is a liberal daily paper in Geneva.

The Neue Zurcher Zeitung considered the pact between the MFA and the political parties to have
denigrated the significance of the elections for the
constitutional assembly . . . they considered it
"revealing a paternalistic orientation, comparable
to that of Salazar . . . ."
    After considering . . . what these votes will
mean for the future . . . the editorialists . . .
conclude:
    "All of the explanations offered by officials
basically utilize the expression 'democracy.'
Democratic self-determination signifies being
able to have opinions that are contrary to their
opinions without being automatically 'antidemocratic'."
    The liberal daily [newspaper] of Geneva
launches grand attacks at Portuguese problems
in the same manner as the wire services that
make up the foreign press. [36]

The journal then focuses on a Belgian newspaper, The Free
Belgian, which had articles and editorials on the nationalization of
the banks and insurance companies and on the pact between the MFA
and the political parties, and quoted the Prime Minister's statements
with regard to a desire for closer relations with the rest of Europe.
On April 14, the same newspaper announced the statement by the
Catholic bishops of Portugal, reminding their communicants that
they cannot vote for the leftist parties:

The Portuguese Church implicitly ordered Portuguese Catholics to vote for the center during the
April 25 elections. The Portuguese bishops also
publicly condemned the recommendations of the
Armed Forces Movement to use a blank vote in

the elections if they could not sufficiently and
seriously understand the programs of the different parties. [37]

The Belgian press was more concerned with the economic
changes and the intransigence of the Bishop than with criticizing the
MFA election structures. The section reporting the U.S. press is
the largest in this important pre-election issue of the weekly.

For your interest and as an example of the thinking and reasoning that guide Information and Analysis, we are translating a small piece which appeared in the American review Newsweek of April
21, in the "Periscope" section.
Ronald Reagan took his non-campaign for
President across the Atlantic last week for a
speech that sent the British Foreign Office into a
tizzy. Addressing the annual dinner of the Pil-
grims of Great Britain in London, the former
California governor inveighed against "the Communist take-over of Portugal" and the opportunity
it gave the Soviet Union to redraw the map of
Europe. London insists that Lisbon has not "gone
Communist" and, with proper NATO support, can
be kept out of Red control. Remarks like Reagan's
the Foreign Office feels, can only hurt non-
Communist parties still active in Portugal. [38]

Also in the issue of Newsweek, April 21, is a piece on the attitudes of the provisional government toward the utilization of the base
at Lajas in the eventuality of a Middle East war. It is illustrated
with a photograph of Vasco Goncalves which carries the legend "New
Friendship Concerns an Old Alliance. . . ."[39]
The bulletin goes on to describe the Newsweek presentation of
Portugal as a possible drop-out from NATO and suggests that the Portuguese attitude about the use of the base at Lajas is prelude to their
further dealings with the Soviet Union. The Portuguese press and
government were angered by such presentations of "either-or" decisions. They wanted their independence and integrity recognized and
their right to their own course respected. The comments in the
International Herald Tribune challenged this capacity:

On the 16th of April, the International Herald
Tribune, which is published in Paris and is the
largest all-Europe newspaper (in distribution)

had an article which stated that the perspective
for the elections was a difficult one and that there
is a lot of interesting conjecture about other aspects, as for instance, the form of socialism that
the Portuguese military are attempting. They
quoted the Armed Forces representatives as arguing that the Portuguese people are "not prepared for the process of political liberty" verified by the "fact that for many years the Salazar
regime had not allowed democracy in the schools"
. . . in order to distinguish between the "diverse
positions of the spectrum of politics" . . . .

It is maintained that they call themselves a
"disciplined organ" secondly, the editorialist of
the Herald Tribune states that the conditions for
"preserving liberty for the assembly" without limiting the liberty and impeding the speech of Socialists to the advantage of Communists or vice-versa.
That would protect Portugal through self-govern-
ment or adopt a constitution that would satisfy
the majority and protect the minority. . . . Moreover, it is the grave judgment of the Herald Tribune,
that the military tends to lack confidence in the
process. . . . "Evidently, the officials do not
give credit to the intellectual awareness of the
masses, but rather only to the military."[40]

The suggestion was clear: the Portuguese people and their leaders
are only capable of formulating a Salazarist or Leninist dictatorship.

The next article reported by the U.S. press appeared in the
New York Times on April 16, written by Henry Giniger. Giniger reported on the same interview with Admiral Coutinho which had appeared in the Geneva Journal. The Portuguese analysts make a point
of mentioning that Giniger refers to Admiral Coutinho as "the principal voice of the Council of the Revolution."

A major spokesman for Portugal's ruling High
Council of the revolution . . . Rear Adm. Antonio
Rosa Coutinho, acting as executive officer of the
council, said in an interview that the armed forces
wanted socialism--he was not sure, he said, what
kind of socialism--and would not be thwarted by
any anti-socialist majority. . . .

"We are going to socialism in the next three
to five years. The country can choose something

else afterward." Asked if the military would yield
at the end of the three to five years, he said: "I
don't know, I don't even know what the situation
will be a year from now. A year ago, I could not
imagine the present situation."[41]

The April 11 French newspapers were citing the words of
Alexander Solzhenitsyn on developments in Portugal. In The Quota-
tion of Paris he said that Vietnam and Portugal "were assassinated
through agreements in Paris--the new Munich." His appraisal of
the political situation in Portugal was contested by publisher Andre
Fabre-Luce in an editorial in the same paper April 14, three days
later and in a discussion on French television.[42]

Perhaps one of the most damaging journalistic criticisms
leveled at Portugal during the several weeks of reports described
in this journal was the article by Nicholas Ashford which appeared
first in the Times of London on April 12.[43] The article, which discussed political prisoners, was subsequently elaborated on in an
article from Flora Lewis (Paris bureau) to the New York Times,
April 23,[44] and was included in the communiques by other Western
media reporters during the rest of the month:

He claims to have affirmed that there are between
twenty and thirty more persons imprisoned (for
political reasons) than there were at the moment
of the revolution on April 25, 1974 . . . he also
refers to the imprisonment of persons from the
far-left movements, asserting that all the prisoners "are being held without charge or trial." . . .
The military claim that there are no political
prisoners and that persons in prison are there
for crimes committed under the old regime or
for their involvement in the planning for September 28 or March 11. By the normal criteria of
Western Europe there have been no detentions
for political reasons since April and there is no
violation of . . . human rights.
     In conclusion, Ashford cites that Minister
for Social Communication who affirmed that the
prisoners had been well treated in flagrant contrast to the situation prior to April 25.[45]

Actually, since April 25, 1974 the prisons at Caxias and
Peniche, as well as the former training center for PIDE/DGS in
Lisbon, have been accessible to journalists. Although the over

1.200 former PIDE/DGS prisoners were finally moved to Monsanto
army base to improve the physical condition of their captivity--more
space for outdoor exercise, fresh air--they received relatively un-
restricted visitation privileges until after the March 11 attempted
coup. So any journalist interested in comparing imprisonment conditions or treatment had the opportunity to do so. Nonetheless, the
political prisoners story initially written by Ashford became exaggerated in the retelling. For instance, in the April 23 New York
Times article, Flora Lewis, speaking of Major Sanches Ossario,
stated,

> Most of the officers with whom he worked are "in
> prison, in Africa, or in exile," he said. He
> charged that there were more political prisoners
> in Portugal today than there were before, in an
> allusion to the rightist Salazar dictatorship. He
> estimated the number at 2000.[46]

Since the estimates by election week had flared to 3,000 political
prisoners being held without charges, it might be useful to place the
issue into perspective. The Commission for the Aid of Political
Prisoners in Portugal, prior to April 25, 1975, had estimated that
as many as 22,000 people had been assassinated or tortured under
the fascist regime. Participation in demonstrations--or suspected
participation in strikes--was sufficient cause for the arrest of 173
people at one time in 1962; in succeeding years, similar massive
arrests combined with prison terms running to ten years and more,
kept the prisons and concentration camp at Terafel full. Furthermore, political prisoners should also include those who were tried
and sentenced for the "crime" of political opposition. Thus while
there were, at any given time, hundreds incarcerated for "interro-
gation" or "investigation" for prolonged periods of time, there were
hundreds more serving long terms.[47]

In answer to questions at a press conference in Lisbon on
April 27, 1975, Brigadier Otelo Carvalho provided the following
statistics (there are overlapping categories):

Total number of prisoners	1,331
Former DGS/Legion	1,226
Arrested for connection with in- surrection of September 28	14
Arrested for connection with in- surrection of March 11	97
Interfering with campaign	69
Incidents in Oporto	47

> Old Regime District Deputies   27
> Economic sabotage (illicit export of
>   capital)   21

The problem with relatively unsensational statements of facts--especially when they tend to desensationalize an escalating rumor--is that such items are not considered "stories." The unwritten "guild" code of the journalistic profession rarely permits such reporting on other reporters. Nor do the news media feel a heavy responsibility for verifying such "facts"--except in cases where such verification will redound to the glory of the particular line which that individual publication or broadcast station has expounded. Thus, despite the clarification of that which had been a banner issue earlier, there was no reportage of the actual count as given by the provisional government.

The press arrangements at Gulbenkien during election week did provide an insight into the etiology of such distortions, however. A typical question, put by the U.S. correspondent for a major newspaper (the Washington _Post_), serves as an example:

> Miguel Accoca: The people who voted, General
> Carvalho, they have rejected the advice of the
> MFA to vote a blank. Does this mean that the
> Social Democratic majority will modify the pact
> you have made? Or the military power will be
> reduced in the immediate future?

The question itself was an extraordinary distortion. The 92 percent of the electorate who voted gave 38 percent of their vote to the Socialist Party--which campaigned as a Marxist party. If PPD and CDS together are counted as Social Democrat parties, then 32 percent of the vote (hardly a majority) went to that ideological position. The 7 percent blank vote could not conceivably be construed as part of the Social Democrat vote, since such a vote was strongly opposed by the Church, and since it represented people who were aware of their own ambivalence as much as people who had taken the MFA alternative as a directive. Considering the total percentage of the vote accorded to PCP and parties identified as Marxist--33 percent, which was slightly higher than the combined Social Democrat percentage--there is no objective information to suggest that there is a "Social Democratic majority." Although the MFA interpretation of the relatively small blank vote had been repeatedly stated--that people wanted to express a political opinion--there seemed a certain fascination for this question on the part of U.S. and British reporters. The answer Carvalho gave did not differ

significantly from previous MFA responses. He said that the MFA
had not "directed" people to vote a blank; that some individuals in
the MFA, speaking as individuals, had offered that as an alternative
for those unable to make an informed choice. As for modification
of the pact or structure of the government, Carvalho reminded the
press that the agreement included maintaining the same distribution
of cabinet posts until the presidential election late in 1975.

Let's see how this journalist reported the answer to his questions. In the May 12 issue of Newsweek Russell Watson, with Miguel
Accoca in Lisbon, wrote:

> Portugal was trying to adjust last week to the fact
> that its radical military government was out of
> step with its people. In the election, Soares's
> Socialists had won 38 percent of the vote, while
> the center-left Popular Democrats amassed 26
> percent. The Communist Party received less
> than 13 percent, and only 6 percent of the voters
> complied with the request of the ruling Armed
> Forces Movement (MFA) to cast blank ballots.
> It was a vote for West European-style democracy,
> but the left-wing officers who run the country tried
> to act as if the election hadn't happened. They had
> required the political parties to agree that the
> military would rule for another three to five years,
> long after the constituent assembly finishes writing
> a constitution.
>   . . . But Soares knows that for the time being
> he will have to accommodate to dictatorship in the
> form of the MFA and the Communist Party. He
> met last week with his former teacher Cunhal, 60,
> and declared: "There can be no democracy in Por-
> tugal without the Communists."[48]

The same press conference elicited a question from Henry
Giniger of the New York Times:

> The MFA has said many times, that the people who
> vote for non-socialist parties are not politically con-
> scious or . . . they are ignorant. Does this mean
> that the CDS and those who voted for it are stupid?

Carvalho responded:

> All who voted for the CDS are not stupid. There
> is a difference between being stupid and being

> politically ignorant . . . we know there are great
> brains who voted for CDS. . . .

Much of the tone of Giniger's election story to the New York Times,[49]
and his story in the International Herald Tribune,[50] dwell on a hypothetical relationship between approval of the MFA and casting a blank
vote or the Socialist Party as an anti-Communist alternative. He
elaborates on the electoral victory of the "moderates," but if the
analysis were done on the basis of votes for the MFA program as
articulated in posters and meetings, then the MFA had a resounding
vote of support. The Socialist Party and all of the parties to the left
of it are Marxist parties. Thus 67 percent of the vote was to the left
of most of the governments of Western Europe. In his meetings in
France during May and June, Mario Soares, general secretary of the
Portuguese Socialist Party, met particularly with those European
socialist leaders whose expressed position is cooperation with the
Communist parties rather than kinship with the social democrats
(the Spanish and Italian parties, for instance). The early election
returns reported by Giniger in the Times of April 26 reflect a peculiar
partial sampling.

> Moderate forces took a commanding lead over
> the Communist Party tonight in the first partial
> returns from the voting for a national constituent
> assembly.
>   Despite the Communists' vaunted organiza-
> tional strength, the party trailed badly in the coun-
> try's north and center areas, getting only 8.2
> percent of the vote, while the centrist Popular
> Democratic party led with 36 percent and the
> Socialists followed with 27. In third place was
> the conservative Social Democratic center, with
> 11.5 percent.[51]

The early returns showed the Socialist Party in first place in Porto,
Setubal, and Lisbon, a fairly representative sample of the geographic
areas--south, north, and center. At that time, CDS and PPD (the
Social Democrat parties, or moderates) were together in the majority in Beja where they ended up with a combined total of under 10 percent of the vote.

U.S. and British media emphasized the MFA's surprise that so
few people took the blank ballot alternative. There is much to suggest, however, that people who over a prolonged period have been
deprived of an opportunity will opt to use it as soon as they can--
rather than waiting to decipher the fine points of its use. There's

an old American Indian anecdote, "If a man floats in a canoe without
a paddle, and he is then given a paddle, he will use it and teach himself the best way to use it." Giniger's observations and analysis reflect his own surprise at the results even while purporting to report
that of the MFA.

> A major surprise was the low vote won by the Social
> Democratic Center, the only conservative party in
> the election. Under constant attack from the far
> left as a "fascist" remnant of the old regime and
> consequently unable to do much campaigning, the
> party registered only 7.5 percent. But for the
> Socialists and the Popular Democrats, this also
> was an advantage since neither the Communists nor
> the military radicals could plausibly charge that
> the country was still under rightist influence.
> It was apparent, however, that both the So-
> cialists and the Popular Democrats had received
> many votes from conservatives who were voting
> essentially against Communism. The Popular
> Democrats, in particular, made a strong showing
> in the North, where conservative and Roman Catho-
> lic Church influences are strong.
> The Socialists took a surprising 44 percent
> of the vote in Lisbon and astonished political ana-
> lysts with their strength in areas generally re-
> garded as Communist strongholds. In the Alentejo
> region, where large landholdings and a numerous
> landless peasants had created a kind of rural Red
> belt, the Socialists were neck and neck with the
> Communists in Evora, the region's capital. In
> Beja, the Communists had 39 percent while the
> Socialists were a strong second with 35. In
> Setubal, an industrial and port city just south of
> Lisbon, the Socialists led with 39 percent against
> 37 percent for the Communists. [52]

Why is it so inconceivable to U.S. scholars and journalists
that the Portuguese electorate is enthusiastic about the MFA and that
they may really prefer socialism? It is an enormous disservice to
both the reading public and policy makers to have an inaccurate appraisal of a regime's popular support. The same error had been
made in earlier writing about Portugal. Then the accepted myth was
that the Portuguese people were lethargic, orderly, and happy under
the oldest dictatorship in Europe. This erroneous impression resulted

in U.S. and British support for the colonial and economic schemes of the Salazar-Caetano regime in many spheres.[53]

The fact is that the Portuguese proletariat, the poorest in Europe, despite heavy pressures from the Church and 50 years of virulent anticommunist propaganda, nonetheless voted 60 percent for parties based on Marxist ideology. If the Socialist Party is excluded from that grouping, there were still 22 percent of the electorate expressing preference for Communist (either Stalinist, Maoist, revisionist, or Marxist-Leninist) parties. If that part of the spectrum was given a choice simply between a Social Democrat and a Communist state, which way would it go? No one is certain, and on this issue the perspicacity of foreign journalists and writers may be taken simply as conjectural.

While Pravda attempted to minimize the significance of the 12.5 percent Communist Party vote, the Soviet news agency counted the leftist vote at 55 percent (they did not count PPD as leftist) and the rightist vote (CDS) at 8 percent.[54]

Journalistic inaccuracies in facts are sometimes innocuous enough (Accoca placed the population at 9 million while it is 8,063,100), but in some cases an error can have serious consequences. A mistake of 10 percent in the estimated illiteracy rate made Accoca, using a 40 percent rate, suggest that only slightly more than half of the population can read--whereas in fact the actual illiteracy percentage is closer to 30 percent. (While Accoca used the exaggerated figure, he did not seem to be able to relate it to the MFA explanation of why the people should be offered the blank ballot option.)

Given these errors in news reporting and the biases which obscure the issues, it is not too surprising then that on April 27, the New York Times summary on Portugal read as follows:

> The Communist party has been decisively defeated
> by moderate political elements in Portugal's elec-
> tion. The result was not unexpected, but it poses
> some difficult questions for the nation's military
> ruling council, which has moved the country left-
> ward and now must contend with an expression of
> popular support for the "moderates," of the sev-
> eral non-Communist parties that have ideologies
> ranging from Socialist to centrist.
>
> Almost complete returns showed the Com-
> munists will receive perhaps 16 percent of the
> vote, the moderate groups more than 70 percent.
> The ruling High Council of the Revolution had
> called the election a "teaching experience." But
> it said the results would not affect the Government's

commitment to transform Portugal into a socialist state. The major parties were required to
agree in advance to military rule for three to five
years.

Whether this will produce confrontations
within the military and between the military and
the civilian rulers remains uncertain. The question will be answered in the coming months by the
actions of the High Council, a Communist-dominated
group of 18 officers, largely nonaristocratic and
nonintellectual, most of whose political ideologies
were developed during the African wars [emphasis
added]. 55

Giniger displays the same problems of numbers and interpretation as afflicts Accoca. There are 24 members of the Revolutionary Council (High Council as he calls it). They may be unaristocratic
but their academic achievement in terms of degrees and professional
experience is not at all "nonintellectual"!

MAY DAY 1975

Events that occurred at the Intersindical May Day rally in Lisbon were politically significant not only because the rally was the
first interparty public appearance following the elections, but because the formation of Intersindical had been the issue that first
shattered the coalition government six months after it took office.
Furthermore, the issues raised by the events of that day have remained sources of contention in Portugal and of speculation by policy
makers of other governments.

The initial reports of the rally in the British and American
media were based more on second-hand reporting by Portuguese
journalists than on actual observation, and this helped to create confusion about what actually happened.

The physical arrangements at the arena placed the press in a
block of bleachers directly under the speakers' platform. At the
time of the seating incident, the Portuguese journalist Miguel Ruis
and I were the only nonparty reporters standing with the Socialist
party leader and his colleagues. They had marched into the stadium
several hours earlier and had been seated in the block of bleachers
next to the PCP supporters. The two groups had been shouting
slogans at each other for at least an hour, when Soares' supporters
began demanding that he be seated on the speakers' platform where
PCP leader Cunhal was already seated. From the place where the

other reporters were seated they could not observe the exodus of the
PS group from their bleachers to the rear of the speakers' platform,
nor could they hear the conversation as Soares' supporters requested
that he be admitted to sit on the platform. Following the rejection of
the PS request, there was a hurried conference and then the orderly
but massive exit of the party from the stadium, followed by PPD
people while the MDP was still shouting for unity. The President
concluded his speech and before the group had departed completely
the theme songs of the revolution, "Grandola" and "Avante Camarade"
were broadcast on the public address system.

The incident was not broadcast that evening on the media re-
plays of the rally. The next morning PS and PPD issued press statements and announced a demonstration to be held that evening in the
Rossio. Giniger filed his story from Lisbon on May 1, headlined
"Portuguese Socialists Invade a Communist Rally." It read as follows:

> Portuguese Communists sought today to prevent
> the Socialist Party from participating in a huge
> May Day Labor Rally in a stadium here. But a
> crowd headed by Mario Soares, the Socialist
> leader, pushed its way in.
>
> The Socialists interrupted a speech by
> Premier Vasco dos Santos Concalves, shouting
> "The people have voted! The Socialists have
> won!"
>
> This was a reference to the elections last
> Friday for a constituent assembly, in which the
> Socialists and the centrist Popular Democratic
> party scored victories and the Communists, with
> only 12.5 percent of the vote, were defeated. The
> two leading parties together received 63 percent
> of the vote.
>
> The Popular Democrats were not invited to
> the rally, but some came anyway. The Socialist
> party was officially invited but when the Socialist
> leaders, including Francisco Salgado Zenha, the
> Minister of Justice, got to the gate the guards
> barred them.
>
> Part of the stadium that was to have been re-
> served for the Socialists was taken over by the
> Communists who, flying their flags, also occupied
> almost the entire front of the field. The Commu-
> nist party leader, Alvaro Cunhal, was on the
> speaker's platform with President Francisco da
> Costa Gomes and the Premier.

During the Socialist demonstration, officers
went up to Mr. Soares and asked him to come to
the speaker's platform. He moved forward, but
returned to his followers. There were boos from
the Communists. The Socialists shouted back,
"Socialism yes! Dictatorship no!"

Later, all three groups--Socialists, Popular
Democrats and Communists--demonstrated and
blew automobile horns in the center of the city,
but there were no clashes. [56]

The weekly news, New York Times, summary perpetuated the confusion with its May 4 statement:

A relatively small event, an attempt by the Communist party to prevent Socialists from participating in a Lisbon May Day rally, may tell a lot
about how things will go in Portugal. The ruling
Armed Forces Movement intervened and forced
the Communists, who were blocking the Socialists' entry into a stadium, to move aside and let
the Socialists in.

The prospect in Portugal seems to be continued rule by the leftist military leaders, contention by an aggressive Socialist-led moderate
group that will control two-thirds of the Constituent Assembly, and a struggle by the Communists to retain the influence they have on the
military.

The country's military rulers reportedly
had hoped that 40 percent or so of Portugal's
voters would cast blank ballots 10 days ago, and
vote for none of the political parties. They expected to use such a vote as a basis for a political movement that would reduce the importance
of the civilian politicians and the elected assembly.

Instead, only 7 percent cast blank ballots
and now the governing High Council of the Revolution, while continuing to transform the country
into a Socialist state, may have to spend much
of its time arbitrating disputes [emphasis added]. [57]

While Time reported the May Day rally without mention of the incident (May 12, 1975), Newsweek reiterated the "Communists eject
Socialists" theme. [58]

In Portugal the effects of this interparty strife were nearly
cataclysmic. For several weeks, vitriolic editorials, reports of
demonstrations, statements by political party leaders, and protests
to the MFA dominated the pages of the Lisbon dailies. Many of these
newspapers are oriented to a particular party ideology, although
each political party also has its own periodicals quite separate from
the mass media. The important weekly, Expresso, is owned and
edited, for instance, by a prominent PPD party leader. A prominent
Socialist party leader edited Republica, a daily which had frequently
taken positions similar to those of A Capital, a newspaper with PCP
orientation.

On May 19, the typographers union struck Republica, demanding that Republica announce itself on its masthead as a PS newspaper.
The typographers closed down the newspaper, the editorial staff protested, and crowds gathered. Armored military vehicles removed
the printers from the building, but the newspaper remained closed
for nearly three weeks, while Soares publicly threatened to withdraw
his party from the government and gained much international publicity
with a trip to meet with other Socialist party representatives in France.
What was not mentioned was the fact that the editor, Rega, had requested in writing that the MFA lock and seal the building. Finally,
even Dr. Garret Fitzgerald, president pro tem of the EEC, announced
that the EEC would withhold any monies to Portugal because of this
example of the undemocratic behaviors by the MFA. Dr. Fitzgerald,
minister for foreign affairs of the Irish Republic, is in a coalition
government with the Irish Labour Party which is a member group
with the Socialist Party in the Socialist International.

PS initiated a court action against the strikers on May 22 and
the MFA minister for social communications, Commander Jorge
Jesuino, stated to the press that the strike violated the Press Law
and that there was no way to force typographers to print the paper
other than a court order. The AP wire service report gave a very
different impression of the events:

> Communists seized control of the Socialist news-
> paper Republica today and armed paratroppers
> barred thousands of Socialists who gathered out-
> side to try to regain control of the paper.
>
> A lieutenant commanding the paratroops
> said he had been ordered to prevent anyone from
> entering the building.
>
> The Socialist party leader, Mario Soares,
> a Minister Without Portfolio, went into the
> streets with party workers to spread leaflets say-
> ing that the defense of Republica was the defense
> of freedom.

> The threat of a confrontation developed as
> the nation's military leaders gathered in a special
> assembly under pressure from hard-liners to do
> away with a strife between the country's political
> parties and bypass civilian politicians altogether.
>
> The Communist printers' seizure of the after-
> noon paper--the only Lisbon daily outside Commu-
> nist editorial control--posed a new problem for
> military men, who are already troubled by a na-
> tional economic crisis and disobedient army units.
>
> The printers who seized Republica told Raul
> Rego, the 62 year old editor, who served three jail
> terms under the former rightist regime, that his
> ideology was all wrong.
>
> There is no more authority in Portugal, Mr.
> Rego declared, as he waited out the crisis in his
> office. . . .[59]

Early in May, several MFA ministers, including those for
social communications and labor, with some of their assistants
(also MFA) had accepted a U.S. State Department invitation to tour
the United States. They were eager to observe American reactions
and present information to the American public and media on the
situation and prospects of Portugal. Other ministers were making
similar visits to the Soviet Union, France, and Cuba.

For Minister of Labor, Major Costa Martins, the State Department arranged a little more than a meeting with George Meany of
the AFL-CIO. Just as he was leaving the United States to return to
Portugal, he learned that during the week he had been in New York,
there was an important meeting of labor officials and organizers,
including Cesar Chavez, which he would have been most interested
in attending.[60]

The Minister for Social Communications, Jesuino, did meet
with James Reston of the New York Times, and with editors from
Time, the Washington Post, the Christian Science Monitor, and UPI.
He also appeared briefly on the Today Show, and met with Portuguese
media journalists, travel magazine editors, a few scholars and pro-
fessors, and on May 5, Arthur Hartman, Assistant Secretary of
State for European Affairs.

Other State Department officials who met with the delegation
were Ambassador Robert McCloskey, Assistant Secretary for Congressional Relations, John Richardson, Assistant Secretary of State
for Cultural Affairs, and James Keogh, Director, United States Information Agency.

These two ministers were prepared and willing to discuss with
anyone their politics and the MFA relationships with political parties.
They were keen to discuss Portugal's relationship and commitment
to NATO and the U.S. air base in the Azores.

The only times they had any chance to address an audience
and speak with it were at the University of New Hampshire, May
9 and a Columbia University seminar on May 12 in New York. Like
their other meetings, these were invitational affairs.

A month after their visit, President Gerald Ford announced on
May 26 his intentions of raising the issue of Portugal at the forthcoming Brussels meeting of NATO. According to press reports, neither
the State Department nor the Department of Defense had arrived at
any degree of consensus with regard to Portugal policy. Yet at the
very time when these two ministers were in the United States this
policy was under review. Despite Ford's statement, the official
position had supported Ambassador Carlucci's thesis that "the only
available option was to work with the Lisbon Government as long as
the appearance of democracy remained extant."

> The debate within the Ford Administration over
> policy toward Portugal's leftist military Govern-
> ment has ended, according to high-ranking officials.
>
> The agreed-on policy, according to the offi-
> cials, is to work with the Lisbon Government as
> long as the appearance of democracy remains in
> Portugal, a view they said was once held by only
> a minority within the Administration. . . .
>
> President Ford declared on May 26 that he
> intended to take up at the NATO meetings the issue
> posed by the evolution of a leftist Government in
> Portugal, which is one of the 15 signatory members
> of the alliance.
>
> Mr. Ford's statement caught the State Depart-
> ment by surprise and caused concern in Social
> Democratic circles in Europe that the President
> might want to bring the issue before a plenary ses-
> sion of North Atlantic Treaty Organization leaders.
>
> But the next day Secretary of State Kissinger
> took the edge off the President's statement by say-
> ing that Mr. Ford was speaking conditionally about
> what his attitude toward Portugal would be "if" the
> Communists took full control of Portugal. He said
> that the United States intended to discuss Portugal
> only in private talks with leaders attending the
> NATO meetings. . . .

Diplomats from NATO countries confirmed that a number of West European heads of government had told Premier Goncalves that, as one put it, "you have had an election and we expect you to take account of it."

Before the election a minority of United States policymakers headed by Frank C. Carlucci, the Ambassador to Portugal, held the view that the only available option was to work with the Lisbon Government "as long as appearances of democracy remained extant," one official recalled.

The overwhelming majority of policy makers, including Mr. Kissinger, Secretary of Defense, James R. Schlesinger and President Ford himself, were weighing another option--"ostracism from NATO"--from mid-March until the April 25 elections, the official said.

"There were rather strong differences of opinion" in this period, the official said. "There were some hair-pulling times, and the possibility of ostracism was at least entertained in the Administration."

He said that while Mr. Carlucci was the highest ranking member ranged against Mr. Kissinger and the others, "there were people from the Defense Department, State and the White House in both camps."

Shortly after the April election Mr. Kissinger ordered a policy review on Portugal and Mr. Carlucci returned to Washington to participate.

The upshot was that in early May the Administration leaders who had favored ridding NATO of Portugal swung behind Ambassador Carlucci's thesis, two United States officials said.

"The alternative appeared after the election to be one of ostracizing Portugal into Communism," one said, "and the difficulty there would be that the European socialists were not going to cut their ties to Mario Soares and his socialists in Lisbon, so that we would have been completely isolated" [emphasis added].[61]

The visit of the MFA delegation as guests of the State Department was timed to coincide with that decision-making process. The MFA delegation had limited access to top decision makers. However it is clear from later developments that they were themselves being carefully scrutinized, as they had believed. [62]

The clear evidence from U.S. media is that news about events in Portugal is a product of policy and, of course, a determinant of policy.

As might be expected, there has been considerably more coverage of Portugal in the British and other European presses than in the American press. Since many more newspapers are involved in its reportage and there is less reliance on wire service accounts, the British press probably reflects the broadest spectrum of perspectives. The Times, The Sunday Times, The Observer, and The Guardian have been very quick to report events, often utilizing free-lance journalists rather than maintaining regular staff in Lisbon. This provides some variety in perspective often within the same newspaper. For instance, in the May 5, 1974, edition of the Sunday Times, the same page carried three articles by three different reporters:

> Portugal Cries for Revenge on Secret Policy
> Denis Herbstein reports from Lisbon
>
> One vengeful cry dominates all the others chanted in the streets of Lisbon since the coup--"Morte a Pide" (Death to Pide, the political police). The full extent of the octopus-like hold of the secret police on the life of the Portuguese will emerge only as the files on the victims and suspects are sifted. But as we viewed the scattered piles of documents at the old Cardoso Street headquarters of Pide last week, a soldier said: "It is as if the whole country has passed through their hands."
>
> Some 2,300 men and women worked for Pide, also known by the initials DGS; fewer than half have so far been arrested. The files may lead to the unearthing of thousands of informers still in Portugal or living among Portuguese communities in Paris, London and other West European countries. Pide agents have even infiltrated the security services of the Portuguese army and navy.
>
> Salazar's political police were formed 40 years ago with the help of a senior Gestapo officer who visited Portugal. During the Spanish Civil War and World War II, when the fascist regime feared attack from the Left, Pide conducted a reign of terror. People were arrested

and shot in prison or sent without trial to the Cape
Verde islands or Portuguese Timor.

Salazar, obsessed by fears of Communism,
encouraged his police to arrest "militants." They
were released after a few days of beatings, which
explains why fewer than 200 political prisoners
were found in Pide prisons last month.

Then there were the political killings. Dies
Coelho, a sculptor and Communist, was shot in the
head by a member of the Pide anti-Communist
brigade while walking along a Lisbon street. Another Pide agent called Seixias, a known killer,
ended up in the bodyguard of the recently deported
President Tomas.

White Pact Against Black Rebels

Examining the files at the former Pide headquarters in Cardoso Street, Lisbon, I found incontro-
vertible proof that Portugal, South Africa and
Rhodesia have been cooperating at top level to
fight the African liberation movement. I saw an
exchange of secret cables about a meeting of the
southern African security "pool" at Luanda,
Angola, in October 1971. Present were Captain
Silva Bais, director-general of Pide until the recent coup; General Hendrik van den Bergh, head
of the South African Bureau of State Security;
General Venter, head of the South African CID,
and a Captain Noppe, as well as two Rhodesians,
A. M. Braes and a Mr. Esler.

Frelimo Will Be Allowed to Form Political Party
Martin Meredith reports from Nampula in northern Mozambique

The war goes on. Portuguese troops carried out
about 1,000 operations against Frelimo guerrillas
during the past week. Occasionally, in the vast,
sparsely populated regions of northern Mozambique,
contact was made: a few dozen Portuguese were
killed or wounded.

But while pressing on as before with their
desultory campaigns with some 65,000 troops and
25 helicopters, army headquarters at Nampula is
prepared to counter any new challenge that might

come from Mozambique's white community, embittered by the radical reforms being suggested by the new order in Lisbon.

Although the fighting continues, the army's role is already being transformed. Its emerging task, officers here say, is to provide the crucial balance between the old autocratic system which favoured the whites and the haphazard beginnings of democracy.

Even the intriguing figure of Jorge Jardin, a powerful Portuguese businessman and newspaper owner who has strong links with black African leaders to the north is believed to favour the idea of Frelimo's entry into the political arena. Nearly all whites, however, long used to years of anti-Frelimo propaganda, remain apprehensive to say the least. A right-wing group of about 80 whites met in Lourenco Marques on Friday night to try to get the Lisbon junta to ban Frelimo activity.

But one vital factor at least may have changed in favour of the army. Portuguese officers consider that now that free political activity is allowed in the country, there is no longer the same justification from Zambia and Tanzania to support the guerrillas. [63]

In a preelection article which appeared on April 12, the Times mentioned the concern expressed at the meeting of the European Parliament in Luxembourg about the progress of Portuguese democracy (or fear of its demise), quoted from interviews with prominent European socialists, and also quoted Lord Reay, a prominent conservative who said that "the indispensable condition for Portugal to enter the Common Market was that the government of Portugal be democratic." He also warned that Europe was watching to see that Portugal's coming elections would be conducted without intimidation and honestly supervised. [64]

The Irish Republic has, through both its political parties--particularly the Irish Labor Party--and its media, been very interested in the Portuguese predicament. Portuguese Socialist Party leader Soares worked with ILP leaders on aspects of the EEC during the years that the PS leaders were in exile in France. Since both countries share some problems--historically they have both been involved in relatively narrow trade arrangements and have both been primarily agricultural, underdeveloped, and Catholic--the Irish government and media have been engaged in observing and aiding the

revolution. RTE (Irish National Broadcasting Company) sent technical experts to Lisbon in late 1974 to help work out some radio trans-
mission problems. Irish radio and television crews have reported
from Lisbon on major events and at least two daily newspapers, the
Irish Times and the Irish Press, gave extensive coverage to the
1975 elections.

Soviet and Eastern European media have been involved in both
on-site reporting from Lisbon and editorial reaction. Having from
the start adopted a public stance of noninterference in the internal
politics of Portugal, the Soviet Union has had to use some restraints
in its support for the PCP, which has been so at odds with the other
leftist parties. In addition, of course, Moscow has had to consider
the effects on detente of the prominence of the PCP in Portuguese
affairs. It is possible that Moscow has acted as a restraint upon
Cunhal, although when journalists ask him about his connection,
Cunhal vigorously denies getting direction from the Kremlin.

Actually, the Soviet Union has been assured naval and air bases
in Guinea-Bissau, and can probably expect a similar relationship with
Angola in the near future. Therefore, it is superfluous for the Soviets
to be concerned with bases in metropolitan Portugal itself. The U.S.
State Department's expressed concern over the matter of Soviet fishing bases seems somewhat misdirected in view of the strategic placement of Soviet bases on the African coast.

There is no question that Portugal is looking east. President
Costa Gomes scheduled a visit to the Soviet Union and managed to
visit Romania after a visit to France. The Soviet-bloc countries are
no less concerned with the political future of Portugal than are the
NATO countries. For example, the following excerpt from a Socialist Party newspaper of Hungarian workers was sharply critical of
Chancellor Helmut Schmidt of the West German government in his
attitude toward Portugal:

> News items have appeared in Lisbon stating that
> the Cabinet of the West German Republic does not
> want to allocate the hundreds of thousands of marks
> in economic assistance promised in Portugal--be-
> cause as explained in Bonn--the political situation
> in that country is uncertain. If the strongest capi-
> talist nation in Western Europe is acting this way,
> against the poorest nation in Western Europe,
> just liberated from fascist oppression for almost
> half a century, it is not an exaggeration to say that
> NATO is exerting pressure on Portugal and that
> the most influential and powerful members of NATO
> are attempting to interfere with Portugal's internal
> affairs.[65]

Moscow does acknowledge a change in its relationships with Western Europe because of its Portuguese connection. On April 25, 1975, Izvestia published an article celebrating the first anniversary of Portuguese-Russian relationship, entitled "Year of Good Relations":

> The Soviet Union constructed its relations with Porgu-
> gal based on the principle of equality and of not inter-
> fering with its internal affairs. The past year opened
> new perspectives between Soviet-Portuguese rela-
> tions which will continue to strengthen and develop
> in favor of the two countries and of the security and
> cooperation between the people. The Portuguese
> consider the establishment of Luso-Soviet relations
> and one of the victories of the April 25 Revolution. [66]

In addition, Soviet Cosmonaut Valentine Tereskova spent six days in Lisbon as the special guest of the Portuguese Democratic Women's Movement in their campaign for equality. Her visit was prominently described in the Portuguese and the Soviet press as still another instance of improved relations between the two countries.

During April-May 1975, an MFA delegation which included members of the Portuguese government also visited Cuba, and were met with considerable fanfare and publicity. When they returned to Portugal, a description of their impressions appeared in the MFA Bulletin of June 17, 1975:

> One aspect of Cuba which constitutes an example
> for all socialist countries . . . the intellectual
> standards . . . Young Cubans in the cities and
> in the countryside, in perfect harmony of the
> sexes, without the exaggerations of the bour-
> geoisie, prepare for the future of their nation
> as students and workers. All of the schools have
> campuses for agricultural work and all of the
> students have daily practical experience in asso-
> ciating their studies with work collaborating in
> the battle for production and seriously cultivating
> healthy habits, like a love and respect for manual
> work. [67]

Thus, in the mirror of the news media, the dimensions of the MFA and Portugal's revolution are clouded by the ideological preference through which each media performs.

NOTES

1. Phillippe Schmitter, writing on the April 25, 1974 revolution in Portugal, said, for instance:

> To my knowledge no scholarly or journalistic
> observer of Portugal foresaw the overthrow of
> Marcelo Caetano, least of all the rapid and com-
> plete collapse of authoritarian rule in Portugal.
> Quite the contrary, the mini-boom in Portuguese
> studies of 1972-73 produced several supposedly
> objective and documented essays by North Ameri-
> can social scientists which emphasized the dy-
> namic, reformist and presumably viable qualities
> of the Caetano regime. Marxist and/or radical
> scholars despite their more critical scrutiny of
> the data and their more or less perennial wish-
> ful thinking about the imminent maturation of con-
> tradictions also failed to predict the overthrow
> of Caetano, much less the extent and profundity
> of political change which has so far accompanied
> it. . . .

"Retrospective and Prospective Thoughts About the Liberation of Portugal," paper prepared for the Mini-Conference on Contemporary Portugal, Yale University, March 28-29, 1975.

2. Ibid.

3. Schmitter (op. cit.) maintains that those who entered the military academies after 1958 formed the dissident party because of their frustrated mobility aspirations. This theme is also reflected in the paper by D. Wheeler, "Days of Wine and Carnations: The Portuguese Revolution of 1974," New Hampshire Council on World Affairs Bulletin (Fall, 1974). The misconception has also been perpetuated in the popular media. Part of the misconception may also have been fostered by the expression "captains' revolution" which was directly translated from the Portuguese, but ignoring the multiple meanings of "Capitao." For example, in naval rankings "Capitao-tenante" means Lt. Commander--a rank considerably higher than the U.S. Captain. Furthermore, because promotions were being delayed, many of the individuals at Capitao ranks were older than would be expected.

4. Antonio de Spinola, Portugal and the Future (Lisbon: Arcadia, 1973).

5. Movimento-Boletim das Forcas Armadas, November 12, 1974.

6. Maria Velho da Costa, Maria Isabel Barrana, and Maria Theresa Horta, New Portuguese Letters (Lisbon: Estudios Cor, 1973). The suppression of this book and the arrest of its authors excited feminist groups to public demonstrations starting in June 1973 with the adoption of a resolution condemning the actions of the Portuguese government, taken at the International Feminist Planning Conference, June 3, 1973 meeting at Lesley College in Cambridge, Massachusetts, sponsored by National Organization for Women.

7. Amnesty International Report on Torture (London: Duckworth and Co., 1973): "Portugal and its Territories," pp. 16, 2-64.

8. People's News Service, London, July 20, 1973.

9. From a headline which appeared in The Observer, London, May 5, 1974; the full headline reads "Caetano's Chamber of Horrors Gives up Its Secrets," by-line Peter Deeley, Lisbon, May 4.

10. Informacao e Analise: Boletim semanal, Lisbon, 24 de Abril de 1975; Sociedade de Estudos e Publicacoes, Lda.

11. A Capital, March 11, 1975. A Capital is one of the major daily newspapers published in Lisbon and circulated throughout Portugal. Their political orientation is considered to be pro-PCP, but like most of the other dailies, they are not reluctant to report inter-party squabbles, accusations, and threats. After the May Day rally, 1975, the daily newspapers devoted three-quarters of the ink to reporting statements issued by the various parties as a consequence of the incident.

12. Povo Libre, the weekly newspaper of the PPD, in the March 11, 1975 issue devoted the entire newspaper to reporting on the attacks on the PPD meeting in Setubal.

13. Expresso "Revista" section, April 25, 1975. Expresso is published once a week. Its editor-publisher is a prominent leader in the PPD. This newspaper itself was attacked by the MFA in their report on the events of March 11, 1975. The MFA felt that Expresso was contributing to dissension and division between the political parties and the MFA.

14. Richard Eder, New York Times, April 5, 1975.

15. Newsweek and Time, May 12, 1975 issues.

16. Speech by President Costa Gomes on the eve of the elections, April 24, 1974.

17. Statements made at the press conference recorded by author.

18. Published in April 25 edition of the Ministry for Social Communication press statements and news.

19. Information and Analysis, op. cit. (trans. by R. Fields).

20. Information and Analysis, April 22, 1975, p. 32 (trans. by R. Fields).

21. Movimento-Boletim Informativo Das Forcas Armadas, November 26, 1974.

22. New York Times, June 7, 1975.

23. Movimento-Boletim Informativo Das Forcas Armadas, March 25, 1975.

24. Henry Giniger, New York Times, March 18, 1975.

25. Henry Giniger, New York Times, March 25, 1975.

26. New York Times, Editorial, March 19, 1975.

27. Newsweek, March 16, 1975.

28. New York Times, March 13, 1975.

29. Ray S. Cline, New York Times, February 27, 1975. Ray S. Cline, executive director of studies at the Center for Strategic and International Studies, Georgetown University, Washington, D.C., was, from 1969 to 1973, director of the State Department's bureau of intelligence and research. He was previously CIA Deputy Director for Intelligence.

Cline, in an article written for the New York Times, presents an argument for sustaining and extending the Covert Operations of the CIA into the present situation in Portugal. The arguments he gives in favor of such action are based entirely on misintelligence. For instance, he says:

> The fall of the decaying authoritarian regime there
> left the country with virtually no organized political
> structure except for the Communist Underground.
> The armed forces are divided between conservative
> and revolutionary wings. The latter seems to be
> dominant and is generally tolerant of Communist
> demonstrations, political strikes, and physical
> harassment of democratic politicians [emphasis
> added].

30. Komsomolskaya Pravda (Young Communists' newspaper), Moscow, April 20, 1975: In an article about the attempted coup, the newspaper described the actions of the MFA as having been effective against the forces of reaction and mentions that the Portuguese government and MFA consider the problem of their continued participation in NATO something to be examined, but that if still another league were formed it would contribute to international discord, that they wanted instead, cooperation with all countries and with adverse societies.

31. New York Times, March 26, 1975.

32. Ibid.

33. Ibid.

34. Newsweek, March 26, 1975.

35. Information and Analysis, April 24, 1975, pp. 32-33 (trans. by R. Fields).

36. Ibid., pp. 33-34 (trans. by R. Fields).

37. Ibid., p. 35.

38. Ibid.

39. Newsweek, April 21, 1975.

40. Information and Analysis, op. cit., pp. 35-36.

41. Ibid.

42. Ibid., p. 37.

43. The Times, London, April 12, 1975.

44. Flora Lewis, New York Times, April 23, 1975.

45. Information and Analysis, op. cit., p. 39 (trans. by R. Fields).

46. Flora Lewis, New York Times, April 23, 1975.

47. Report by Amnesty International Investigative Study, May 1975 (unpublished).

48. Russel Watson and Miguel Accoca, Newsweek, May 12, 1975.

49. Henry Giniger, New York Times, April 27, 1975.

50. Henry Giniger, International Herald Tribune, April 28, 1975.

51. New York Times, April 26, 1975.

52. New York Times, April 27, 1975.

53. New York Times correspondent Giniger emphasized the vote as the "defeat" of Communism. This kind of analysis in the case of the African colonies proved disastrous for U.S. and British policy makers, cf. J. Duffy, Portugal in Africa (Baltimore, Md.: Penguin African Library, 1963), pp. 208-09, 217-18; and William Minter, Portuguese Africa and the West (London: Penguin African Library, 1972), Ch. 2, 5, and 6.

54. Pravda, April 27, 1975.

55. New York Times, April 27, 1975.

56. New York Times, May 2, 1975.

57. New York Times, May 4, 1975.

58. Newsweek, May 12, 1975.

59. New York Times, May 20, 1975 (AP wire service).

60. Personal communication from Maj. Costa Martins. I had conveyed his interest to Linda Fisher, executive assistant to the President of the New York City Council. By the time she talked with Costa Martins (a few hours later) it was too late for him to get to the meeting.

61. New York Times, June 14, 1975.

62. The nature of their program and the events which instigated their being placed under secret service guard had made Commander Jesuino feel that the delegation was being examined and tested, rather than, apropos of the invitation, allowed to examine the United States (personal communication).

63. <u>Sunday Times</u>, London, May 5, 1974.
64. The <u>Times,</u> London, April 12, 1975.
65. <u>Pravda</u>, February 27, 1975.
66. <u>Izvestia</u>, April 25, 1975.
67. <u>Movimento-Boletim das Forcas Armadas</u>, June 17, 1975.

8

IN THE CONTEXT OF
REVOLUTIONS

There is little unanimity among social theorists on what constitutes a "revolution" as distinct from "social and political change, "
"evolution, " "progress, " and "transformation. " The MFA defines
itself as a revolutionary movement. However, U.S. scholars and
journalists, as we have seen, frequently refer to the MFA ascen-
dancy as a "coup, " or a nonviolent transfer of legitimate power and
authority.

The American colonial struggle from 1775 to 1783 has also
been variously described as the Revolutionary War and the War for
Independence.[1] In this case, there is no question that violence was
the mode of action, but there is serious scholarly debate about
whether the objective and outcome were actually revolutionary in
terms of social and political change. Many believe the war simply
separated the colonial society from a dominant other, without significantly altering the social structure or political system of either party.

There is no question either that violence guarantees or even
portends revolution. The big question, particularly in the case
of Portugal, is whether revolution can occur without violence. Much
sudden and rapid sociopolitical change might well be labeled "progress, " and in fact some theorists conceive of the revolutions of the
twentieth century particularly in terms of "internal war." Certainly
the national liberation struggles of Portuguese Africa, as well as the
movement groups that developed in the United States during the 1960s
and were defined as revolutionary, can be understood in this sense.[2]
Germany's National Socialist Third Reich was clearly an internal
revolution as well. Revolution does not necessarily imply a "progressive" shift, or liberalization, or even a change in the ownership
of the means of production. Yet liberalization, economic upheaval,
and progressive social change may be achieved objectives--as was

the case in the United States during the New Deal--without the existence, strictly speaking, of a revolutionary situation.

After one year of government by the MFA, the Portuguese
people appear to be convinced that they are involved in a revolution.
Apart from the rhetoric, however, is there a revolutionary sub-
stance to these events?

The change in power in Portugal was accomplished swiftly.
Caetano formally surrendered the government to Spinola on April 24,
1974 without a violent confrontation. While in a sense the MFA had
illegally usurped power, legitimacy was officially conferred upon
them by Caetano's deliberate refusal to resist at the headquarters
of the Republican Guard. There was at the time a relatively small
military force in Portugal itself--8,000 people, including one under-
manned armored division.[3] Admiral Tomas and his far-right allies
would have been only too happy to don the warriors' mantle to defend their corporate state, and yet the peaceful transfer of power
was very like the abdication of an aging monarch in favor of his son.
This was certainly no manifestation of revolution: the behavior of
all parties suggested nothing so much as a palace coup.

If the initial acquisition of authority did not itself betoken revolution, neither was the MFA Program a revolutionary one in the sense
of reordering either the social or economic structure of the country.
It did promise some progressive reforms of a New Deal nature--to
create a welfare state--but the program was a modest proposal
rather than a call to arms. Even the behavior of the MFA provisional government toward members of the old regime--only the most
active leadership of PIDE/DGS was imprisoned pending trial by the
still to be developed new jurisprudential code; Caetano, Tomas, and
their high colleagues were exiled to the Azores; there were no venge-
ful executions--indicated change, not revolution.

However, there was in the program an explicit intention to re-
organize and restructure the society by changing the power structure, insuring free expression, improving living conditions, and
instituting economic reforms; it is clear that the kind of social and
economic change which has occurred in the first year of this regime
has radically restructured the social and political life of Portugal.

The revolutions of the twentieth century have become increasingly complex in comparison with earlier revolutions. The complex-
ity stems in part from the proliferation of ideologies, particularly
Marxist ideologies. Can the antiideological bias of the MFA be interpreted as a Guevara-type approach to revolution (as suggested by
his maxim "action precedes ideology"[4]) or is it, as many western
journalists have suggested, a prelude to the kind of fascism exemplified by National Socialism, which is antiideological to the extent
that its only ideology is action?[5] The fear of the latter development

has often proved justified in the emerging African nations, which originated in wars for national liberation and soon formalized governmental structures based on military rule.

If the MFA officers are to be characterized as Guevara-style revolutionaries, they have very different points of origin. The Cuban revolutionary elite, which became guerrilla warriors in opposition to a strong military, were revolutionists when they initially came together. They fought their way into Havana and forged a unique ideology after an experience of violent struggle against a common enemy. The MFA, on the other hand, had its origins as a movement rather than as a band of revolutionary guerrillas. Even as a corps of career officers the MFA was a more numerous and diverse group than would be found in a guerrilla army. Even while they existed as a movement, they were not in isolated groups, but rather the products of and colleagues to civilian movements and liberation armies.

Movements originate as vehicles for social change through the experience of shared oppression; they lead to political action and there is accompanying violence if the process is blocked. Depending, then, on the nature of the opposition and the size of the movement, violence may grow from revolt to revolution. One of the unique features of the MFA was that its membership controlled the means for violent opposition and hence had little need to use violence.[6]

The Portuguese revolution fits the model of the contemporary revolution (in contrast with the classic revolutions) as a "Leninist" transformation which emanates from internal developments not imposed by a foreign power. Boris Goldenberg, writing on the Cuban revolution, included in this class of revolution those of Russia, Yugoslavia, Albania, and North Vietnam:

> All have been brought about by a radical elite in underdeveloped countries; in none has the purpose been to break the fetters which an overmature capitalism had imposed on further social progress; in none did the preconditions exist which Marx considered essential for the establishment of socialism; and in none did the revolution come from the more or less conscious will of a popular majority composed of impoverished and embittered proletarians.[7]

Goldenberg goes on to say that such revolutions tend to establish a totalitarian system of rule with the consent of a considerable part of the population:

What is meant is a social and political system imposed, shaped and controlled by a revolutionary
elite, which finds its legitimization in some ideology, monopolizes all power, prohibits all opposition, reduces the private sphere of men's lives,
indoctrinates the population, and maintains it in a
state of constant mobilization. [8]

While the description of the etiology of Leninist revolution fits the
Portuguese situation, Goldenberg's analysis of the subsequent direction taken by the Cuban revolution has no relationship to it at all.
The first year of the provisional government has been marked by an
ongoing development of multiparty activity; neither prohibition of
opposition nor mobilization has been evident. The Leninist political
groups who have advocated these steps have been ignored or viewed
as threats to the revolution.

Portugal may move in a more totalitarian direction as the MFA
grows increasingly impatient with interparty rivalries and disruptions: the MFA as military men are hardly tolerant of inefficiency
and chaos. Yet it is conceivable that the totalitarian direction taken
by the other Leninist revolutions was a product of narrow base
rather than their initiation by an elite as such. The MFA, on the
other hand, is a movement with a broad popular base emanating out
of a national identity which included experiences of popular revolution. It is quite probable that this difference could swing the revolution far from totalitarianism.

Movement groups and revolutionaries share some social and
psychological dynamics. One of the strongest bonding elements
among such groups is a conviction of rectitude and a tendency which
increases across the spectrum from movement to revolution, toward
united action and self-sacrifice. [9] Eric Hoffer discusses the simi-
larities and differences between mass movements and armies to illustrate the psychological and philosophical development of movements into action groups--and thus, for our purposes, into revolutionaries. Since the MFA is both a mass movement and an army,
it is useful to examine his thesis.

Both mass movements and armies are collective
bodies; both strip the individual of his separate-
ness and distinctness; both demand self-sacrifice,
unquestioning obedience and single-hearted allegiance; both make extensive use of make-believe
to promote daring and united action . . . and endure an autonomous existence. . . .

> The differences are fundamental: an army does
> not come to fulfill a need for a new way of life; it is
> not a road to salvation. It can be used as a stick in
> the hand of a coercer to impose a new way of life
> and force it down unwilling throats . . . the army
> is mainly an instrument devised for the preserva-
> tion or expansion of an established order--old or
> new. It is a temporary instrument. . . . The mass
> movement . . . seems an instrument of eternity,
> and those who join it do so for life. The ex-soldier
> is a veteran . . . the ex-true believer is a renegade.
> The army is an instrument for bolstering, protecting
> and expanding the present. The mass movement
> comes to destroy the present. Its preoccupation is
> with the future. . . . The popular army, which is
> often an end product of a mass movement, retains
> many of the trappings of the movement--pious
> verbiage, slogans, holy symbols; . . . it is held
> together less by faith and enthusiasm than by the un-
> impassioned mechanism of drill, esprit d'corps. . . .[10]

Given some of the contradictions between armies and movements, it
is difficult to place the MFA in either category. Yet the very fact
that the military people who comprise the movement were career
officers, not draftees, nor enlistees, may suggest some psychological dynamics of a movement. Indeed in Portugal a military career
did fulfill a need for a new way of life and a kind of salvation--at
least for those who chose it as a career prior to the mid-1960s. They
joined it, as Hoffer describes membership in the mass movement,
"for life." The MFA as military men have focused on bolstering and
reinforcing the present, and that is precisely why they have exerted
and continue to exert their authority in the government. At the same
time, however, they formed a movement and then catalyzed a mass
movement to "destroy the present." The MFA has become institutionalized as a popular army--a complete reversal of role. But, as
Hoffer describes it, the popular army eventually maintains itself by
instituting the same procedures as any other army.

Leadership, tactics, and attitudes toward the masses differ
between armies and movements. Hoffer says:

> Being an instrument of the present, an army deals
> mainly with the possible. Its leaders do not rely on
> miracles. Even when motivated by fervent faith,
> they are open to compromise. They reckon with the
> possibility of defeat and know how to surrender. On

the other hand, the leader of a mass movement has
an overwhelming contempt for the present--for all
its stubborn facts and perplexities. . . . He relies
on miracles. His hatred of the present (his nihilism)
comes to the fore when the situation becomes desperate. . . .

The spirit of self-sacrifice within an army is
fostered by devotion to duty, make-believe, esprit
d'corps, drill, faith in a leader, sportsmanship,
the spirit of adventure or the desire for glory.
These factors, unlike those employed by a mass
movement, do not spring from a deprecation of the
present and a revulsion from an unwanted self. . . .
The analytical soldier is usually a fanatic turned
soldier rather than the other way around. . . .

To the typical general the mass is something
his army would turn into if it were to fall apart. He
is more aware of the inconstancy of the mass and
its will to anarchy than of its readiness for self-
sacrifice. . . . He knows how to suppress the mass,
but not how to win it. . . .[11]

The MFA has no contempt for the present. In fact, the Bulletin is
very specific about the need to maintain discipline in the armed
forces in order to accomplish democratization:

Conscientious Discipline and Dynamic Hierarchy

1. The success of the Revolution in which we are engaged succeeds through the efficiency of the Armed
Forces--the People in Arms. Only the Armed Forces
are operationally capable of acting with determination
against the multiple heads of the hydra reactionary
(from the unconscious "leftisms" to the retrograde
and/or nostalgic "rightisms"), which constitute, effectively, the powerful support of the revolutionary
right.

The effectiveness of the Armed Forces has as
its primary condition--Discipline! Discipline understood as the quality according to which an order
emanated from the superior organs of the Revolution
re-echoes itself in the various echelons in a way that
it will be totally accomplished by the bases. Not as
charismatic discipline, but rather a conscious discipline, a consensual discipline.

2. Discipline exists in all types of organized society and constitutes the first condition of their effective reactive functioning. Without discipline it is anarchy and chaos. This is true in business, in school, in the Armed Forces.

Discipline, unity and hierarchy are constant in all armies of the world, whatever forms of government there are that govern the country where they are situated. Without discipline there are no Armed Forces. We have the horde, and this differs so much from the Armed Forces, as a pile of rocks differs from a house.

The designation of "Command" (and not of ordering) contains in itself the idea of intervention of the group. This participation, must begin in the very staffs of the various echelons and go all the way to the soldier, generates a feeling of freedom, responsibility, and leads to the spirit of body.

Among the democratic processes (processes of democratic command) to be developed in the Armed Forces, that lead to a valid discipline, are primarily: existence of a climate of mutual respect; definition of responsibilities, elimination of the abuse of authority; participation, by the articulation of opinions, suggestions, feelings and desires; concern about the problems that interest the group.

A static hierarchy leads to stagnation, to stoppage, to death. A static hierarchy is a break, functions as a dead weight, detains the historical march of societies.

The existence of hierarchization in an organism is a necessary condition but not a sufficient one. It is a dynamic hierarchy; a motive (driving) hierarchy; a hierarchy in action. A hierarchy that has as base the constant interaction among its various echelons.

In the present Armed Forces, it is imperative that the relation of chief-subordinate proceeds with a base in persuasion previous to the order, so that this will initiate the immediate execution. "Previous" does not mean immediately before; it means that there must be a constant work of elucidation, aiming at that, in the difficult moments, the inferior reacts without hesitations to the order of

the superior, conscious that, with his attitude, he
is collaborating significantly in the success of the
Revolution. [12]

On a more general level, comparison of the events in Portugal
with other cases of what Harry Eckstein terms "internal wars"[13]
might provide us with another kind of information with which to
clarify the nature (and prospects) of the MFA revolution. Eckstein
lists 21 hypotheses and generalizations about the etiology of internal
war. Of these 21, 11 seem particularly pertinent to Portugal's position prior to the revolution:

Internal wars result from the failure of a regime
to perform adequately the function of political
socialization.
Internal wars are caused by the alienation
[desertion, transfer of allegiance] of the intellectuals. Internal wars are generated by growing
poverty.
Internal wars are caused by a combination
of long-term economic improvement and short-
term setbacks.
Internal wars are due to the inadequate cir-
culation of elites (that is, inadequate recruitment
into the elite of the able and powerful members of
the non-elite).
Internal war is a reflection of frustration
arising from little general social mobility--from
general social stagnation.
Internal wars are due to the estrangement of
rules from the societies they rule.
Internal war is simply a response to bad government. . . .
Internal wars are due, not to the attacks of
the governed on those who govern, but to divisions
among the governing classes.
Internal wars are responses to oppressive
government. . . .
Political violence is generated by rapid social
change. . . .
Internal war occurs when a state is somehow
"out of adjustment" in society. [14]

All of these conditions existed in Portugal, and the level of repression measured in both personal restrictions and actual bloodshed

had increased even while the rhetoric promising and declaring greater freedom escalated. Nonetheless, Portugal is/was not a Marxist revolution in the classic sense, although it does have some similarity to the Russian Revolution. These points of commonality are in the disaffection of the military from the political policy of external warfare; the precedent of an earlier thwarted popular rebellion (providing both martyrs and a revolutionary cadre); disaffection of the bourgeoisie and intelligentsia; and development of a leftist mass movement.

There are some special problems connected with the comparative study of revolutions apart from disagreement about definitions. In the case of Portugal, we are dealing with a relatively small, homogeneous population in a society which has for at least a thousand years identified itself as a nation-state. The same description does not hold true for the majority of other contemporary revolutionary states cited in the literature. None of the African, Asian, or Latin American revolutions has these qualities. If we look back to the French Revolution, we find some of these characteristics, but set in a very different context of world events. Where the French and English Revolutions, and to some extent the American and Russian Revolutions, transpired as wars within a relatively isolated geographic context, the Portuguese revolution happened in the midst of the era of geopolitics.

Without being explicitly articulated, the "spheres of influence" model played some part in the American Revolution. For economic and territorial reasons France, and to a lesser degree Spain, took a great interest in aiding the colonists. And again, this was less an internal war than a war against foreign dominance.

Since the end of World War II, geopolitics--resting on the theory of spheres of influence--has guided the strategies of the major world powers in their relationships with revolutionary movements. The epitome of this strategy was the liberation struggle in Angola into which each power bloc has become involved with opposing liberation armies. This strategy becomes more difficult to implement, except through economic interventions, in an established nation-state: in such a case, civil war may result, as was the case in Spain. While there were no contributions--either direct or indirect--from other powers to the movement of April 25, 1974, Portugal has since become a test ground in a "hearts and minds" kind of battle between contending ideological forces--each providing material and verbal support to particular political parties.

It is this kind of politics that can promote a civil war in Portugal. The situation is particularly complex because the MFA as a nonpartisan but dominating force in the government is continually pressed into arbitration over issues resulting from interparty

disputes. This tends to impinge on the integrity and cohesion of the
MFA itself and to promote antiparty sentiment within the movement.
If the MFA is forced to use its muscle during the revolutionary process itself, there is some prospect for the Portuguese revolution to
become like its contemporaries in Africa, Asia, and Latin America.

But one of the distinguishing characteristics of the Portuguese
revolution has been its peculiar revolutionary process. As the MFA
and political party leaders define it, the revolution really began after
the ouster of Spinola. If revolution is radical change in the social
and economic life of a society, then the events of April 25, 1974
constituted a military coup; October 1, 1974, with the appointment
of the new president, Costa Gomes, reflected the victory of the revolutionary forces within the MFA and marked the beginning of the
revolution. Furthermore, by that date the elite-initiating movement
had been transformed into a mass movement which enacted a revolution by its resistance to reactionary forces. The "movement" character of the MFA was further elaborated after the second attempted
coup. This was pragmatic as well as progressive: given the Portuguese people's prolonged period of repression. The sudden lifting
of restrictions on April 25, 1974 could have resulted in a violent
revolution by an opposition movement had these not been incorporated
immediately into the new government.

The move of the MFA to institutionalize itself into a major
branch of the new government has already evidenced its shift from a
movement to an army--albeit a "people's army." The Cultural
Dynamization Program has its counterparts in the efforts of the
People's Liberation Army in China and in Cuba, but it can only serve
as a supportive element for a mass movement, rather than a mass
movement itself.

Another problem common to Leninist and other leftist revolutionary movements which have in the mid-twentieth century resulted
in new nations, is the activization of the agricultural population into
the radical reform of their own sector. This was the major thrust
of both the Cuban and Russian Revolutions.

Almost invariably revolutionaries have risen from the urban
born or have been unconventional (often disreputable) villagers.
Agrarian reform is a primary objective for the revolutionary government of an underdeveloped society--which is the kind of society in
which such revolutions have been occurring. In Portugal there was
a strong revolutionary movement among a sector of the agrarian
population during the past two decades. The southern agricultural
region--dominated by huge latifundi with absentee owners, seasonally
employed underpaid laborers, and a decline in population and production over the past 50 years--was not only largely sympathetic to the
Communist Party, but was also the scene of violent revolt. The

martyrs of Alentejo and of the village of Grandola are part of the revolutionary tradition forming the basis for the present regime.

On the other side of the coin are the provinces in the north and northwest, a region composed of small subsistence family farms. Although many of the MFA men themselves were born and raised in this region, as were other prominent persons in the political parties and the government, the region itself has been apolitical. It also has had the highest rate of emigrant labor. Agrarian reform is a frightening prospect to the farmers of the north and northwest because they have identified as property owners, despite their poverty. In this, they resemble similar populations caught up in the Cuban and Russian Revolutions. Since the revolution itself is not a military victory with an immediate change of society, but rather a process which over time incorporates the change of each sector of the economic and social life of the society, different groups enter the mass movement for different reasons--or fail to enter it at all.

With the revolution having already begun to change the social and economic ordering of the society and with the revolutionary movement having already institutionalized itself, the MFA and the political parties maintain that the revolution is continuing. This is not unusual in itself. We have the examples of the Chinese and Cuban Revolutions, in both of which the threat of counterrevolution and a series of economic crises were used to provide greater incentive to the continuity of the revolutionary regime. So long as the government maintains itself in the style of a movement and continues to incorporate the masses in the process of change--either through hopes of advantage or through threats of incipient disaster--emergency centralization of power in the MFA becomes consolidated. This has been the sequence after each coup attempt, whether rightist or leftist.

It is this prospect in Portugal which alarms political party leaders. Yet, like their counterparts in the Cuban and Peruvian cases, the political parties among themselves frequently initiate these crises, by inciting their following to antigovernment or anti-other party actions.

In Cuba, the revolutionary leadership had to develop a mass movement behind them. In Portugal the MFA spontaneously catalyzed a mass movement. As the political parties attempt to develop a mass movement basis themselves, they at one and the same time threaten the revolution and support it. They threaten the revolution through divisiveness, but strengthen the ultimate objective of the revolution, which is to produce a politically pluralist society. The MFA and Portugal are completely unique in this revolutionary thrust of such a delicate balance.

The failure in political socialization of the previous regime did not automatically ensure a population socialized for democratic socialism. Lenin pondered the same problem in Russia. He found that even the trade unionism of the working-class movement was more often an instrument for bourgeois ideology than a step toward "social democracy."[15] Thus the ideological aspirations of the Portuguese people in their political parties and as a mass movement behind the MFA are betrayed by their behaviors. Their socialization into fascism leaves them, much as the Russian trade unionists of Lenin's time (whom he criticized for their homage to "spontaneity"), willing parties to absolutism in partisan championing of their particular political party.

Brinton[16] and other political theorists describe progressive stages of revolution. Brinton's scenario of stages--the rule of the moderates, the accession of the extremists, the reigns of terror and virtue, and the thermidorian period--suggests that there are successions of elite leaderships which embody for their time the spirit of the revolution. Each is replaced by the priorities created among the masses by their respective positions. The French Revolution lasted about 40 years as it underwent these stages. The Chinese Revolution, however, has been gathering momentum over a 40-year period and moves no further than back and forth between the extremists and the reign of terror and virtues which Brinton would attribute to the flexibility and longevity of Mao Tse Tung, perhaps.

It would be difficult after only one year of the revolutionary regime in Portugal to consider it as having progressed beyond Brinton's first stage. The earliest stage in Portugal was of course not really revolutionary, but rather a coup. October marked the commencement of the revolution as a reign of moderates. Since that point there has been a steady hammering away at the revolutionary fabric by extremists--particularly leftist extremists. While the mass movement seems quite capable of dealing with rightist counter-revolution attempts, the groups to the left of the Communist Party have been organizing opposition movements which have forced the government into measures not initially contemplated--such as the internment of the MRPP leaders, the forceful arrest of AOC demonstrators, and the utilization of military teams for political education in the rural district. (That is, the use of military teams rather than student teams as initially undertaken. Many of those in the student teams were more intent on organizing in behalf of their movement than in providing genuine nonpartisan political education.)

There is some similarity between the Portuguese Revolution and the ascent of the Allende regime in Chile. In both cases, there was a nonviolent accession to power of a leadership committed to socialism and pluralism. Allende's popular vote and the MFA's

popular support have more in common with each other than with the
Peruvian or other military revolutions to the left. Both regimes
maintained the objective of a pluralistic society with an active civilian political party component, and thus placed themselves in similar
jeopardy. MFA and party leaders in Portugal are very conscious of
the parallels. Yet the MFA did not choose either the Peruvian model
of leftist revolution through military dictatorship, nor could they expect in Portugal an elected leftist government.

In summary, while there are many parallels between the MFA
revolution and other contemporary revolutions, there are no direct
correlations. The MFA leaders had evidently thoroughly studied
revolutionary history and theories and from that and their knowledge
of their own country developed a unique model. While they cannot
totally assure its future or control within the government, they are
increasingly viewing it as the "MFA and People's Revolution"--an
integral entity unique unto itself.

NOTES

1. Although in the United States it was generally referred to
as the Revolutionary War, Britain frequently referred to it as the
War of Independence. Historians and political scientists debate definitions, but they generally conclude that "such social and economic
changes as took place were the consequences rather than the purposes of the war . . . one of the most remarkable aspects of the
American Revolution was that its social change was relatively so
modest. The estates of conspicuous Tories were indeed confiscated,
but this was done to provide a lesson (and a warning) . . . there was
no intention of redistributing property to the landless. . . . New
laws abolished the old European practices of creating large hered-
itary estates through entailment and primogeniture . . . the reforms
did not prove too consequential. Some patriots undoubtedly fought
the war to rid themselves of debts owed British merchants. . . .
(Richard B. Morris, The Making of a Nation [New York: Time, Inc.,
1968], p. 39). Crane Brinton points out, however, that "The American Merchants were really aiming to reverse the whole new imperial policy of Westminister. . . ." (Crane Brinton, Anatomy of Revolution [New York: Vantage Books, 1965], pp. 41-42).

2. Eric Hoffer, The True Believer (New York: Harper & Row,
1951), or for descriptions of contemporary social movements described in America as "Revolutionary," see John Howard, The Cut-
ting Edge: Social Movements and Social Change in America (Phila-
delphia, New York, Toronto: J. P. Lippincott Co., 1974).

3. Kenneth Maxwell, "Portugal: A New Revolution," The New York Review of Books, June 13, 1974.

4. Ernesto "Che" Guevara, "Notes . . ." from Studies on the Left, vol. 1, no. 3 (San Francisco: Agenda Publishing Co., 1960).

5. Naziism as antiideology, see Hadley Cantril, The Psychology of Social Movements (New York: John Wiley & Sons, 1941), p. 237, or Hoffer, op. cit.

6. Hoffer, op. cit.

7. Boris Goldenberg, "The Cuban Revolution: An Analysis," in Revolution: A Reader, ed. Bruce Mazlish, Arthur D. Kaledin, David B. Ralston (New York: Macmillan Co., 1971), p. 399.

8. Ibid., p. 389.

9. Cantril, op. cit.

10. Hoffer, op. cit., pp. 83-84.

11. Ibid., pp. 84-85.

12. Movimento-Boletim das Forcas Armadas of the 25th of April, MFA, December 24, 1974.

13. Harry Eckstein, "On the Etiology of Internal Wars," in Revolution: A Reader, op. cit.

14. Ibid., pp. 27-28.

15. V. I. Lenin, "What Is To Be Done?" in What is To Be Done? (Moscow: Progress Publishers, 1969).

16. Brinton, op. cit.

9

THE PRESENT PURCHASES
THE FUTURE: CONCLUSIONS

"The MFA is the army of the people: the MFA is the people in arms." So say the posters and graffiti, and the people, from the streets of Lisbon to obscure fishing villages, turned out repeatedly in the new government's first year to cheer "their MFA."

But there are others--political party leaders, intellectuals, and shopkeepers--who criticize the MFA and argue against its assumption of a prominent place in the government. By the end of the Freedom Year One, leftist extremists were campaigning abroad to garner sympathy for their imprisoned colleagues and to protest their suspension from the ballot. Originally among the leaders of the MFA, General Spinola and Major Ossario, in Brazil and Paris respectively, were publicly proclaiming that the MFA was forming a dictatorship of the left. Socialists in Portugal and abroad were warning that democracy was again on the wane in Portugal.

The red carnations showered on the celebrants at the stadium in Lisbon were crushed on the ground as members of two of the parties in the government angrily departed the May Day rally. And in Luanda, despite the Algarve agreements signed in January by the leaders of MPLA, FNLA, and UNITA, the three rival liberation movements were still killing each other and innocent bystanders.

Is the MFA going with the revolution or is the revolution going away with the MFA?

One year of very public behavior from the unsteady seat of Portuguese government has provided data, guidelines, and shifting definitions of the MFA. We have examined how they developed; the actions they took and the circumstances under which decisions for action were made; programs they have initiated and how these have been enacted; and finally, to what degree they have been successful in attaining their objective--a pluralistic socialist democracy.

There are serious limitations to this kind of assessment. Regardless of their efforts and intentions, the MFA did not appear on some kind of a blank slate or tabula rasa on April 24, 1974. The crises already devastating Portuguese economic and colonial systems did not start or stop with the MFA revolution. Instead they entered into responsibility for dealing with the most severe economic crisis the nation had ever faced, a chaotic educational system on the verge of collapse, three unresolved colonial wars, and a desperate financial situation. What did the members of the movement, collectively so diffident about a permanent political role, expect to accomplish?

It is difficult at a distance and in retrospect to speculate on what expectations they had of the effects of their revolution for themselves or for the larger society. Considering the diversity among them, it is probable that each man had his own set of anticipations and that reality as it evolved matched no single set of expectations. With the exception of the Spinolists, who acted in opposition to what appears to have been the constant majority consensus, there is no real evidence of internal struggles for power and control. There is considerable evidence (from my conversations with the MFA) that those who were out of step with policies as they evolved tended to withdraw from the arena. Expansion of membership in the MFA to enlisted men and some noncareer officers also accounts for the changing cast of characters and of mind in the movement.

What of the Portuguese people? They were ready for popular rebellion, but required the appearance of a strong deliverer. The Caetano regime had promised reforms and had then continued the Salazar program. The liberalization was rhetorical rather than real. The advent of the MFA meant, for the people, the beginning for freedom. In an astute and important article about the Portuguese revolution, Jane Kramer wrote:

> Freedom has curious meanings in a place where
> no one under the age of seventy has had any adult
> experience of it. Freedom to most Portuguese,
> born in the Salazarist state, is more apt to begin
> with the simple privilege of speaking openly.
> People of Lisbon, convinced by the examples of
> Chile and Brazil and Greece that the United States
> will try to subvert the revolution, were outraged
> when the European edition of Time described the
> revolutionary movement as not advocating "any
> major changes in Portuguese life," except an end
> to the war and a restoration of civil liberties.
> Civil liberties mean everything to the Portuguese.
> People here have lived for so long in fear and

> silence that the right to talk, to assemble, to
> demonstrate, to strike--even to shroud a statue
> of Marcello Caetano, Salazar's deposed successor,
> or scrawl a protest on the shantytown wall--is quite
> literally the beginning of their political education.
> In some of the provinces they have had to start with
> lessons in "What is a party?" and "What is voting?"
> Political meetings which began here on April 25th,
> still go on, night after night, in farms and factories,
> theatres and apartments, bullfight rings, taverns,
> and the new party offices. Everybody goes to them.
> In the vast farming province of Alentejo, in the
> south, where landowners' agents have started threat-
> ening peasants who talk about land reform or better
> wages, the meetings are a source of encouragement
> and reassurance, an antidote to threats about the
> terrible things that will happen to them "when
> Marcello comes home."
>   In the cities, the meetings are something of
> a cross between classes in politics and celebra-
> tions of the human voice. Half of Lisbon seems
> to have laryngitis and the other half seems to be
> suffering from nervous exhaustion.[1]

The happy, bloodless revolution with slogans emphasizing the joint commitment of the MFA and the people was consistently misinter-preted by the rest of the world while the revolutionaries themselves struggled to define their own relationship to their successful cam-paign. Initially they viewed themselves, as they put it, as "the flea on the sleeping elephant."[2] But after the elephant awakened on April 25th the flea took on enormous tasks. As the alternatives for the people, the MFA, and the combination itself expanded, the issue be-came "whether the elephant could fly and the flea would stay immobile."

As the year proceeded and the problems and crises multiplied, the MFA increasingly focused on economics as the priority arena for consolidating their gains. This was a result of their knowledge of the Chilean economic disaster which only a year before had destroyed Chilean democracy. These awful economic conditions had been a fes-tering but hidden sore under the Caetano regime. Despite the appear-ance of a relatively balanced budget, there was a serious money drain out of the country. Payments on the large international loans during the latter period of the Salazar regime created a serious financial out-flow masked, however, by new loans. The increased foreign industry contributed to the flow of profits out of the country. Unemployment had been ignored because the availability of factory jobs in Western

Europe provided a temporary solution, while the prolonged African wars contributed further to the attrition of the labor force. The house of cards thus constructed was bound eventually to collapse.

The MFA turned rapidly toward a program of nationalization and agricultural reform. The internal political economy would be irrevocably socialistic, but external priorities remained: NATO membership and prospective EEC membership.

In July of 1974, the MFA entered into a unique program of mixed civilian-military government. Where their original design had called for military supervision with civilian governance, they moved with alacrity to place their trusted leaders into key ministerial positions. Still somewhat idealistic, they viewed their role as temporary--as catalysts, caretakers, mediators, and defenders of the fragile democracy their revolution had initiated. They became known as "the sleepless ones"*--the serious-faced, conservatively garbed youngish men whose offices never seemed to close and who, after long days in meetings, worked longer nights at their desks. Mixing ideas from scientists, intellectuals, philosophers, and political systems east and west with their knowledge of their homeland and people, they shaped a program. They intended to accomplish in one year the rebirth of a pluralistic society.

But democracy in Portugal had not only been pushed underground, it had been interred in leaden caskets. The new political parties all wanted to prove to their constituents that they had power, legitimacy, and the MFA in their hand. Those who had under the previous regime been politically repressed were too often ready to abrogate the political rights of groups which they saw as politically tainted. The PCP and PS were lumped together as "social fascists," a new term of abjuration. To prove their point, the ultra-left continued to violate the few rules which the MFA had decreed for the preservation of political pluralism--and thus proved that even under conditions of free speech they could be interned.

On the other end of the political scale, excolonialists and major profit takers, frightened of the new legitimacy of Communism, began to look for ways to restore a regime which would preserve their interests. Assuring themselves that there was a leftist plot for an "Easter massacre" (a planned attack by the leftists in power on centrists and rightists to imprison, exile, or kill them),they planned a counterattack. They were convinced that once their battle started the cause would attract widespread support because a majority of the military and the masses were as disenchanted as they were with the

---

*This phrase--a description--is used by people in Lisbon, particularly in describing the MFA leaders in the government.

leftward drift of the government. Instead of joining their rising, however, the crowds gathered to jeer those soldiers who had been de-
luded into taking the plotters' orders seriously. In two small aircraft, the leaders of the plot ignominiously fled to Brazil.

The world press argued about the meanings of these events and
some prophesied an early demise to the newly proclaimed democracy.
Anticipating violence, journalists flocked to Lisbon to cover the April
25 elections. Some, encouraged by the first manifestations of freedom to appear in the Iberian peninsula in their lifetime, wrote en-
thusiastically. Others were cynical. There was little to suggest
that the Portuguese people were unable to deal with the ballot or even
with the proliferation of political parties--which were as extensive
as those in the much older French democracy. With great attention
to detail, an electoral system had been devised that assured even the
illiterate of a way to differentiate among the parties.[3]

Even as the new Portugal celebrated the First of May--the international celebration of the rights of workers--the rumblings of
interparty rivalries grew into a roar and overwhelmed the amplified
voices of the MFA leaders. The two political parties from whom the
MFA had expected the closest cooperation and support--PCP and PS--
had articulated their mutual animosity and become engrossed in the
issues of power which had for 50 years, and in nations throughout
the world, made Communists and Socialists enemies. The split on
the left grew wider and less amenable to conciliation. The unity
which would be essential to prevent a rightist counterrevolution
seemed impossible.

Some within the MFA grew impatient with the maneuverings of
party leaders and began to argue for forming a government by the
MFA, not unlike the leftist military regimes of Nigeria, the Sudan,
and Peru. For social scientists as well as for the MFA, the most
crucial issue continues to be whether a government of military and
civilian collaboration is possible in a multiparty system. The second
major issue, an aspect of the problem of political socialization, is
whether or not after years of single-party governance, a whole people
can move rapidly to a pluralistic democracy.

Dealing with these questions in the context of cases in Thailand
and Turkey, David Morell says:

> The feature of greatest single importance is civilian
> weakness, not military strength. If civilian leaders
> and non-military institutions are embroiled in bick-
> ering and factional competition, transition from a
> military regime cannot succeed. This is true what-
> ever the extent of manpower or weaponry available
> to the armed forces. If civilians--probably the

largest residual category in the social sciences--
are unable to pull themselves together and to devise coherent structures for national governance,
the resultant chaos and instability produce a
power vacuum into which the armed forces quickly move. . . .

[Those] . . . concerned with the transition
process . . . must assess why civilian political
structures are weak as well as why armies are
strong. The length of military rule, the degree
to which the military has coopted or subverted
potential rivals, inherent divisions between civilian groups, and the nature of the military's
own strategy for civilian rule must be evaluated
. . . political leaders in developing countries
facing the transition challenge must devote attention to the development of effective political parties which reach beyond the capital city into the
provincial periphery; to creation of relatively
powerful legislative institutions which offer a
modicum of access for demand articulation,
political participation and grievance resolution;
and to procedures to improve the capabilities
of the civil bureaucracy as a principal institution for governance and interactions between the
governors and the governed. [4]

Morell, from his examination of the Thai and Turkish experiences,
maps out five "phase lines" for accomplishing civilian transition
under such circumstances:

(1) a second set of national elections.
(2) a gradual elimination of appointed members of
    the legislature.
(3) establishment of provincial branch offices for
    political parties.
(4) gradual expansion of the political roles of the
    legislature and other extra-bureaucratic insti-
    tutions; and
(5) eventual separation of powers and establish-
    ment of executive branch accountability. [5]

Keeping in mind that the MFA set out from the opposite direction to the countries described by Morell, let's see how it deals with
such phases.

(1) A second set of national legislative elections was scheduled for late 1975. The MFA described the elections for a constitutional assembly as "an exercise in democracy." They seemed thus well aware that the intensity of a single campaign could heighten tensions between parties, promote violence or a countercoup, and, for an inexperienced electorate, result in frustration and voter apathy.

(2) There will be no members appointed to the legislature directly. Instead the MFA will function as part of an executive council, and the appointed positions like those in the cabinet, will be eliminated. PPD, PS, and CDS wanted even the pro tem cabinet to be changed to reflect the party choices of the constitutional assembly electorate, despite their having signed a preelection pact of agreement to maintain the cabinet as it was first constituted until legislative elections. The outcome of the elections for the legislature will, whenever they are finally held, determine the composition of future cabinets and thus will accomplish the elimination of appointed members. In effect, however, the MFA positions in the cabinet and on the Revolutionary Council had been "appointed" on the basis of election processes within the MFA itself.

(3) As for establishment of provincial branch offices for the political parties--that was accomplished by the parties themselves within weeks of the revolution. Such branch offices have been greatly aided by the financial contributions of foreign political parties in sympathy with their respective "candidates" in Portugal. While the contributions from outside sources to the Portuguese Socialist Party were made a matter of public record, the alleged extensive funding of the Communist Party by its Moscow confederates has been neither proven nor disproven. Of all the parties, PCP seemed to have garnered the largest number of full-time staff and provincial offices. If Moscow money did go into their campaigning, Moscow's silence and posture of "distant approbation" of PCP was a smokescreen intended to obscure the well-known relationship between them. Besides the branch offices of political parties, the MFA had, through its Cultural Dynamization program, ensured that its own versions of branch offices are also available to the rural population.

(4) As for gradual expansion of the roles of the legislature and other extra-bureaucratic institutions--the MFA has established workers' councils, which take active part in determining policy for their particular place of employment. But rather than having expanded the role of the legislature, their constitutional outline sets specific limits to it for the next three to five years.

(5) The constitutional agreement also provided for eventual separation of powers and thus, establishment of executive responsibility. In the interim, such accountability was practiced but is directed to and through the MFA assembly. That body described

itself through a cabinet minister as the only democratically elected
functionaries, and therefore accountable. [6] It seems that they will
continue to provide such accountability, but to a broader base.

The MFA has also provided itself with a format to exercise
some control over politics to ensure, in the MFA's own words, "protection of the political process." That such protection is necessary
has been subject to debate and challenge by several of the parties--
with the notable exception of the PCP, which seems content to have
the MFA protect their continued and expanded role in government.

A natural possible collision between the MFA, advocating political pluralism, and the Communist Party, with its traditional position of one-party rule, has been delayed and perhaps averted by this
strategy. If the PCP increases its proportion of popular support--
as it may well do through its support of the MFA--there may be both
economic sanctions and prospects of foreign intervention against the
Portuguese government. All political parties and the MFA are very
aware of that prospect. On the other hand, it seems unlikely that,
left to its own devices and free of external pressures, the PCP could
garner the support of more than 20 percent of the population over the
next five years. This will be especially true if the adverse economic
situation can be remedied.

Snarled knots of decolonization remain to plague the MFA and
whatever new government emerges from the constitutional assembly
and the legislative elections. While Mozambique and Guinea-Bissau
have been sorting themselves out as new and unified nations, Angola,
Cape Verde, and the Azores, remain thorny issues.

If the bloody turmoil in Angola had been totally a product of
disputed political ideologies, compromise solutions might be effective in formulating a system of government, at least temporarily.
However, in the long process of their liberation struggles, the three
movements, MPLA, UNITA, and FNLA have assumed particular
tribal loyalties and close ties with proponents of conflicting political
ideologies. The Angolan prize is a rich one. The chaos there has
further undermined the economy of both Angola and Portugal. But
the MFA have resolved that they will not jeopardize either their
forces nor their fragile new democracy in metropolitan Portugal in
order to achieve Angolan independence. They withdrew their troops
as promised on November 11, 1975.

There is no question that, while emigration from the overseas
territories has been increasing, the emigration seems headed toward
Brazil more heavily than Lisbon. Other emigrants have moved on to
South Africa and Rhodesia. While there are no precise figures, by
April 1975 it was estimated that at least 200,000 whites had departed
from Portuguese Africa. [7]

Meanwhile, the provisional government has disptached technical and educational personnel to Guinea-Bissau at the new nation's
request. Massive efforts are under way to increase literacy in that
country and in Mozambique. New textbooks originally produced for
their liberated territories by indigenous revolutionary groups are
being reproduced in Portugal and delivered to the former colonies.

Foreign policy for the first year has been based on expanding
economic options as well as encouraging cultural exchange with many
countries from whom Portugal had been shut off for 50 years. The
government has also made considerable effort to reassure their colleagues in NATO of their continued interest in membership.

The Portuguese attitude toward the U.S. air base in the Azores
has been to attempt to maintain the agreements, which were anyway
due for renegotiation. This base was the major refueling center for
U.S. shipments to Israel during the October 1973 Mideast War. As
a result, Arab oil producers cut off the supply of petroleum to Portugal, undermining the economy and particularly the balance of trade.
Consequently, the provisional government's stance on continued U.S.
usage of the base includes a prohibition against it being used to provide future aid to Israel. This seems to have triggered a series of
warnings from the United States that Portugal could be ostracized
from NATO, that such bases would be obtained in Spain, and that
there might be a decline in the U.S. contribution to the economy of
Portugal. For its part, the provisional government has reinforced
its stance by rapidly initiating trade agreements with the Arab countries. In one instance, the production of a U.S.-owned steel plant
has been contracted to Saudi Arabia, and Portuguese technicians are
being employed in that country to construct the product.

MFA spokesmen have in some instances described their sense
of relationship with the Arab countries based on Arabic antecedents
in the Iberian peninsula. Since the original impetus to Portuguese
nationhood and empire was an anti-Arab vendetta, this is somewhat
paradoxical. The revolution in Portugal came at a time when its
Spanish neighbors had become more explicitly hostile to the fascist
regime of Franco than ever before in its 35 years of existence. The
Portuguese provisional government and the Spanish government have
tried to avoid antagonizing each other. Don Juan, designated by his
father, King Alfonso IV, as heir to the Spanish throne, lives in
Estoril, Portugal. From there he now publicly articulates a leftist
line and has gathered support for his claim to the throne from the
Spanish Communist Party and other leftist underground opposition.
His son, Juan Carlos, has been designated by Franco as king. In
June 1975, Don Juan was informed by the Spanish ambassador to
Portugal that he would not be permitted to cross the frontier into
Spain. Don Juan's public statements indicate total accord with the

leftward move of the Portuguese revolution. And more Spaniards than ever seem to be visiting Portugal on political party business, or, as a Spanish medical student put it, "to breathe the air of freedom."

This has, of course, raised questions about the possibility of revolution in Spain. Asked about their influence and attitudes on that subject, the MFA remark that they are not trying to revolutionize the world, only one small country. They are not, they say, exporting their revolution. When North African nations pressured Spain to give up claims to the Spanish Sahara, the Spanish government did not repeat the experience of Caetano in Africa. In May 1975, the Spanish relinquished the territory, and in November after a confrontation with Morocco, Spain agreed to cede the territory to that country.

The French Revolution could provide no recipe for Portugal, and the MFA does not consider that the Portuguese revolution can provide a model for anyone else. Like the French Revolution, the MFA revolution may one day stand as an example of what can be accomplished through a leftist military coup. Such models provide the inspiration for other revolutions, but, as Morell notes, modeling a revolution after a successful one in some other place may in itself be sufficient to induce its disaster. [8]

It is doubtful that the revolution would have happened in 1974 either if there had been a brief and glorious war in Africa or if Caetano had succeeded in his proposed reforms in metropolitan Portugal. But either circumstance would have simply put off for a time a viable revolutionary impetus. For the world had been rapidly changing, and in 1974 the Portuguese people were clamoring to get back in it.

By 1975 it often appeared that the direction of the Portuguese revolution itself could totally change the delicate balance of power which had been keeping that world turning. Not since the fifteenth century had events in Portugal been so central to the future of Western Europe.

NOTES

1. Jane Kramer, "Letter from Lisbon," The New Yorker, September 23, 1975.

2. Movimento das Forcas Armadas Boletim, September 9, 1975.

3. The ballot for the Constitutional Assembly elections printed symbols as well as names. There was also an illustrated brochure, widely distributed, which gave step-by-step directions in words and pictures, for obtaining a ballot, marking it, and returning it to the ballot box.

4. David Morell, "Alternatives to Military Rule in Thailand,"
<u>Armed Forces and Society</u> 1, no. 3 (May 1975): 298.

5. Ibid., p. 299.

6. Commander J. Correa Jesuino, Minister for Information
in the 3rd, 4th, and 5th Cabinet, made this analysis at a press conference, April 25, 1975.

7. Estimates given at a press conference, April 25, 1975.

8. <u>Armed Forces and Society: An Interdisciplinary Journal
on Military Institutions, Civil-Military Relations, Arms Control and
Peacekeeping and Conflict Management: Special Issue on Political
Participation Under Military Regimes</u> 1, no. 3 (May 1975), eds.
Henry Bienen and David Morell. Published by the Inter-University
Seminar on Armed Forces and Society.

The Portuguese revolutionaries seem to have sown the seeds of their own destruction as they showered red carnations on their countrymen. Two months after the elections which marked the first anniversary of the MFA revolution, the fragmentation of the MFA was evident in the Program for Popular Participation (PAP), and the departure from the cabinet of Mario Soares and his Socialist Party colleague, Francisco Zenha, then Minister for Justice.

From January 1975, when he raised the issue of the Intersindical as a manifestation of Communist intent to subvert the revolution, Mario Soares had begun courting allies in the international arena to support his anticommunist stance. The confrontation which logically should have ensued between the Portuguese Communist Party (PCP) and the MFA over the incorporation of a pluralistic democracy never surfaced. Instead, as the months progressed, the only party consistently supporting the MFA and hence the provisional government's programs was the PCP.

The delicate balance between revolutionary ideologies and the broad based popular front needed to provide support for revolutionary programs faltered and collapsed under the weight of a devastated economy and the interpolation into internal politics of European political party alliances. The MFA carried within itself the chinks that would widen into caverns when democratization became a reality.

If one examines the progress of the first year in the context of other revolutions--particularly those enacted by military officer corps--the unique quality of the MFA program for partnership with civilian political parties seems in retrospect an omen of disaster. The MFA's recognition of the problems of political socialization of a politically inexperienced populace was reflected in the Program for Partnership with the People, which was produced 14 months after the revolution. This realization proceeded from their analysis of the voting behavior exhibited in the Constitutional Assembly elections, but it ought to have been apparent from their own personal experience of political socialization.

Unlike the revolutionary military regimes of Libya, Western Nigeria, Egypt, and Chile, the MFA did not eradicate its prospective foes by imprisonment or execution. Instead, it attempted to incorporate within a year the entire spectrum of ideologies into a unified leftist popular front--and they strove to achieve this integration not on the periphery of European economic and political commitments but within Western Europe itself. Thus, an analysis of the first year of revolutionary Portugal must be also an analysis of Portugal's role as a Western European, colonialist state.

The vast majority of Portuguese people had never, before the revolution, experienced democratic decision making. Fifty years of fascism and a relatively brief history of participation in party politics had left the majority of the people with a limited capacity to appraise programs and ideologies, and a strong sense of reliance on interpretations presented by figures in authority. Thus, the persons within an electoral district who had traditionally held positions of economic or clerical authority retained their influence even after members of PIDE/DGS and the Portuguese Legion were discredited. Many such persons of influence, particularly in northern and eastern Portugal, became dominant figures in the Center Social Democrats (CDS), Popular Democrats (PPD), and, to a lesser extent, the Socialist Party (PS). The relationship between the subsistence peasantry and these not-so-new elites had its basis in tradition and the basic insecurity that was the fabric of life for such rural inhabitants. The urban dwellers of Oporto, many of whom labored in less-than-thoroughly unionized industrial enterprises that had been dominated by management, had a similar relationship to their "superiors." Furthermore, the impoverished north, which had long suffered from unemployment and forced emigration, had become more susceptible to the interests of their employers, especially after their last bloody stand against the Salazar regime in 1929 and the repression of all dissident political parties.

In addition to the political inexperience of the majority of the Portuguese people, there are two further conditions which must be explored to understand why, by the end of 1975, the revolution was beset by internal factionalization to such an extent that the fifth and sixth cabinets were installed within a period of two months.

One condition is other nations' foreign policies toward Portugal in the geopolitics of "detente." Portugal's own foreign policy has not been the dynamic factor, but instead a reaction to the impact of other ideologies embodied in European political parties.

Portugal's NATO membership is the key factor here. This membership did not evolve out of a common action against the Axis powers, but because after the victory of El Alamein in 1942, the Allies were able to persuade Salazar to provide them limited use of bases in the Azores. Thus, Portugal's leadership, which had demonstrated a clear preference for the Axis powers until 1941 and had not fulfilled the democratic prerequisites demanded of other members, was invited to be a charter member of NATO while Spain was not.

NATO membership promoted Salazar's prestige at home and abroad, although it did little to promote the economic growth of Portugal. Salazar's strictures against foreign investment, based on the desire of the Portuguese landed aristocracy to maintain their corporate state, were finally dropped in 1963 in the face of increased budgetary demands for defense spending on the colonial wars. The foreign investment which then entered Portugal was highly concentrated.

The colonial wars contributed to the isolation of Portugal as well. The NATO allies criticized the colonial policies in the United Nations in 1961 and later, but continued to provide the military means to continue them. Furthermore, at the start, Portugal was not important to the defense of Central Europe, and it was not until the NATO concern extended to the southern Atlantic, later in the 1960s, that Portugal's strategic potential broadened. Even then, Portugal's contribution to NATO remained minimal. As one authority described it: "We can sum up the role of Portugal in NATO by saying that she has been performing the dirty jobs within the community in exchange for political and economic support for the corporate regime."[1]

Given this marginal role in NATO, there would seem to be little reason for the concern articulated by the United States and other NATO states about the MFA's internal policies. Portugal certainly is not as crucial to NATO dominance in the Mediterranean as is Italy, which has undergone a stronger electoral move toward Communist Party dominance. Even the radical shifts in Greece and Turkey, which had a more immediate effect on NATO strength in the Mediterranean, did not evoke the concern in regard to NATO security that the United States directed at Portugal.

Despite repeated assurances by the Minister for Foreign Affairs, Melo Antunes, and President Costa Gomes that the revolution would be an internal matter of social and economic change rather than a shift in bloc loyalties, President Ford and Secretary of State Kissinger remained unappeased until July, when Kissinger began to place his emphasis on the maintenance of "democracy" and "parliamentarianism" in Portugal.

Yet the real source of European and American anxieties about Portugal's position in detente is doubt about Portugal's economic and political ties throughout Europe.

The foreign policy prospects for revolutionary Portugal revolve around three basic options, each with a different implication for detente. As suggested by d'Oliviera e Sousa:

> The first one is a West European Portugal progressively integrated in Europe as a poor member from southern Europe. This option is supported by moderate elements within the MFA and by the Socialist Party, PPD, and CDS. The second option is an East European style communist Portugal integrated into the East European Community and economically supported by the Soviet Union. Only the somewhat archaic Portuguese Communist party supports such a vision. The third option envisioned is a nationalist Portugal, as a non-aligned country, serving as a "bridge" between the Third World countries and Europe. This nationalist orientation has the support of leftist groups and of a considerable number of prominent members of the MFA.[2]

It is conceivable that Portugal's position at the NATO periphery, as well as its central position in the African periphery of European Imperial Centers, make it a likely location for the exportation of intersystemic conflicts. (Intersystemic conflict refers to the NATO and Warsaw Pact Systems as the parties to detente.) This interpretation may explain the otherwise peculiar warnings to the Soviet Union, issued by President Ford and Secretary Kissinger during April and May 1975, in regard to Moscow's alleged support of the PCP and its February bid for fishing harbors. It also explains the financial outlay to their respective political allies in Portugal by the major powers, that is, the Socialist International support to PS, and U.S. support to PPD.

Senator James Buckley and other American political figures were so outraged at the prospect of a shift in global balance because of Portugal's internal changes that in March they publicly argued for CIA and military intervention.[3] Money channeled through the CIA to the PPD and PS was acknowledged to have been conveyed by European political parties and figures--particularly from West Germany.[4] On the other side of the detente line, the probable financial aid to PCP came from Moscow rather than from the various European Communist parties. The Communist parties of both East and West Germany appear to have been split on the issue of support for Cunhal and his party. The German Democratic Republic appears not to have directed anything more than propaganda support to Portugal until June of 1975.[5] The French, Italian, and Spanish Communist parties were reluctant to collaborate with Cunhal probably because of his pro-Moscow orientation.

The development of the far left--Maoists and others--was meanwhile aided by "ideological tourists" from other countries who seldom provided money, but often provided physical presence and work. There is some reason to suspect that besides gaining moral support from China and Cuba, these various far leftists acquired substantive funding from foreign organizations considerably to the right of the PCP, like the CIA.[6] Thus, in July and August 1975, when Soares and PS, allied with PPD, were demanding the resignation of Goncalves, there was a tentative alliance forged with the far left in the interests of dislodging PCP. Many of the actions attributed by the Western press to the Communists such as the seizure of Radio Renascenca, were in fact the actions of far leftist groups.

It is peculiar that the flames fanned by CDS, PPD, and PS against the PCP and MDP/CDE during their numerous rallies and demonstrations in July and August seemed never to spill over to touch these more leftist, more violent groups. Not until early October do we find open antagonisms erupting between these two factions. This suggests that there was a concerted international effort against the Moscow-oriented left.

There would seem to be no explanation more likely for this internecine conflict than the function of Portugal at the periphery of the NATO bloc. A similar argument could be made for the exacerbation of violent factionalist warfare in Angola. Besides the function of Angola as the warring edge of bloc relationships (including Peking), the lack of a peaceful resolution to conflict in that country served to further exacerbate political factionalization in metropolitan Portugal as over 200,000 refugees streamed into Lisbon in daily airlifts and another 100,000 waited for transportation to refuge in their homeland or among rapidly forming pockets of antirevolutionists mobilized in Spain, Brazil, and France. Their presence in Lisbon with no negotiable funds (Angolan escudas were frozen and the banks rejected them in Lisbon), no jobs, no homes, and a strong antagonism for the MFA, contributed to the explosive potential. The Angolan refugees were strong allies for the right-wing counterrevolutionary mobilization which had begun in earnest after the failure of the attempted coup on March 11.

Other counterrevolutionary forces began building in the Azores and Cape Verde, while the Portuguese colony of Timor erupted in violent conflict between the underground forces which represented the three ideological contestants in July. The provisional government, besieged at home and abroad, abandoned Timor to its fate.

The revolution and the European economy, along with the strains on detente posed by Portugal's membership in NATO and the sudden disengagement from the south Atlantic and Portugal's relationships in the European economy, also made its internal politics of high interest to certain other European countries.

West German interests in Portugal had expanded with the quadrupling of German business investment between 1971 and 1973. (See Table 10.1.) This foreign investment by West German industrialists was not entirely unprotected by their government's political party leadership. They were well aware that Caetano's hold on the loyalties of his countrymen was a fragile one. They were also aware of the strong opposition movements building underground and even in the open--such as the Movement for a Democratic Portugal. Until 1972, the only well-organized opposition party, however, remained PCP, even despite the arrest, torture, and execution of many of its leaders and members and the exile of its dominant charismatic figure, Alvaro Cunhal.

TABLE 10.1

Foreign Investment in Portugal
(thousands of escudos)

	1971	1972	1973
Federal Republic of Germany	237.1	589.0	815.4
United States	391.6	300.3	238.9
France	72.6	74.7	109.6
United Kingdom	156.2	298.6	552.3

Source: Salgado de Matos, Investimentos estrangeiros em Portugal (Lisbon: Serra Nova, 1973).

The nucleus of opposition leadership which had formed the backbone of the electoral campaign of General Humberto Delgado still existed, either underground in Portugal or abroad in exile, and was planning for the eventual democratization of Portugal. Prominent among the exiles was Dr. Mario Soares. His efforts in forming the new Portuguese Socialist Party were aided considerably in 1972 with the financial support of the Friedrich-Ebert Foundation of Bad Godesburg (FRG). [7] This foundation is a functionary of the West German Social Democratic Party, which belongs to the Socialist International. After April 25, 1974, the Popular Democratic Party

(PPD) became a contender for membership in that group, and thus a further tool for the discipline of PS. The development of PS's electoral campaign, moreover, was increasingly dependent upon the funding and the international backing generated by these parties. Some of the contradictory behavior of Soares and PS--specifically their articulated intention to work in coalition with PCP and their presentation of themselves to the electorate as Marxist allies of the MFA and PCP, coupled with their disavowal of MFA and PCP programs in the international arena--is explicable only through the focus of this dependency.

Following the abortive March 11 coup, the provisional government accelerated its program for nationalizing the financial resources of Portugal. This move evoked cries of alarm from the leaders of those countries with major business investments in Portugal. It also heralded the acceleration of mobilization to protect those interests and a slowing of the rush toward a revolutionary regime.

The U.S. State Department funded investigatory expeditions and channeled contributions through U.S.-Portuguese immigrants to PPD. There are allegations that the CIA funded the build-up of the Portuguese Liberation Army (ELP) in Spain. Some of the interviewers of ELP officers asserted that they have alluded to their having "Anglo" surnames and U.S. passports. [8] There is ample precedent for attributing accuracy to these allegations.

Through confidential sources in the Portuguese American community, I had become aware in March 1975 of U.S. State Department sponsored visits to Portugal by Portuguese Americans who were ostensibly visiting business enterprises with which there were American contracts. However, they were also acting as emissaries for the distribution of funds to the Center parties--CDS and PPD. Considerable fund raising from private sources amongst the Portuguese-American community was enhanced by indirect contributions from CIA sources.

During the first two weeks in May 1975, I was an unofficial part of the MFA/Ministry for Social Communications delegation which was touring on the east and west coasts at the invitation of the U.S. Department of State. There were two incidents of violent attacks on the delegation which were ostensibly engineered by Cape Verdians who opposed PAIGC activity in Cape Verde for which they blamed the MFA decision to grant independence to Guinea-Bissau's leftist PAIGC dominated de facto government. The delegation suspected CIA instigation to these attacks as a consequence of which the delegation was then sequestered and put under close security guard.

However, there is yet another indirect channel through which the Movement for the Liberation of Portugal (MDLP), a rightist army based in Spain and supporting General Spinola may be a conduit for CIA operations. Colonel Santos e Castro who has raised a mercenary force to support Holden Roberto's FNLA in Angola, is also an operational chief of MDLP. Roberto's support includes U.S. aid through Zaire as well as the Chinese. The latter are supporting the MDLP's base in Spain. Colonel Castro may be the link for support for the FNLA from the United States.

Although the Portuguese Liberation Army (ELP) is Salazarist, according to a statement given in a press conference on March 23 by the Chief of Staff of the Porta military region, Col. Enrico Caruvacho, they supported the March 11 coup attempt by Spinolists. According to the Minister, their headquarters are in Madrid and the leaders have U.S. passports and Anglo names, Morgan and Castor.

Robert Moss, writing in Harper's December 1975 issue, claims that the leader of the ELP is Barbeeri Cardoso, former deputy chief of PIDE/DGS.[9] If this is the case, then he would have had access to various facilities for forging passports and identification. He may also have had access, through Portugal's affiliation with the International Chiefs of Police organization, to securing such materials and possibly aid, as well.

But it was European political leaders who met with Soares and his confederates on a monthly basis, who provided direct financial infusions and strategy directions. By July the lines were clearly formed between those groups which identified themselves as victims of the new regime's "perversion of the revolution" and those who supported the MFA. The Radio Renascanca case* had cemented the alliance between PS (an avowedly Marxist party forbidden to the Catholic voters by the Bishops Council April edict) with the Catholic hierarchy. PS and PPD had walked out of the cabinet and included both Republica and Radio Renascanca in their demands for redress.

In the north they had allied with CDS, which had its only support amongst the rural subsistence farmers and the Church. For this population, the monied interests and the Church were the authorities to which they had become accustomed. These small farmers were exposed to constant rumors that their holdings would be collectivized (as in the Soviet Union) and their homes and cars taken from them. Since many are illiterate, they could not read and interpret for themselves the land reform program which had been issued by

---

*In May, Radio Renascanca, the broadcasting arm of the Catholic hierarchy in Portugal, was taken over by leftist workers in that station. These workers then broadcast political news and views of the Front for a Leftist Communism (FEC), far-left Marxist-Leninist and Maoist parties. The problem was already fomenting in March but the takeover came three months later.

the provisional government that guaranteed their right to maintain
their small holdings. The continued economic hardship, which resulted in further price escalations and shortages of food staples in
June, seemed to them still another omen of incipient decline. With
the exception of the MFA Cultural Dynamization teams, these people
had no recourse to information except through their traditional
sources, the Church and the monied interests. Antigovernment leaflets, speeches, and rallies began to proliferate in the north during
early July. On July 18, a demonstration in Oporto threatened a
march on Lisbon to unseat Prime Minister Goncalves, who was accused of being a Communist. That weekend PCP and MDP offices
near Oporto were razed by angry mobs, and at the last minute Soares,
yielding to the implorations of the MFA, denounced any plan to march
on Lisbon. Meanwhile, the barricades went up and teams of MFA
and armbanded civilians searched cars entering and leaving the city. [10]

That same weekend, however, a complement of Europeans invited by PS to participate in a seminar on Portugal found themselves
on display at a Lisbon rally as representatives of various allied
European socialist parties. The rally drew over 10,000 spectators
and featured speeches by Soares, Zenha, and Rega, with the crowd
prompted for appropriate cheers--"Out with the Communists," "Down
with Goncalves," and "We want Socialism, not Communism." Military men were hissed, an army helicopter was greeted with clenched
fists, and the reporting team from Radio Renascanca was beaten up
and their equipment smashed. The same night in another part of
Lisbon, a group of anarchists held a somewhat smaller meeting,
while a demonstration by far leftists demanded the termination of
the constitutional assembly. [11]

No deaths resulted from these Lisbon demonstrations, but in
the countryside two soldiers had already been killed by angry mobs.
The tempo and ferocity of these rallies increased during July. Within
the MFA itself new problems emerged as even officers began to take
sides in the larger politics. The Assembly had a hurried meeting on
the subject of discipline, and found themselves caught up in the incom-
pletion of the democratization program and the divisiveness of political party polarization. To this maelstrom was added the newest plan
for administering the government without a cabinet--a troika executive which placed Brig. Otelo Saraiva De Carvalho alongside Costa
Gomes and Goncalves in the leadership. Carvalho, then in Cuba,
rushed home to assume his new responsibilities and promptly fell
into dispute with Goncalves on the selection of a new cabinet as well
as on his own duties.

The fifth cabinet, initially announced as a temporary arrangement by Costa Gomes, contained fewer civilians than had the fourth
cabinet, and included only civilians who had renounced political party

affiliations. Many MFA ministers who had served in the second, third, and fourth cabinets stayed on in this one, for example, Minister for Labor Costa Martins, and Minister for Social Communication Jeşuiho.

Meanwhile PS leadership began to crumble and the small Popular Socialist Front (FSP) which prior to the elections grew into a new force in Portugal, swelled to new proportions. But the lines were hardening and the Common Market was reaffirming its disinclination to provide funds for the new government unless the cabinet was restored with PS in it. For the political parties of Western Europe and for the U.S. government, the PAP program--which bypassed political parties but built on the kinds of face-to-face relationships most consistent with Portuguese patterns--was an even greater threat than had been the nationalization of banks and finance companies. Each new directive issued by EEC or by Olof Palme, the Prime Minister of Sweden, restated that support for the Portuguese government depended upon the security of a multiparty political system and the representation in the cabinet of those parties proportional to their votes in the April elections. They all seemed to have forgotten that the elections, by agreement, were for the constitutional assembly, not for a legislature.

As the lines hardened, discussion focused on Goncalves' survival in the political arena. He had become the symbol or the scapegoat for each group. The struggle took on new violent proportions in August with apparently coordinated actions in Lisbon and the northern countryside. On August 4, a bomb went off outside the Ministry for Agriculture in Lisbon. The one death in the explosion was Ricardo Perreira, who had apparently planted the bomb and who was identified as a leading member of ELP and a former member of the Portuguese Legion. Yet, even though the bomber had been publicly identified, Western news reports described him as a "passerby."

During the evening of the same day, a crowd of about 200 people attacked the office of the PCP in Villa Nova de Famalicao. Residents later claimed that these people were strangers and that they did not know from where they had come. The attack was consistent with the leaflets distributed by CDS and PPD, which urged their members to "attack the Communists." The crowd, refusing to listen to the disbursement orders of the military unit protecting the premises, rushed the building, and in the ensuing warning volley, one member each of CDS and PPD was killed.

Later that evening the mob, still including a large portion of outsiders, went to the homes of Lino Mima, a lawyer, and Vierra Da Carvalho, a dentist, both members of MDP/CDE; they then broke into the homes and set fire to them.

PPD and CDS announced then that the following day, during the funerals of the two who had died that evening, they would again attack the PCP office. They buttressed this call to arms with leaflets which stated that "militant members of the Communist Party of Portugal have . . . killed two staunch democrats by cruelly murdering them with shots in their backs." This report was sufficient to arouse more townspeople, so that the next day there were at least 2,000 people attacking Communist Party headquarters. Fearful of another death, and unable to restore order, the soldiers spread their arms and leaned forward to push the crowd back. Western press captions on photos of this event gave such distorted interpretations as "Army fraternizes with antigovernment protestors."[12]

Ten persons were finally arrested as a result of the violence. They all proved to be members of the former Portuguese Legion (the Salazarist version of the Nazi SS) and at least one was a leader of the former powerful fascist party, ANP.[13]

By early September, Costa Gomes, acceding to the violent demands of the antigovernment forces, named a new prime minister, Admiral Jose Pinheiro Azeveda, a member of the Revolutionary Council who had the support of various factions within the council and the MFA Assembly. He tried to name Goncalves to the post of Chief of Staff of the Military, but faced with serious opposition from military figures including Carvalho, Goncalves declined the position. Meanwhile Azeveda with great difficulty formulated a sixth cabinet, which included four members from PS (not including Soares), two from PPD, one from PCP, and three independents.

Some of the first attempts by the new government to restore Radio Renascanca to the Church hierarchy failed; soldiers from a select unit, Copcon, occupied the radio station, but failed to oust the leftists who had taken it over. The same thing happened with other radio and television stations; in some cases the military failed to even half the vituperative antigovernment propaganda which issued from the far leftists in control of these media.[14]

Demonstrations and counterdemonstrations ensued, and mutual charges by the far left and the coalition of PPD, PS, and CDS reached a peak in the first week of October. At that time Soares said he expected a leftist antigovernment coup. The factual basis of that apprehension was never clearly demonstrated, but the implied threat was sufficient to have military security units sent into position to neutralize far leftist military units such as the First Light Artillery Regiment located in Lisbon.

General Antonio Spinola had announced in mid-July that he would return to Portugal by the end of August. That would appear, in retrospect, to have been the only avowal of antigovernment intention which did not achieve fruition. However, during Spinola's July and August tours of the United States and Western Europe, he met with Soares and leaders of PPD and CDS. When questioned about the rumors of such a meeting, Soares not only admitted to the contact, but expressed his intentions of cooperating with Spinola. Whether these intentions included the deployment of ELP forces in the campaign to topple the fourth cabinet, or suggested the formation of a united front group composed of PS, CDS, PPD, and Christian Democrats in a broadly social democratic framework, is uncertain. The implication, however, was that Spinola was likely to reemerge on the Lisbon political scene if the centrist coalition could hold on to the reins of power long enough to stabilize its hegemony through elections for the legislative assembly, which were promised for November 1975, but which never materialized.

Whatever else may emerge to unbalance detente in Africa or Asia, the NATO and EEC powers will not permit the kinds of internal shifts in the social and economic order of Portugal which might translate into am imbalance in the intersystem framework. The situation is faintly reminiscent of the Warsaw Pact bloc interventions in Czechoslovakia in 1968, although with a distinct social democratic flavor.

This second-year events also raise some serious questions about the possibility for mobilizing mass support for a revolution or liberation struggle without undergoing either a reign of terror or a war against an outside colonial power. And circumstances again raise the spectre of similarity with the counterrevolutionary build-up of 1972-73 in Chile. The economic boycott enacted against the regime in Portugal has parallels extending even to the ITT withdrawal of late August 1975, the freeze on Portuguese currency in Western Europe which occurred in early September, and the international vocal and financial support provided for the regime's opposition.[15]

As the various political factions proceed to polarization and become armed groups, the possibility of civil war in Portugal is enhanced. The outbreak of armed struggle in neighboring Spain, interacting with the political factionalization in Portugal, portends a bitter time for the Iberian peninsula. The factionalization of the left in both countries has provided a strong base for the mobilization of rightist forces--and this is not unlike the circumstances of 1926 in Portugal or 1938 in Spain. However, in this present crisis, the economic strategies of Western Europe, combined with the political necessity of detente, make it impossible for the Iberian struggle to proceed again in isolation.

NOTES

1. Jorge d'Oliviera e Sousa, Portugal and Detente, paper presented within the framework of the Inter-University Centre Post Graduate Course: European Security and Cooperation; Dubrovnik, Yugoslavia, April 7 to May 2, 1975.
2. Ibid., pp. 11-12.
3. New York Times, March 22, 1975, "Senators Issue Warning."

> Two United States Senators urged today that the
> Ford Administration pay closer attention to the
> Portuguese political situation which they said
> was becoming a threat to the North Atlantic
> Treaty Organization.
> Senator James L. Buckley, Conservative-
> Republican of New York, said President Ford
> should call Secretary of State Kissinger home to
> decide what was to be done in the Portuguese
> emergency.
> Senator Hubert H. Humphrey, the Minnesota
> Democrat, said in a separate statement that the
> United States had "missed numerous opportunities
> to support democratic elements in Portugal" and
> should do more to help them now.
> Mr. Buckley, who said a Communist take-
> over was being "planned, supported, armed, and
> guided by the Kremlin," asserted that the Admin-
> istration might have to "consider options" of an
> air-naval action to protect the United States mili-
> tary base on the Azores. He added that while he
> was not suggesting specific measures, "if the
> Communists solidify their rule, they should be
> thrown out of N. A. T. O."
> The Senator said he based his estimates of
> Soviet involvement on reports "from intelligence
> communities here and abroad," and from friends
> of Portuguese political exiles.

New York Times, June 1, 1975, Portugal: "Hour of Peril."

> To the Editor:
> It is abundantly clear that Mario Soares'
> Socialist party is the major hope of freedom and
> justice in Portugal. Now that this party, and with

it the hopes of Portuguese democracy, is threatened by a wing of the Movement of the Armed Forces and by the Portuguese Communist party, we are proud to affirm our solidarity with it.

It is precisely because of this solidarity that we are disturbed by recent reports that President Ford and Secretary Kissinger are preparing to intervene in Portugal. The United States was all too happy to welcome Portuguese fascism into the camp of the "Free World" for an entire generation. And what concerns Washington now is not so much the democratic and social rights of the Portuguese people but the fear that a dictatorship of the authoritarian left will opt out of or subvert the NATO alliance.

So intervention on the part of the Ford Administration in Portugal, be it open or covert, can only serve one of two equally unacceptable ends. Either it will be directed toward a coup and the restoration of a dictatorship of the fascist right or it will discredit the socialist and democratic forces by associating them with the foreign friends of Salazar and Caetano. In either case, Ford and Kissinger can only hurt the democratic socialists in the forefront of the struggle.

It is not an accident that Olof Palme of Sweden, who so forthrightly condemned the war in Vietnam, and Willy Brandt, who moved toward detente in Eastern Europe, are so active in support of the Portuguese freedom movement. They have the credentials to mobilize the kind of support that the Portuguese Socialists need in this hour of peril. In America, the democratic left must speak out, not the least because it is one more tragic consequence of Washington's support of fascist dictatorship in the name of an indiscriminate anti-Communism that it has forfeited the right, and the very ability, to do so. Michael Harrington, Irving Howe, New York, May 26, 1975

New York _Times_, February 28, 1975, Op. Ed. page article by Ray Cline cited in Chapter 7, footnote 21.

4. _Portugal Blatter_, April/May 1975, p. 5. See also New York _Times_, October 12, Leslie Gelb wrote on CIA funneling funds through West Germany.

5. From author's analysis of East German propaganda, the first direct relationship between an official agency of the Democratic Republic of Germany and the PCP occurred in April 1975. Within the next two months workers' delegations were exchanged between the two parties and in June and July 1975 workers' delegations from the Norwegian and West German Communist parties also visited Portugal.

6. This is suggested in a pamphlet, A Farsa dos pseudo radicais em Portugal, Jose Manuel Jara, Edicoes Socais (pub.) May 1974.

7. Portugal Blatter, op. cit.

8. Irish Times, March 24, 1975, p. 6.

9. Robert Moss, "Portugal's Civil War," Harper's Magazine, December 1975.

10. I personally witnessed these events, tape recorded them and interviewed participants during July 1975.

11. Stephan Metreveli, "Mobilization for Counter-Revolution," paper presented at Commission II, International Peace Research Association annual conference, Turku, Finland, August 1975. His paper was half of a joint presentation with this author on Portugal: "Mobilization for Revolution and Counterrevolution."

12. Stephan Metreveli, Siege in Portugal (West Berlin: Druck und Verlag, 1976).

13. Ibid.

14. New York Times, October 23, 1975 (AP), "Leftists Occupy Lisbon Radio Unit," October 22.

15. Portugal Blatter, July/August 1975.

THE MFA PROGRAM

November 1974

Considering that at the end of 13 years of fighting overseas, the existing political system has not succeeded in objectively concluding the fighting or developing a politics that leads to peace among Portuguese of all races and beliefs;

Considering that the replacement of these political systems will have to transpire without adversely affecting the peace, progress, or well-being of the nation:

The Movement of the Portuguese Armed Forces in the deep conviction that it expresses the desires of the great majority of the people and that its action justifies itself in the salvation of the motherland with the strength given to the nation by its soldiers, proclaims and commits itself to guarantee the adoption of the following measures, the platform it believes necessary in order to resolve the great crisis of Portugal's adversity:

A. Immediate Measures

1.   The exercise of political power by the Junta of National Salvation in regard to the formation of a Provisional Civil Government will be the choice of a President and Vice-President whose beliefs are characteristic of the Junta.
2.   The Junta of National Salvation decrees:
     a.   The immediate destruction by the President of the Republic of the National Assembly and the Council of State followed by the public announcement of the convening, within months, of a National Constitutional Assembly elected by universal election and secret vote according to the electoral law to be developed by the Provisional Government.
     b.   The removal from office of all civic governors on the continent, governors of autonomous districts, and governors of overseas provinces, as well as the immediate extinction of National Popular Action.
          1) The general government of the overseas provinces will be immediately assumed by the general secretaries invested with the functions of the temporary government until the

naming of the new government by the provisional government.

2) The current affairs of civil governments will be undertaken by the respective substitutes while the provisional government is nominating new governors.

c. The immediate extinction of the DGS, the Portuguese Legion and their political youth organizations. Ultimately the DGS will be restructured and cleansed. Meanwhile the military police will serve when militant operations are required.

d. The delivery to the armed forces of the individuals culpable of crimes against the political orders that are installed. The Junta of National Salvation will give instructions on processing and judgment.

e. Measures which would permit rigorous vigilance and control of all foreign economic and financial operations.

f. The immediate amnesty of all political prisoners with the exception of those guilty of common crimes, and their return to their former homes, the voluntary reintegration of civil servants who were removed from their positions for political reasons.

g. Abolition of censorship and previous examination system. Recognizing the necessity for protection of military secrets and providing for the protection of public opinion from ideological aggressions of the malevolent reactionaries, there will be created an ad hoc commission for the control of the press, radio, television, theater and cinema to be of a transitory nature and directly dependent on the Junta of National Salvation, which will maintain these functions until publication of the new laws on the press, radio, television, and cinema by the provisional government.

h. Measures for the reorganization and cleaning up of the armed forces and related military organization.

i. Measures that will lead to efficient control over corruption and speculation.

B. Short-Term Measures

1. In a maximum time of three weeks for the consolidation of power, the Junta of National Salvation will choose from among its members the one who will exert the functions of President of the Portuguese Republic, who will have similar functions to the ones outlined in the present constitution. The remaining members of the Junta of National Salvation will assume the functions of Chief of Staff and Major General of the Armed Forces, Vice Chiefs of

Staff to the Major of the Army, Navy, and Air Force, and they will be part of the Council of State.

2. Upon assuming his functions, the President of the Republic will name the civilian provisional government, composing it of persons representing current political groups and independent persons who identify themselves with the present government.

3. During the period of the provisional government, imposed by the historical necessity of the political transformation, there will be maintained the Junta for the National Salvation to insure the safety of the objectives. This exceptional period will be completed as soon as a new constitution is completed and a new president of the republic is elected by the legislative assembly.

4. The provisional government will govern by decree, which is necessitated by the period of the present proclamation.

5. The provisional government, keeping in mind that the great and and deep reforms will only be adopted through the future national constitutional assembly, will nonetheless be obligated to immediately promote

   a. The application of methods to prepare and guarantee the formal applications of measures of a material character--economic, social, and cultural--that guarantee the future liberty of the citizens' political life.

   b. The freedom of unions and associations. The application of these principles will permit the formation of political associations to evolve into political parties and guarantees of freedom for unionization in accordance with special laws to regulate their exercise.

   c. The liberty of expression of new forms of thoughts.

   d. The promulgation of the new forms of thought on radio, television, theater, and cinema.

   e. Measures and dispositions to insure the independence and dignity of the judicial power.

      1) The extinction of special tribunals.

      2) The crimes committed against the state in the new regime will be handled by judges or ordinary tribunals with all the ordinary guarantees of arguments for the defendants.

6. The provisional government will disseminate the foundations of:

   a. The new economic policy to be put to the service of the Portuguese people, in particular to the levels of the population which have up to now lacked opportunities, with immediate concern about the fight against inflation and the excessive rise in the cost of living.

   b. A new social policy that will have as its objective defense of the interests of the working classes and the acceleration of improvement in quality of life for the Portuguese people.

7. The provisional government will maintain itself in external pol-
    itics by the principles of the independence and equality among
    all nations, non-interference in the internal problems of other
    countries, and diversifying the international relations and en-
    larging the basis of friendship and cooperation with other nations.
8. The politics of the provisional government will be guided by the
    following principles in the overseas provinces:
    a. Finding a political solution rather than a military one for the
        war.
    b. The creation of the conditions for bringing debate to the na-
        tional level on the problems of the overseas provinces.
    c. The development of foundations for the overseas policy which
        will lead to peace.

C. Final Considerations

1. As soon as the new government is elected by the nation and by
    the legislative assembly and the new president of the republic,
    the Junta of National Salvation will be dissolved and the armed
    forces will return to its specific mission of defense of the na-
    tional welfare.
2. The Armed Forces Movement, convinced that the principles and
    objectives herein proclaimed are imperative, declare our com-
    mitment to the country in order to serve the highest interests of
    the nation, address to all Portuguese our vehement appeal to the
    sincere participation in the national public life, and exhort them
    to guarantee by their efforts in whatever circumstances they oc-
    cupy and in the shortest possible period of time, that they will
    develop a political schema which will deal with these grave, na-
    tional problems with harmony and progress in social justice--
    indispensable to the health of our public life--which will obtain
    for Portugal its place among the nations.

Cited from: Proclamation of the Armed Forces Movement. Ministry
of Mass Communication, April 25, 1974. (Translation from the
original Portuguese by R. Fields and M. Froes.)

ANGOLA: THE INDEPENDENCE AGREEMENT

January 1975

The Portuguese State and the Angolan National Liberation Movements--the National Angolan Liberation
Front (FNLA), the People's Movement for the Liberation of Angola (MPLA) and the National Union for the
Total Independence of Angola (UNITA)--having met at
Alvor, in the Algarve, from January 10 to 15, 1975,
to negotiate the procedure and the calendar of the
access of Angola to independence, have agreed the
following:

Chapter 1

On the Independence of Angola

Art. 1--The Portuguese State recognizes the Liberation Move-
ments--National Angolan Liberation Front (FNLA), the People's
Movement for the Liberation of Angola (MPLA) and the National Union
for Total Independence of Angola (UNITA)--as the sole legitimate
representatives of the people of Angola.

Art. 2--The Portuguese State solemnly restates its recognition
of the right of the people of Angola to independence.

Art. 3--Angola forms one indivisible unit, within its present
geographical and political boundaries, and in this context Cabinda is
an unalienable component part of Angolan territory.

Art. 4--The independence and full sovereignty of Angola shall
be solemnly proclaimed on 11 November 1975 in Angola by the President of the Portuguese Republic or by a specially appointed representative of the President.

Art. 5--Until independence is proclaimed, the power shall be
wielded by the High Commissioner and by a Transitional Government
which shall take office on 31 January 1975.

Art. 6--The Portuguese State and the three Liberation Movements formally affirm, under this agreement, a general ceasefire,
already being observed de facto by their armed forces throughout
Angolan territory.

After this date, any use of force other than as decided by the rightful authorities to prevent internal acts of violence or acts of aggression from outside the country shall be considered to be illicit.

Art. 7--After the ceasefire the armed forces of the FNLA, the MPLA and the UNITA shall take up positions in the regions and places where they are at present stationed, until such time as the provisions laid down in Chapter IV of this Agreement shall be put into practice.

Art. 8--The Portuguese State undertakes to transfer progressively, no later than the terms of the transitional period, all the powers it enjoys and wields in Angola to the Angolan organs of sovereignty.

Art. 9--With the conclusion of this Agreement, an amnesty is held to be granted to cover all the effects of the patriotic acts performed in the course of the national liberation struggle in Angola which would have been considered to be liable to punishment under legislation in force at the time of their performance.

Art. 10--The independent State of Angola shall exert its sovereignty fully and freely, both internally and on the international plane.

Chapter 2

On the High Commissioner

Art. 11--During the transitional period the President of the Republic and the Portuguese Government shall be represented in Angola by the High Commissioner, who shall defend the interests of the Portuguese Republic.

Art. 12--The High Commissioner in Angola shall be appointed and released from office by the President of the Portuguese Republic, by whom he shall be sworn in and to whom he is politically responsible.

Art. 13--It is for the High Commissioner to:
    a) Represent the President of the Republic, ensuring and guaranteeing, in full agreement with the Transitional Government, the observance of the law;
    b) Safeguard and guarantee the physical security of Angolan territory, in close co-operation with the Transitional Government;
    c) Ensure the fulfilment of this Agreement and of such others as may come to be made between the Liberation Movements and the Portuguese State;
    d) Guarantee and promote the process of decolonization of Angola;
    e) Ratify all acts which concern, or refer to, the Portuguese State;

f) Attend the meetings of the Council of Ministers, when he thinks fit, where he may participate in their discussions but without the right to vote;

g) Sign, approve and have published the decree-laws and the decrees drafted by the Transitional Government;

h) Ensure, together with the Presidential Committee, the direction of the National Defence Committee, and to direct the foreign policy of Angola during the transitional period, aided in this by the Presidential Committee.

Chapter 3

On the Transitional Government

Art. 14--The Transitional Government is chaired and directed by the Presidential Committee.

Art. 15--The Presidential Committee comprises three members, one from each liberation movement, and its main task is to direct and coordinate the Transitional Government.

Art. 16--Whenever it thinks fit, the Presidential Committee may consult the High Commissioner on matters concerning the work of the Government.

Art. 17--The decisions of the Transitional Government shall be taken by a majority of two-thirds; the members of the Presidential Committee shall chair it in turn.

Art. 18--The Transitional Government shall comprise the following Ministries: the Interior, Information, Labour and Social Security, Economic Affairs, Planning and Finance, Justice, Transports and Communications, Health and Social Affairs, Public Works, Housing and Town-Planning, Education and Culture, Agriculture, Natural Resources.

Art. 19--The following Offices of Secretaries of State are hereby instituted:

a) Two in the Ministry of the Interior,

b) Two in the Ministry of Information,

c) Two in the Ministry of Labour and Social Security,

d) Three in the Ministry of Economic Affairs, to be known respectively as the Secretary of State for Trade and Tourism, the Secretary of State for Industry and Power and the Secretary of State for Fisheries.

Art. 20--The Ministers of the Transitional Government shall be appointed in the same proportion by the National Angolan Liberation Front (FNLA), the People's Movement for the Liberation of Angola (MPLA) and the National Union for the Total Independence of Angola (UNITA), and by the President of the Republic and shall be sworn in by the High Commissioner.

Art. 21--Bearing in mind the transitional nature of the Government, the distribution of the Ministries shall be as follows:

a) The President of the Portuguese Republic shall appoint the Ministers of Economic Affairs, of Public Works, Housing and Town-Planning and of Transports and Communications;

b) The FNLA shall appoint the Ministers of the Interior, of Health and Social Affairs and of Agriculture;

c) The MPLA shall appoint the Ministers of Information, of Planning and Finance and of Justice;

d) The UNITA shall appoint the Ministers of Labour and Social Security, of Education and Culture and of Natural Resources.

Art. 22--The Offices of the Secretaries of State provided for in this Agreement shall be distributed as follows:

a) The FNLA shall appoint one Secretary of State for Information, one Secretary of State for Labour and Social Security and the Secretary of State for Trade and Tourism;

b) The MPLA shall appoint a Secretary of State for the Interior, a Secretary of State for Labour and Social Security and a Secretary of State for Industry and Power;

c) The UNITA shall appoint a Secretary of State for the Interior, a Secretary of State for Information and the Secretary of State for Fisheries.

Art. 23--The Transitional Government may institute further posts of Secretary and Under-Secretary of State, but in their distribution the rule of political heterogeneity shall be observed.

Art. 24--It is for the Transitional Government to:

a) Further, and co-operate in, the successful management of the process of decolonization until total independence is reached;

b) Superintend the whole field of public Administration, ensuring its functioning and promoting access of Angolan citizens to posts and positions of responsibility;

c) Conduct internal politics;

    d) Prepare and guarantee the holding of general elec-
        tions for the Constituent Assembly of Angola;

    e) Perform through decree-laws the legislative func-
        tion and draft decrees, regulatory decrees and
        instructions for the proper implementation of the
        laws;

    f) Guarantee, in co-operation with the High Com-
       missioner, the safety of persons and property;

    g) Carry out the judicial reorganization of Angola;

    h) Define economic, financial and monetary policy
        and create the structures needed to ensure the
        rapid development of the economy of Angola;

    i) Guarantee and safeguard individual or collective
       rights and freedoms.

Art. 25--The Presidential Committee and the Ministers are jointly responsible for the acts of the Government.

Art. 26--The Transitional Government may not be dismissed on the initiative of the High Commissioner; any change in its composition shall be effected by agreement between the High Commissioner and the liberation movements.

Art. 27--The High Commissioner and the Presidential Committee shall seek to solve all the difficulties arising from the work of the Government in a spirit of friendship and through reciprocal consultations.

Chapter 4

On the National Defence Committee

Art. 28--A National Defence Committee is hereby set up, composed as follows: the High Commissioner, the Presidential Committee, a Unified General Staff.

Art. 29--The High Commissioner shall inform the National Defence Committee of all matters concerning national defence, both internally and abroad, so as to:

    a) Define and carry out the military policy arising
       from this Agreement;

    b) Ensure and safeguard the present frontiers of
       Angola;

    c) Guarantee peace and security and public law and
       and order;

    d) Promote the safety of persons and property.

Art. 30--The decisions of the National Defence Committee shall be taken by a simple majority; the High Commissioner, who will chair the Committee, shall have a vote.

Art. 31--A unified General Staff is hereby set up, which shall comprise the commanders of the three branches of the Portuguese Armed Forces in Angola and three commanding officers of the liberation movements.

The unified General Staff shall be placed under the direct authority of the High Commissioner.

Art. 32--Armed forces belonging to the three liberation movements shall be integrated to the same total number with the Portuguese forces in the mixed military forces, on the following numerical basis:

8,000 men belonging to the FNLA,

8,000 men belonging to the MPLA,

8,000 men belonging to the UNITA,

24,000 men belonging to the Portuguese Armed Forces.

Art. 33--The National Defence Committee shall effect the progressive integration of the armed forces in the mixed military forces specified in the previous article; in principle the following calendar should be respected.

Between February and May, inclusive, and per month a total of 500 men from each of the liberation movements will be integrated and 1,500 men of the Portuguese Armed Forces.

Between June and September, inclusive, and per month, a total of 1,500 men from each of the liberation movements will be integrated and 4,500 men of the Portuguese Armed Forces.

Art. 34--Such Portuguese Armed Forces contingents, as exceed the quotas laid down in Art. 32 shall be evacuated from Angola by 30 April 1974.

Art. 35--The evacuation of the contingent of the Portuguese Armed Forces integrated in the mixed military forces shall begin after 1 October 1975 and shall be completed by 29 February 1976.

Art. 36--The National Defence Committee shall organize mixed police forces to maintain public law and order.

Art. 37--The unified police command shall have three members, one from each of the liberation movements, and leadership shall be put in commission, the chair being taken by each member in turn. The force shall be placed under the authority and supervision of the National Defence Committee.

Chapter 5

On Refugees and Displaced Persons

Art. 38--Immediately after the swearing-in of the Transitional Government, mixed equal-representation committees shall be set up, on nominations by the High Commissioner and by the Transitional

Government, to plan and prepare the structures, means and procedure necessary to deal with Angolan refugees.

The work of these committees will be supervised by the Ministry of Health and Social Affairs.

Art. 39--Those persons housed in the "Peace Villages" may return to their own villages and homes.

The mixed equal-representation committees shall propose to the High Commissioner and to the Transitional Government social, economic and other measures to ensure a speedy return to normal ways of life of displaced persons and the reintegration of their various forms of activity in the economic life of the country.

Chapter 6

On General Elections for the Constituent Assembly of Angola

Art. 40--The Transitional Government shall organize general elections for a Constituent Assembly within not more than 9 months from the date of its installation, that is, 31 January 1975.

Art. 41--Candidatures to the Constituent Assembly shall be put forward exclusively by the liberation movements--FNLA, MPLA and UNITA--as the sole legitimate representatives of the people of Angola.

Art. 42--Once the Transitional Government is installed, a Central Committee shall be instituted, with equal representation of the liberation movements, to draft the Basic Law and to prepare the elections to the Constituent Assembly.

Art. 43--When the Basic Law has been approved by the Presidential Committee, the Central Committee shall:

    a) Draft the Electoral Law;
    b) Organize lists of voters;
    c) Register the lists of candidates for election to the Constituent Assembly put forward by the liberation movements.

Art. 44--The Basic Law shall remain in force until the Constitution of Angola comes into force, but it may not run counter to the terms of this Agreement.

Chapter 7

On Angolan Nationality

Art. 45--The Portuguese State and the three liberation movements--FNLA, MPLA and UNITA--undertake to co-operate to eliminate all the consequences of colonialism. On this topic, the FNLA, the MPLA and the UNITA stress their policy of non-discrimination, according to which the quality of Angolan citizenship is definable by birth in Angola or by domicile therein, always provided that those domiciled in Angola identify themselves with the aspirations of the Angolan Nation through a conscious choice.

Art. 46--The FNLA, the MPLA and the UNITA hereby undertake to consider as Angolan citizens all individuals born in Angola, provided that they do not declare, on the terms and within the time-limits to be laid down, that they wish to maintain their present nationality or to choose another one.

Art. 47--Individuals not born in Angola but settled there may seek Angolan nationality in accordance with such rules governing Angolan nationality as come to be laid down in the Basic Law.

Art. 48--A mixed committee with equal representation will study special agreements to regulate the forms of concession of Angolan citizenship to Portuguese citizens domiciled in Angola, and the status of Portuguese citizens resident in Angola and of Angolan citizens resident in Portugal.

Chapter 8

On Economic and Financial Topics

Art. 49--The Portuguese State undertakes to regularize with the State of Angola the situation arising from the existence of property belonging to the latter outside Angolan territory, so as to facilitate the transfer of such property, or the equivalent value, to the territory and ownership of Angola.

Art. 50--The FNLA, the MPLA and the UNITA declare themselves ready to accept the responsibility arising from the financial undertakings assumed by the Portuguese State on behalf of, and relating to, Angola, always provided that they have been assumed in the real interest of the people of Angola.

Art. 51--A special mixed equal-representation committee, composed of experts appointed by the Provisional Government of the Portuguese Republic and by the Transitional Government of the State of Angola, shall list the property mentioned in Art. 49 and the credits referred to in Art. 50, shall effect such acts of valuation as it thinks fit and shall put before the two Governments such solutions as it holds to be just.

Art. 52--The Portuguese State undertakes to provide the Committee specified in the previous article with all the information and data at its disposition and which the Committee may need in order to reach well-thought-out conclusions and to propose equitable solutions within the principles of truth, respect for the legitimate rights of each party and the most loyal co-operation.

Art. 53--The Portuguese State will aid the State of Angola in setting up a Central Issue Bank. The Portuguese State undertakes to transfer to the State of Angola the powers, the assets and the debits of the Angolan Department of the Bank of Angola, on conditions to be agreed in the mixed committee for financial topics. This committee will also consider all questions related to the Portugal Department of the same bank, proposing just solutions to the extent that they concern and affect Angola.

Art. 54--The FNLA, the MPLA and UNITA undertake to respect the property and the legitimate interests of the Portuguese citizens domiciled in Angola.

Chapter 9

On Co-Operation Between Angola and Portugal

Art. 55--The Portuguese Government on the one hand, and the liberation movements on the other, agree to set up between Portugal and Angola links of constructive, lasting co-operation in all fields, specifically in the cultural, technical, scientific, economic, commercial, monetary, financial and military spheres, on the basis of independence, equality, freedom, mutual respect and reciprocity of interests.

Chapter 10

On Mixed Committees

Art. 56--Technical mixed equal-representation committees will be set up by the High Commissioner, in agreement with the Presidential Committee, to research and propose solutions for problems arising from decolonization and to lay down the foundations of active co-operation between Portugal and Angola, especially in the following spheres:

a) Cultural, technical and scientific;
b) Economic and commercial;
c) Monetary and financial;
d) Military;
e) The acquisition of Angolan nationality by Portuguese citizens.

Art. 57--The committees mentioned in the previous article shall carry out their work and negotiations in a climate of constructive co-operation and loyal spirit of compromise. Their conclusions shall be put as quickly as possible before the High Commissioner and the Presidential Committee for their consideration and for the drafting of agreements between Portugal and Angola.

Chapter 11

General Provisions

Art. 58--Any questions arising as to the interpretation and application of this Agreement which cannot be solved on the terms of Art. 27 above shall be settled by negotiation between the Portuguese Government and the liberation movements.

Art. 59--The Portuguese State, the FNLA, the MPLA and the UNITA, true to the social and political ideas repeatedly stated by their leaders, reaffirm their respect for the principles enshrined in the Charter of the United Nations and in the Universal Declaration of Human Rights, and also actively repudiate all forms of social discrimination, especially apartheid.

Art. 60--The present Agreement shall come into force immediately after it has been approved by the President of the Portuguese Republic.

The delegation of the Portuguese Government, the FNLA, the MPLA and the UNITA stress the climate of perfect co-operation and cordiality in which the negotiations took place and feel great satisfaction at reaching this Agreement, which will meet the just aspirations of the Angolan people and of which the Portuguese people are rightly proud; henceforth, they will be linked by ties of profound friendship and common desire for constructive co-operation for the progress of Angola, of Portugal, of Africa and of the world as a whole.

Signed at Alvor, Algarve, on 15 January 1975, in four copies in Portuguese.

NATIONAL EMPLOYMENT PLAN

March 1975

<u>Aims</u>

1. The National Employment Plan (PNE) will aim to improve the
    use made of available human resources through:
    a. A reduction of the trend towards the elimination of economi-
        cally and socially effective jobs, in the general framework
        of an economy moving towards socialism;
    b. The creation of productive paid jobs through economically
        and socially effective plans and programs;
    c. Programs to further the occupational transformation and
        training of Portuguese human resources;
    d. Programs to damp down the pressure of job demand.
    The aim of full employment entails transformation of the eco-
nomic structure. In this transitional phase of our economy, we
shall take into account the solution of the most serious employment
problems through a policy of active intervention in the labor market.
But it will not be possible in this manner to eliminate unemployment
in the short term, in an economy the material basis of which it is our
intention to transform.

<u>Programs to form part of the PNE and its phased development</u>

2. The first phase, to be completed within 60 days, entails an
    undertaking to effect the following:
    a. Launching of programs or projects for the creation of new
        jobs as to which there are no technically and economically
        significant doubts, with an indication of the organs or bodies
        responsible for their execution.
    b. Publication of a general scheme of incentives and forms of
        support (fiscal, technical and credit), arranged in order of
        priority, to be provided for new investment programs and
        plans likely to have a greater, faster impact on the job mar-
        ket, without detriment to their economic effectiveness, es-
        pecially such as refer to forms of association of small and
        medium-scale entrepreneurs or to production cooperative
        ventures.

c. Publication of legislation intended to:
    1) eliminate existing obstacles in the public sector on the
       rapid taking of decisions affecting public sector and
       local authority initiatives and programs;
    2) reinforce the executive, technical and financial capacity
       of local authorities, especially in social equipment
       projects.
d. Publication of a law on the general bases of structure of
    public corporations, the powers superintending their crea-
    tion to be transferred to the area of competence of the min-
    istry presiding over this area. The creation of such jobs
    will take place, after appraisal by the economic council, by
    a decree countersigned by the prime minister, the minister
    of economic planning and coordination, the minister of
    finance, and the minister of the respective department.
e. Issue of legislation to keep active productive units and their
    jobs which are of economic importance to the country, but
    which the respective firms are unable to continue managing.
    This legislation will include the following, above all:
    1) revision of Decree-Law number 660/74;
    2) publication of a basic law on production cooperatives;
    3) revision of the bankruptcy procedure;
    4) transformation of the unemployment subsidy;
    5) revision of criminal law as it affects companies.
f. Adoption of measures to permit solution of problems arising
    from delays in payments to suppliers by the public sector.
g. Steps to reduce the pressure of job demand, especially by
    reducing the voluntary retirement age, together with the
    system of unemployment subsidy.
h. Drawing up of an Occupational Transformation and Training
    Program as the first step for the National Program for the
    Development of Human Resources, to coordinate the transi-
    tional economic system with the education system and the
    development of the labor market. The Occupational Trans-
    formation and Training Program will also be progressive
    and will accompany the development of the PNE. This pro-
    gram should be linked with concrete needs, plans and prob-
    lems calling for solution within the labor market and, when-
    ever possible, should be productive in nature. Total exist-
    ing occupational training facilities in Portugal will be mobi-
    lized. This program should also be integrated with the
    civic service program and with compulsory military ser-
    vice regulations.
3. The government will appoint the persons and bodies responsible
    for drawing up, carrying out, and supervising projects and other
    forms of action.

4. Apart from the projects to be initiated in the first phase, those
    projects which are technically and economically badly or incom-
    pletely drafted will be revised, in toto or in part.
5. An urgent examination is being effected at present into the allot-
    ments made under the Extraordinary Expenditure Budget so as
    to determine the likelihood of the physical and financial execution
    of such allotments in order to guarantee total mobilization of
    available public resources.
6. The competent minister or ministers will appoint the technical
    teams, to include a representative of the Ministry of Economic
    Planning and Coordination, which will research alternative op-
    tions and will lay down the programming of decisions to be taken
    on the following national or regional projects:
    a. Project for the Sines industrial area;
    b. Iron and steel plan;
    c. Program for industrial estates;
    d. National cold storage network;
    e. Project for the Alqueva Dam;
    f. Cachao industrial area;
    g. Urban and suburban transport program for the Greater Lis-
        bon and Greater Oporto zones, including, above all, exten-
        sion of the underground railway network, modernization of
        the Lisbon and Oporto bus fleets and the Tagus river ferries,
        complementary work, etc.;
    h. Surface transports program linked with the planned, inte-
        grated development of railways and highways;
    i. Air and sea transports program, entailing the major options
        on infrastructures;
    j. National information policy program;
    k. Master plan for central and specialized hospitals.

    The Economic Council has powers to add another national or re-
    gional project to this list.
7. The PNE will be effected in close cooperation with the cultural
    extension programs of the Armed Forces Movement, the work-
    ers, and small and medium-scale entrepreneurs.

Means to be mobilized for the National Employment Plan

8. Apart from support at the local level, already specified, the
    PNE will be able to count on the following forms of support:
    a. Budget allotments for extraordinary expenditure already
        assigned for 1975 and concerning identified programs or
        projects;

b. Allotments for extraordinary expenditure diverted from projects or programs which manifestly cannot be begun in 1975 or which do not enjoy priority;

c. Mobilization of the financing capacity of the nationalized insurance companies through taking up of treasury bonds assigned to them;

d. Mobilization of revenue of the Unemployment Fund, especially for projects of regional or local importance. The creation or maintenance of jobs through the Unemployment Fund will be done in the framework of the PNE; the Management Bureau of the Unemployment Fund shall henceforth be represented in the Permanent Executive Committee of the PNE;

e. Mobilization of necessary human resources by means of requisitioning or transferring or commissioning personnel from the armed forces, the private sector and other state departments;

f. Apart from the support for the PNE which the Government departments are obligated to provide, this program will be given specific support by the technical and human resources of the Ministry of Economic Planning and Coordination, the Ministry of Labor, especially the Office of the Secretary of State for Employment, and the departments dependent on the Director General of Employment and the Director General of Job Promotion.

Institutional means of definition, attribution of responsibility, and execution of the National Employment Plan

9. The PNE will be defined by the Economic Council, in the terms of this law, and will be coordinated and controlled by the Ministry of Economic Planning and Coordination, in collaboration with the other ministries.

10. Within the Ministry of Economic Planning and Coordination the execution of the PNE will be done by the Office of the Secretary of State for Planning Human Resources. A permanent Executive Committee will also be set up to provide operational directions for the PNE, especially as regards the collaboration between the several ministries and the coordination and control of the Program. This committee will gather the technical means it requires and may set up support groups, making use of all of the available technical and human means of the Ministry of Economic Planning and Coordination. The composition of the Interministerial Permanent Executive Committee will be defined by order of the prime minister, acting on proposals made by the

minister of economic planning and coordination. It will work in direct collaboration with the organ that, in the context of the revised version of Decree-Law number 660/74, is eventually set up in the Ministry of Economic Planning and Coordination to coordinate state intervention in firms.

11. Job initiatives, projects, and problems will be identified and solved through two channels:
    a. At the central level, through the central planning organ and government departments;
    b. At the local and regional levels, these projects, initiatives and problems will, in essentials, arise from contact with the population. In this direction, Regional and Local Employment Committees will be progressively set up, including representatives of the MFA, local authorities, the trade unions, and local offices of government departments, and associations of small and medium-scale entrepreneurs. Regional technical support teams will be set up to make up for the shortcomings of local technical means to solve problems affecting employment. These teams will also serve as a coordinating link between the Permanent Executive Committee and the Regional and Local Committees.

12. The PNE will be supported by the following steps, among others:
    a. Improved means of collection and analysis of data on the development of the labor market;
    b. Immediate acceleration of research into the reorganization of industrial and other sectors which employ large numbers of personnel;
    c. Creation, at the central planning organ level, of a suitable employment forecasting unit to which the technicians who have worked in this field in government service, especially in the Ministry of Labor, will be transferred at once.

PRICES PROGRAM: ESSENTIAL FOODSTUFFS

March 1975

Within the context of an economy in the transition to socialism, that is, with the aim of placing the economy at the service of the workers and peasants, an immediate necessity is to guarantee the purchasing power of the population as regards essential foods and to meet the difficult situation of small- and medium-scale farmers who have benefited little from the changes that have taken place since April 25, 1974.

But we should stress that increased income for countrydwellers only be in conjunction with the stabilization of the cost of living through a governmental subsidy program to seek a rapid redistribution of incomes, benefiting the types of consumption of the least favored classes and burdening those of the better-off classes of the population.

Thus, the present policy of essential foodstuffs prices has as its main aims:

1. To guarantee the purchasing power of the workers;
2. To increase the income of small- and medium-scale farmers. On this basis we guarantee stabilization of prices of a range of essential foods which, while affecting the whole population, play a basic role in the budget of the working classes.

At this time, after analyzing the situation of the main current consumer foodstuffs, we can guarantee that until the end of this year there will be no increase in the present price levels of a series of products, especially important among them being bread, meat, milk, sugar, olive oil, flour products, chicken, salt cod, and margarine. In view of the changes in world prices of ground-nut oil, the price can be brought down. There will also be a slight fall in the price of butter.

Other essential products, such as fish, wine, fruit, and vegetables, are being analyzed; stabilization of price levels in these cases depends on clearing out the distribution channels, especially through the work of the public corporations that are to be set up in these sectors.

As regards the incomes of small- and medium-scale farmers, and bearing in mind their main crops, it has been decided to:

1. Increase at once the price of milk paid to the producer to esc. 6.40 and esc. 5.20 (grade A and grade B, respectively), backdated to March 1, 1975;
2. Increase at once the price of beef paid to the producer by about 10 percent;
3. Increase, at the time of the next harvest, the minimum guarantee price for millet to esc. 4 per kilo, plus a subsidy of esc. 1 per kilo delivered to the Cereals Institute, thus totalling esc. 5 per kilo for the producer.

It should be pointed out that these price rises will not be passed on to the consumer.

This prices program has been defined in conjunction with the agrarian reform program to be carried out by the Ministry of Agriculture and Fisheries.

AGRARIAN REFORM PROGRAM

January 1975

The agrarian reform to be effected is oriented in two main directions: to support small and medium-scale farmers, and to solve the serious matter of the ownership and farming of land in southern Portugal. The constant background to this orientation will be the concern to associate farm workers and small and medium-scale farmers closely with the work and actions of the state. Over the short term the following measures will be taken:

1. Overall nationalization of rural property totally or partly situated within the areas of hydro-agricultural and irrigation projects carried out with public funds and belonging to persons or to firms which, taking such areas together, own land over 50 hectares in area, this figure being adjustable according to the differences of return from the various irrigated areas.

Guarantee of ownership for those affected by these intervention measures, for an area of up to 50 hectares.

2. Expropriation of unirrigated landholdings over 500 hectares of average land, adjustable according to yield, with a guarantee of ownership for those expropriated of an area up to 500 hectares.

3. Expropriation of irrigated landholdings of an area in excess of 50 hectares, adjustable on the basis of the return, with guarantee of ownership for those expropriated of an area up to 50 hectares.

4. Agricultural credit. Creation of a system of emergency agricultural credit, personal and in kind, to meet the needs of small and medium-scale farmers, facilitating the acquisition of fertilizers and correctives, seeds and propagules, pesticides, animal feedstuffs, supplementary food products for animals, and small items of equipment necessary for high productivity of farms and with the basic aim of increasing output.

5. Common lands. The principle has been adopted of handing back common lands to their legitimate users, who will in future manage them through their associations, either alone or in collaboration with the state. A preliminary step will be to mark out and define the common lands and, inside them, the area belonging to each parish. Management will be based on management units subject to utilization plans and managed through an organic structure supported by state departments, after they have been reformed.

6. State intervention in processing cooperatives where considerable sums of public capital are invested and where the risk capital accounts for a very small proportion of total investments, so as to guarantee full use being made of equipment and fittings, to coordinate the production of the different units and to promote effective management.

7. Abolition of the system of game preserves and the adoption of measures for a census of game stocks.

8. Publication of legislation to define eligibility and non-eligibility with a view to the immediate removal of undesirable elements from the managing bodies of cooperatives.

9. Launching of Agrarian Support and Development Teams to work at the level of groups and rural districts, with the following aims:

  a. To promote the setting up of leagues and trade unions and aid the consolidation of existing ones; to supply farmers with data and information on the associative principle, credit and all legislation affecting them, especially the Rural Leasehold Law; to take steps to cleanse local institutions (cooperatives, farmers' associations, etc.) and to make them serve the needs of small and medium-scale farmers;

  b. To channel the technical aid provided by the Ministry of Agriculture and Fisheries to benefit small and medium-scale farmers;

  c. To act as a fixed center and a base for all campaigns (culture and health, run by the MFA; literacy, as part of the civic service duty, etc.) in a total process to invigorate rural communities and bring them fully into the current democratic process.

10. Promotion campaign for the increased production of forage crops, especially millet, to reduce our dependence on imports. The aim of this campaign is a substantial increase in annual output and will concentrate on areas of smallholdings; it will include operations to improve technical levels of cultivation and will give support to agrarian associations.

11. Anti-brucellosis campaign; where animals have to be slaughtered, the owners will be compensated.

12. Reorganization of the fresh meat processing and dealing circuit.

PROGRAM FOR THE CONTROL OF BASIC SECTORS

A Program for the Control of Basic Sectors will be launched. Apart from immediately ensuring the mobilization, to the general interest, of vast resources still controlled by the monopolies, this program will enable us in future to:
1. Neutralize the main bases of monopolistic accumulation;
2. Ensure closer links with other sectors;
3. Create opportunities and the necessary conditions for an industrial development process oriented towards a policy of true national independence;
4. Intervene in undertakings ruled by special economic statutes or which depend on exceptional forms of aid-- subsidies or others--from the public sector.

The situation of the various sectors as regards the attainment of these specific objectives will determine the nature and the degree of control to be wielded, bearing in mind the special position of foreign investments, in accordance with the suitable guarantees to be laid down in the forthcoming Code of Foreign Investment.

On the other hand, questions arising from the application of the principles expressed in the present program and connected with the interests of the former Portuguese colonies now undergoing decolonization, shall be the object of negotiations between the Portuguese government and the freedom movements participating in the transitional governments of the territories concerned, bearing in mind the general principle, recognized by the Portuguese state, of the legitimacy of transfer to such territories of the assets and property of nationalized undertakings or those in which the Portuguese state acquires a majority of the risk capital.

On these terms, preparation of the phase of transition to socialism calls for the immediate taking of the following measures:
1. Nationalization:
   a. Of electricity production and high-tension distribution, simultaneous with steps to control distribution of low-tension electricity and effect its later nationalization;
   b. Of Portuguese oil refining and distributing companies, and also of Portuguese capital in the company engaged in the transportation of crude oil;
   c. Of the Portuguese Iron and Steel Corporation (Siderurgia Nacional, SARL).

2. Research and subsequent application of control measures, including nationalization, where suitable, to the main mining enterprises and the following industries: tobacco, beer, cellulose, chemical fertilizers, sodium and chlorine products, petrochemicals, cement, heavy engineering, shipbuilding, and pharmaceutical products, the latter to be in conjunction with steps to be taken by the Ministries of Social Affairs and Foreign Trade and the National Defence Department;

3. Examination of the policy of concessions for on-shore and off-shore oil prospecting and greater supervision of existing contracts or of such new contracts as come to be drawn up; the Portuguese state will continue to honor in their entirety all obligations arising from contracts previously signed with foreign enterprises, without detriment to the possible review of such contracts by agreement between the two parties after negotiations;

4. Such acts of prompt intervention as are made advisable by the proven existence of reasons arising from certain concrete situations, under Decree-Law number 660/74.

The development of the Program for the Control of Basic Sectors will make it easier to clarify the field open to private enterprise. In this domain this clarification is essentially restrictive in nature and will be completed by other positive measures to be integrated in a Program of Support for National Production, which will cover both the public and the private sectors.

TRANSPORTS AND COMMUNICATIONS PROGRAM

March 1975

The main features of the transports and communications sector
of our life as a nation are:
1. Great political, social, and economic importance;
2. For many of its operations, considerable strategic value;
3. Large volume of investment entailed;
4. Considerable job provision capacity;
5. High degree of sensitivity to labor conflicts.

The present stage of the current revolutionary process makes
it both possible and vital to define such general orientations as will
guarantee in this domain the consolidation and development of the
revolution in Portugal. The need is to lay down the principles and
guidelines to orient the work to be carried out, with a calendar and
a hierarchy that will guarantee any necessary corrections, and which
will promote the indispensable participation of the workers in the recovery of this important sector of our national life.

1. Planning Policy
The planning policy for transports and communications will put
into practice the following basic principles:
a. In the fields of internal transports and communications:
Integrated, well-informed and selective planning (for each
method and type of transport and communication) so as to
ensure the unity of the national system, both economically
and politically.
b. In external transports and communications: redefinition
and adaptation of the systems concerned to new economic
and political facts, so as to permit better integration in the
international community and to gain the maximum advantage
from the geographical position of the country, and will also
take into account the following objectives:
c. Full employment: which implies a reconsideration of the
use of manpower in this sector, with the aim of eliminating
underemployment and sham employment and their social
and economic consequences.
d. Accessibility: which implies the intervention of transports
and communications in a better occupation of the territory

by the community, on the economic, social, and political
planes, to achieve a recovery of the most backward zones
of the country;

e. Austerity: which implies an inventory and appraisal of
the bottlenecks in capacity and the overlapping of services
and the correction of such defects to bring about a more
economic utilization of existing equipment and resources.

2. Exploitation Policy

The exploitation or running policy should seek, over the short
term, to prepare the conditions indispensable to achieve that system
of integrated planning mentioned in the previous chapter, within the
following context:

a. Nationalization of the major transportation and communication operators;

b. Concentration of small-medium-scale operators, both by
the encouragement of co-operatives and by setting up transport communities or sole-operator systems.

c. Correction of the weight of participation of public and private means of transportation in the overall system, giving
absolute priority to the public transport system;

d. Patterns of safety and levels of quality of service, defined
on the basis of realistic criteria applicable to Portugal as
a whole;

e. Full information for the public's benefit, to guarantee
their comfort and the full use of the public transports
system.

3. Economic and Financial Policy

Economic and financial policy in the transports and communications sector must be based on the following basic principles:

a. A sole system of financing the sector, which might include
the industries that produce and repair the equipment used;

b. Non-reimbursable financing of long-lasting fixed assets;
and will also take into account the following orientations:

c. Priority for small, high-return investments under two
years and contention of larger-scale investments;

d. Tariffs and costs linked by clear-cut criteria of relationship;

e. Costs calculated through a coherent series of rules to be
introduced into the standardized system of national account-
ing.

4. Administrative Policy

Administrative policy in transports and communications will consist in rethinking the structure, the functions, and the relations of the administrative organs of the Ministry of Transports and Communications in the new sectoral context determined by the orientations set out above, more specifically by the weight of the major operators of nationalized communications and transports, bearing in mind:

a. Functionality: through a clear definition of the functions and relations among the several organs;
b. Operationality: through the laying down of criteria and means of decision and information;
c. Economy: through the elimination of overlapping forms of competition and shortening the circuits of decision and data provision;
d. Communicability: through the creation of machinery to ensure permanent two-way communication between users and sectoral organs.

5. Short- and Medium-Term Actions

From the list of general orientations there arise certain urgent needs for action. By their nature they can be grouped in three categories:

a. Those of a predominantly political content;
b. Those to stop the worsening of the sector and to initiate its recovery;
c. Those to condition medium- and long-term operations.

The measures proposed are not exhaustive but suppose a listing of priorities imposed by a diagnosis of the sector. These measures will enable us to:

a. Re-appraise the situation so as to lay down a complete, coherent series of operations;
b. Speed up the draft of an integrated, selective, well-informed plan, considered to be the long-term aim.

Over the immediate and medium terms the implementation of these measures will lead to improvements in the transport and communications services made directly available to the public, with considerable effects on the integration of the activity of this sector in the political, social, and economic aims defined in the programs of the MFA and the provisional government. These measures are as follows:

a. Nationalization, reconstitution and recuperation of the major operators in rail, road, air, and sea transports, and in communications.

b. Nationalization, reconstitution and recuperation of large-
    scale public,urban and suburban transports in Greater
    Lisbon and Greater Oporto.
c. Formation of co-operatives and transports systems, given
    priority over private transports.
d. Review of the safety patterns and levels of quality of
    service.
e. Laying down of norms of public information so as to
    promote rational use of available forms of transport.
f. Issue of suitable legislation to ensure co-ordination of
    the various participants--local authorities, management
    bodies, users, and workers in the sector under the aegis
    of the Ministry of Transports and Communications.
g. Adoption of a sole system of financing the sector of trans-
    ports and communications, which might include the indus-
    tries that produce and repair the equipment used.
h. Creation of a Transports and Communications Planning
    Bureau, directly dependent on the minister's office, and
    bringing together all the planning organs in the sector.
i. Fixing of a calendar for the series of measures held to be
    indispensable for the recuperation and reconstitution of
    the sector.

THE PRESS LAW

March 1975

The aim of the Press Law is to prepare a measure necessary to fulfill the Program of the Armed Forces Movement which is, at the moment, the premier constitutional law of our country. That program laid down that, as an immediate measure after the victorious revolution of April 25, there should be decreed "the abolition of the censorship and previous examination system" (A. Immediate Measures, number 1, subsection g), and an "ad hoc committee set up to supervise the Press, Radio, TV, Theatre and Cinema, on a transitional basis, directly dependent on the Junta for National Salvation"; its aims would be to "safeguard military secrets and prevent disturbances in public opinion caused by the ideological acts of aggression of the more reactionary areas of thought" (ibid., 1-g-I).

Among the short-term measures incumbent on the provisional government is the "publication of a new law for the press, radio, TV, theatre, and cinema; once this law is approved and enacted, the work of the ad hoc Committee shall cease."

The government has decided to draft a law applicable only to the written press. It is believed that this decision resulted from the view that this orientation would be swifter and more practical, from the very specific nature of the current problems of the radio and, even more, of the TV; from the Portuguese legislative tradition itself; and finally, from the possibility that the future democratic institutions will at any given moment revise the present law in the light of its implementation over a period in which it could be our desire to maintain a legislative void or any kind of arbitrary, confused juridical system. Moreover, this orientation is also referred to at one stage in the MFA Program.

The purpose of the present law is to regulate the press as a whole, in such a way as to resume the tradition of freedom of expression which, with short periods of exception, was current in Portugal between 1821 and 1926, while at the same time inserting it in the context of present-day Portuguese society and bearing in mind the need to build up and consolidate a true democracy in our renovated Portugal.

The return to respect for the freedom of expression of thought through the press and the building of a juridical system, the Universal

Declaration of the Rights of Man,is undoubtedly a landmark in the journey towards the construction of a democratic society, made possible and necessary for all Portuguese by the Revolution of April 25. In seeking to make good and correct the mistakes and abuses committed over the last half-century against the press, and, by this means, against citizens in general, it has not been forgotten that it would not be enough to restore previous systems, which were possibly suited to periods of history different from ours. The aim has been to innovate, to define, and distinquish the possible, free, responsible avenues open to a press in a democratic country.

The MFA Program states explicitly that the Press Law must embody, in all its purity, the basic principle of the freedom of the press as a qualified form of the freedom of expression of thought. To complement and parallel it, more modern forms of legislation, especially the Universal Declaration of the Rights of Man (1949) [safeguard] the right to information, stressing the social significance of distributed information and its responsibilities as regards veracity and independence.

Thus the first article of the draft lays down certain aspects of the right to provide information proper to a pluralist democracy, and citizens are guaranteed, as is public opinion, the right to be informed through objective information and its social control by those for whom it is intended. In this light, in Chapter 1, some of the most important institutions of our press law are developed, which gives them a deeply innovating character.

Effective regulation of press freedom must prohibit any and all kinds of deposit or prior qualification and administrative censorship, or equivalent institutions, both as regards the setting up of journalistic undertakings and in editing and publishing. A system of broad liberty is laid down in setting up journalistic, editorial and news-agency undertakings which, bearing in mind the needs of national control and the different nature of the activities associated with each, aims at preventing administrative interference in the constitution of firms, without detriment to the definition of objective requirements in the public interest, which must be met.

Faculties complementary to the freedom of expression include freedom to work as a journalist, with all its corresponding professional guarantees and responsibilities, the freedom to publish and distribute in all its forms, the right of access to information and a very clear-cut system of protection of professional secrecy, suitably protected in spite of its subjection to the general system. The limits established in all these domains are, as far as possible, objective and precise, and merely seek to protect that minimum imposed by the public interest and individual rights in a state where law and justice prevail.

The right to reply, as an essential means of defending the good name and reputation of citizens, has been the object of particularly careful regulation, extending the respective civil and criminal law tutelage; but measures have also been included against misuse or sometimes the mere invocation of this faculty, restricting its aim as the public defence of those who consider themselves to be harmed by concrete, specific imputations.

On the other hand, there will be a transitory organ, working in close collaboration with the Ministry of Mass Communication, set up to watch over the defence of the freedom of the press and the way the latter performs its public function by informing objectively, truthfully, and from different angles. This is the Press Council, set up on the British model. An original formula has permitted the attribution to this organ of a position of rare independence, without which it would be unable to gain prestige. It has been conceived as an organ whose authority will be essentially moral and political, as is the case with the British Press Council; it will possess wide critical and advisory functions and the power to take concrete decisions, which must be printed in the publication concerned.

Independence of the press as regards the political and the economic powers leads to multiple implications which should be taken into careful account, as far as they are susceptible to juridical regulation. In this field, particular importance has attached to the anti-monopolistic legislation, in seeking to preserve the Press from the interference of the political arm or of any social forces which might wrongfully try to limit it or place it firmly in the service of private or partial interest.

The social function of the press has made it necessary to lay down several juridical systems inspired by its duty to provide truthful, objective information: the obligation to publish official notes and communiques, where there is real public importance attached to them, a careful regulation of publicity, which should be responsible and identified, the subjection of periodical publications to the duty to publish a statute defining its informative status for the enlightenment of the public and of third parties.

One absolute innovation in this law is the inclusion of a chapter defining in very general terms the organization of the journalistic undertaking. Formerly, the fact that legislation had not been passed on the topic gave rise to an excessive predominance of owners over workers in the orientation of newspapers, leaving the participation of the workers dependent either on the employer's favour alone or in the strictly legislative domain, this subject is broadly innovatory compared with most other democratic countries. Thus institutional recognition is given to the Editing Council, made up of journalists elected by all the professional journalists of each publication, which will enjoy broad participation in the orientation of publications, taking more specific concrete shape in approval of the choice of director, collaboration with him in defining the guidelines of the publication, and deliberations on all matters affecting the exercise of the professional activity of the journalist.

Another important innovation in this law is the statement of the general principle that civil or criminal responsibility will be made exclusively through jurisdictional channels, in the firm intention of putting an end to a past characterized by absorbing, arbitrary administrative interference which violated the freedom and the independence of the press; in future it will be exclusively for the courts to assess punishable facts and to punish the culprits.

This removal of press offences to the jurisdictional channels has meant the inclusion of provisions whose sole aim consists in accelerating and simplifying judicial procedure, which is sometimes slow and easily held up. We have avoided concentrating the power to appraise such cases in one ordinary court, because of the risks of discrimination which might result; the absolute rule has been defined of the powers of the ordinary court of common jurisdiction, and the attempt has been made to avoid unnecessary delays, on the initiative of the courts as of the interested parties, without any falling-off in the basic guarantees.

We feel sure that this legislation is a solid item in the democratic order now arising in Portugal, to be improved and consolidated in the future by democratic practice and by the revision of our legal system as a whole.

Ministry of Mass Communication
March 1975

CONSTITUTION OF THE PROVISIONAL GOVERNMENT

February 1975

A. Introduction

    1. The revolutionary movement begun by the Armed Forces on April 25, 1974 has progressively grown in dynamism, the better to meet the just desires of the Portuguese people and also to offset the successive, ever more violent acts of aggression engineered by the forces of reaction.

    2. The serious counterrevolutionary acts of March 11 have made it an imperative, urgent need to give the Armed Forces Movement an institutional framework. Thus Constitutional Law Number 5/75 set up the Council of the Revolution, which has been endowed with the powers formerly wielded by the Junta for National Salvation, the Council of State, and the Council of the Chiefs of the General Staffs of the Armed Forces.

    3. Law 5/75 does not in any way seek to replace or to crowd out the authentically democratic political parties that are sincerely engaged in carrying out the MFA Program; its intention is to reinforce and watch over the revolutionary process, which will at all times be carried out in the closest possible alliance with the people of Portugal and with those political parties that defend their most legitimate interests.

    4. The MFA, represented by the Council of the Revolution, hereby lays down a public political platform with the parties that are determined to carry out the principles of the MFA Program and to consolidate and broaden those democratic gains that have already been made.

    5. In drafting this agreement, we have borne in mind the results of conversations held with the various parties and also the situation arising from the crushing of the counterrevolutionary coup of March 11.

B. Aims of the Agreement

    1. The aim is to establish a common political platform to enable us to continue the political, economic, and social revolution begun on April 25, 1974 within a context of political pluralism and a

socializing trend which will permit us to carry out, in freedom, but without sterile, destructive political strife, a common plan of national reconstruction.

2.   The terms of this agreement shall be incorporated in the future political constitution to be drafted and approved by the Constituent Assembly.

3.   This agreement shall be valid for a period known as the "period of transition" with the duration fixed for it in the new constitution of between three and five years, and which shall terminate with a revision of the constitution.

C.   Elections to the Constituent Assembly,
     Its Working, the Drafting and Publica-
     tion of the Political Constitution

1.   The Council of the Revolution restates its determination to carry out all that has been promised as regards the holding of truly free and responsible elections for the formation of the Constituent Assembly.

2.   During the work to draft the future political constitution, a committee of the MFA will be set up which, in collaboration with the parties signing this agreement, will accompany the deliberations of the Constituent Assembly so as to facilitate cooperation between the parties and to activate the work of drafting, within the spirit of the MFA Program and this agreement.

3.   Once the new constitution has been drawn up and approved by the Constituent Assembly, it shall be made public by the President of the Republic, after seeking the advice of the Council of the Revolution.

4.   Until the new organs of sovereignty defined in the new political constitution begin to operate, the Council of the Revolution, the MFA Assembly and the provisional government shall maintain their present functions.

5.   Bearing in mind that the forthcoming elections are intended solely for the formation of a Constituent Assembly, whose exclusive mission shall be to draw up and approve the constitution, any alterations in the make-up of the provisional government, until a legislative assembly be elected and, as a consequence, a new government formed, shall be made on the sole initiative of the President of the Republic, after seeking the advice of the Prime Minister and the Council of the Revolution.

6.   The parties signing this agreement undertake not to question the institutionalization of the MFA, on the terms set out below, and to include it in the new constitution, together with the other issues agreed in this document.

D. Future Structure of the Organs
    of Authority and Their Powers

    1.   Organs of sovereignty.

The organs of sovereignty of the Portuguese republic during the transitional period shall be the following:

    a.   The President of the Republic
    b.   The Council of the Revolution
    c.   The MFA Assembly
    d.   The Legislative Assembly
    e.   The Government
    f.   The Courts

    2. The President of the Republic

2.1 The President of the Republic shall be, ex officio, Chairman of the Council of the Revolution and the Supreme Commander of the Armed Forces.

2.2 The President of the Republic shall enjoy the powers and carry out the functions ascribed to him by the Constitution, among which shall be included the following:

    a.   To chair the Council of the Revolution;
    b.   To act as Supreme Commander of the Armed Forces;
    c.   To choose the Prime Minister, after seeking the advice of the Council of the Revolution;
    d.   To appoint and dismiss the members of the Government, on the terms of proposals made by the Prime Minister;
    e.   To dissolve the Legislative Assembly, when the Council of the Revolution so determines, setting a date for new elections within a period of 90 days;
    f.   To publish and make public the Laws of the Council of the Revolution and of the Legislative Assembly, as well as the decree laws drawn up by the Government.

2.3 The President of the Republic shall be elected by an electoral college made up for the purpose by the MFA Assembly and the Legislative Assembly.

2.3.1 Declarations of candidature must be signed by not less than 80 members of this college.

2.3.2 Election shall be by absolute majority in the first round, or by a simple majority in the second round; only those candidates who obtained not less than 20 percent of the votes cast in the first ballot shall be eligible to enter for the second ballot.

2.4 Should the President of the Republic die in office or become permanently disabled his powers and functions shall be taken over by a person chosen for the purpose by the Council of the Revolution, and a new election shall take place within 60 days.

3.   The Council of the Revolution

3.1   The make-up of the Council of the Revolution shall be that defined in Constitutional Law Number 5/75 of March 14, 1975.

3.1.1   Any change in the composition of the Council of the Revolution may only be made through legislation of the council itself, in accordance with the decisions of the MFA Assembly.

3.2   The functions of the Council of the Revolution shall be to:

   a.   Define, within the spirit of the constitution, the necessary programmatic orientations of home and foreign policy, and to see that they are respected.

   b.   Decide, with general obligatory force, on the constitutionality of laws and other items of legislation without detriment to the powers of the courts to appraise their formal non-constitutionality.

   c.   Appraise and sanction legislation emanating from the Assembly or from the government when it concerns the following topics:

      1.   The general guidelines of economic, social and financial policy;

      2.   Foreign relations, especially with the new Portuguese-speaking countries and the overseas territories still under Portuguese administration;

      3.   The enjoyment of basic freedoms and rights;

      4.   The organization of national defence and the definition of the duties arising therefrom;

      5.   The regulation of political activities, above all as regards elections.

   d.   Carry out legislative powers on matters of national interest calling for urgent solution, where the Legislative Assembly and the government are unable to do this.

   e.   Make sure that ordinary laws are obeyed and appraise the acts of the government or the administration.

   f.   Propose for the consideration of the Legislative Assembly alterations to the constitution in force.

   g.   Wield legislative powers in military matters; where such legislation involves an increase in expenditure which cannot be met from approved budget allotments, it must be countersigned by the Prime Minister.

   h.   Authorize the President of the Republic to declare war, in case of actual or imminent aggression, and to make peace.

   i.   Express its options in consultation with the President of the Republic on the choice of Prime Minister and those ministers who must enjoy the MFA's full confidence.

j.   Deliberate on dissolution of the Legislative Assembly, when it considers this step necessary for the solution of situations of political impasse.

k.   Authorize the President of the Republic to declare a state of siege and express its opinion on all emergencies that are of grave import for the life of the nation.

l.   Express its views on the temporary or permanent physical disability of the President of the Republic.

m.   Choose the person to carry out the duties of the President of the Republic for the time being in the case of of the latter's death or permanent disability.

3.3 The Council of the Revolution shall function on a permanent basis, according to its internal regulations, which it will draw up.

4. The Government

4.1 The Prime Minister shall be chosen by the President of the Republic after seeking the advice of the Council of the Revolution and such political forces and parties as he thinks fit.

4.2 The government shall be chosen by the Prime Minister, bearing in mind the representation of the parties in the Legislative Assembly and possible coalitions, and shall be empowered by the President of the Republic.

4.3 In the cases of the initial formation or a ministerial reshuffle affecting not less than one-third of the ministers, the new government shall submit to a vote of confidence of the Legislative Assembly at its first session.

4.4 The Prime Minister is politically responsible to the President of the Republic and to the Legislative Assembly.

4.5 The Legislative Assembly may vote motions for censure against the government. Approval of two such motions at not less than 30 days' interval shall make a ministerial reshuffle obligatory.

4.6 The government shall enjoy powers to legislate through decree-laws on topics not reserved to the Council of the Revolution or to the Legislative Assembly. It may also, on its own initiative, put forward bills to the Legislative Assembly.

4.7 The ministers of defence, of home administration, and of economic planning must enjoy the full confidence of the MFA, so that they should not be appointed before the Council of the Revolution has been consulted on their appointment.

5. The Legislative Assembly

5.1 The Legislative Assembly shall be elected by direct, secret universal suffrage and shall have a maximum of 250 members.

5.2 The legislative powers of the Assembly shall be limited only by the necessary sanction of the Council of the Revolution in the issues detailed in 3.2; it may not legislate on exclusively military topics.

5.3 If a state of siege is declared, it may not be prolonged beyond 30 days without ratification by the Legislative Assembly.

5.4 The Legislative Assembly, with all its elected members, forms part of the electoral college for the election of the President of the Republic.

5.5 The Legislative Assembly may enjoy constituent powers on the decision of the Council of the Revolution, when the Council itself proposes alterations to the constitution.

5.6 Items of legislation emanating from the Assembly which do not gain the approval of the Council of the Revolution may be issued in their original form if, on a second vote, they are approved by a majority of two-thirds of the total number of members.

6. The Assembly of the Armed Forces Movement

6.1 The Assembly of the MFA shall be made up of 240 representatives of the Armed Forces, as follows: 120 of the army, 60 of the navy and 60 of the air force. Their composition shall be determined by a law of the Council of the Revolution.

6.2 The MFA Assembly, into which the Council of the Revolution is incorporated, shall be chaired by the latter through the latter's chairman, or by his legal substitute.

6.3 With all its members of the MFA Assembly forms part of the electoral college for the election of the President of the Republic.

6.4 The MFA Assembly shall function on a permanent basis, according to its own internal regulations, which shall be part of the legislative powers of the Council of the Revolution.

E. Sundry Provisions

1. The Constitution, its terms and revisions:

1.1 The future constitution to be drawn up by the Constituent Assembly shall remain in force for a period equal to the period of transition, which will be set at between three and five years.

1.2 At the end of the period of transition the Legislative Assembly will be dissolved and a new Assembly elected, which will begin its mandate with constituent powers and will then revise the constitution. Only when this revised constitution comes into force will the period of transition be considered to have ended.

2. Programmatic issues to be included in the Constitution:

Apart from the provisions which form the basis of this Agreement, the constitution shall also embody the principles of the Armed Forces Movement, the gains legitimately made throughout the process and also the developments and extensions of the program imposed by the dynamism of the revolution, which has openly and irreversibly placed our country on the original path that leads to a Portuguese form of socialism.

3. The Armed Forces

3.1 Throughout the period of transition the military power shall be kept independent of the civil power.

3.2 The Commander in Chief of the Armed Forces shall be the Chief of the Joint General Staffs of the Armed Forces, who is directly dependent on the President of the Republic.

3.3 The Chief of the Joint General Staffs of the Armed Forces shall be aided by a Vice-Chief of the Joint General Staffs of the Armed Forces, who shall stand in for him when he is unable to act.

3.4 Each branch of the Armed Forces shall be headed by a Chief of its General Staff.

3.5 The Commander in Chief, the Vice-Commander in Chief, and the Chiefs of the General Staff of the three branches of the Armed Forces shall have ministerial powers.

3.6 The Armed Forces will guarantee and will provide incentive for the revolutionary process, leading to the building up of a true political, economic, and social democracy.

3.7 Apart from their specific mission to defend national independence and territory, the Armed Forces will participate in the economic, social, cultural, and political development of the country within the framework of their movement.

FINAL PROGRAM OF DEFINITION OF MFA

June 1975

1. <u>Political definition</u>
1.1   The MFA is the liberation movement of the Portuguese people;
       it stands above party and its essential aim is that of national
       independence. The MFA recognizes that this national indepen-
       dence involves a process of domestic decolonization, which
       can only be achieved by means of the construction of a socialist
       society.
1.2   By "socialist society," as the final aim to be attained, we un-
       derstand a classless society, obtained through the collectiviza-
       ation of the means of production, eliminating all forms of ex-
       ploitation of person by person, in which all individuals will be
       given equal opportunities of education, work and promotion,
       without distinction of birth, sex, religious beliefs or ideology.
            The transition from our present society to a socialist
       society must necessarily entail several stages, the first of
       which will cover the period of transition laid down in the con-
       stitutional agreement platform, the stages of which will be de-
       termined by the socio-economic and political development of
       the Portuguese people.
            But the MFA has already made it quite clear that this
       aim will be reached along a pluralist path.
1.3   Pluralism means freedom of expression and discussion of
       opinions, and also experiments in building the new society, by
       means of a permanent, open dialogue with the whole of the
       Portuguese people.
            Socialist pluralism includes co-existence, both in theory
       and in practice, between various forms and concepts of the
       building of the socialist society. Thus the MFA repudiates the
       implantation of socialism by violent or dictatorial means.
            Party pluralism, as laid down in the constitutional agree-
       ment, implies recognition of the existence of various political
       parties and currents of opinion, even though they do not neces-
       sarily defend socialist options. It thus makes allowance for an
       opposition, whose criticism may well be beneficial and con-
       structive, provided that its activity is not opposed to the build-
       ing of a socialist society by democratic means.

The MFA will enjoy the natural support and backing of those parties which, by their political programs and practice, do show a real interest in adopting and concretizing objective measures called for by the transition towards socialism, and with them it will establish the necessary alliances and coalitions.

1.4   During the period of transition to socialism, the political parties should play a very valuable role, not only through their pedagogical work in making the masses politically aware and ready to act, but also as vehicles to transmit the will of the people, by tuning in to their needs and aspirations in all possible ways, including elections.

But elections, to be held and developed through the transitional period, must be consciously integrated in the revolutionary process; they cannot in any sense be allowed to constitute an obstacle to it.

1.5   In accordance with the express vocation it has taken on itself as a national liberation movement, the MFA wants all the Portuguese people to play an active part in their own revolution, so that it will decisively support, and will establish links with, all base units, whose aims form part of the concretization and defence of the MFA Program for the construction of the socialist society.

These people's organizations will form the embryo of an experimental system of direct democracy, through which we believe we can achieve the active participation of the whole nation in public administration and in national political life, in connection with the local and regional organs of the central power. They will also have the advantage of encouraging, starting at the base, concentration of the efforts of the various parties, through unity in concretizing common aims.

But no armed civilian organizations, party-organized or not, will be allowed, although people's organizations may, on the initiative of the MFA itself and under its control and as an extension of its work, carry out, in cases of national emergency, tasks of self-defence of vital objectives.

Within the armed forces no politico-military organizations will be permitted, whether party-based or not, outside the MFA, and all military personnel should be progressively integrated into this movement, which is theirs.

1.6   The MFA restates its determination to carry out, and ensure that others carry out, in their entirety, the terms of the constitutional agreement platform, freely laid down with Portuguese political parties, and solemnly states that it will denounce and will take action against all attitudes which, openly or covertly, seek to question and undermine that pact.

1.7   In accordance with the principles laid down, the MFA considers
       that it is its duty to make it publicly explicit that the sole power
       of the Constituent Assembly is to perform the patriotic mission
       of drawing up the political constitution of the Portuguese nation,
       and it is forbidden to indulge in any other form of official inter-
       ference in national political or administrative life.
1.8   In foreign affairs the MFA will go on with a policy of national
       independence and of contribution to peace and cooperation in
       Europe and the world at large.
            Within this context we shall respect already established
       alliances and undertakings, specifically Portugal's participa-
       tion in NATO, so as not to endanger the political and military
       balance of Europe.
            In the political field Portugal will follow a strategy of
       readiness to maintain relations with all countries of the world,
       without interfering in their domestic affairs, or allowing them
       interference in ours; she feels she possesses a historical vo-
       cation to serve as a link between the European peoples and
       those of the Third World, especially with the sister Portuguese-
       speaking countries.
            In the economic sphere, our foreign policy will be ori-
       ented towards a progressive diversification of trade relations
       and we shall not permit any country or bloc to seek to impose
       on the Portuguese people, by means of economic relations,
       any form of domination.

2. The exercise of authority
2.1   Analysis of the present political situation and its likely devel-
       opment reveals the need to strengthen the revolutionary author-
       ity of the MFA, as an indispensable basis for a state power to
       allow a normal, pacific development of the path of transition
       to socialism.
            There are in fact threats of counterrevolutionary activ-
       ities encouraged from other countries and supported inside
       Portugal by agents of national capitalism and colonialism, now
       being uprooted, which, unless firmly and exemplarily eradi-
       cated, would represent a grave danger for disturbance of public
       order and the safety of persons and property, and could create
       a climate very propitious to the return of a right-wing fascistic
       regime.
            On the other hand, certain manifestations of pseudo-
       revolutionary leftism, even though sometimes well intentioned,
       tend to create situations of potential anarchy, which thoroughly
       disturb a coherent revolutionary process, the objective result
       being a strengthening of the declared aims of those whom they
       say, or whom they would have us believe, they are fighting.

We thus conclude that only the exercise of a firm, though not necessarily repressive, authority can guarantee the success of the revolution in which the MFA and the Portuguese people are engaged.

2.2   We thus re-affirm our intention of ensuring that all the laws that contribute to the aims of the Portuguese revolution shall be obeyed, until the process of history shows that they are unsuited to the concrete circumstances in which our society finds itself.

To further this firm exercise of authority, apart from the revolutionary legislation already published, new laws will be published to bring about the desired aims.

2.3   The need to put down, with the necessary firmness, the possible activities of groups or clandestine armed organizations forces on us the publication of a special law, now being drafted, which will enable us to punish with severe penalties, those who participate in such counterrevolutionary organizations.

2.4   We consider that the struggle against leftism should be waged essentially in the ideological field, by seeking to recuperate its well-intentioned supporters for the aims and tasks of the revolution.

But different kinds of repression will be employed, including armed action if necessary, against those groups or organizations whose actions and practices systematically disturb law and order and which disregard the rules laid down for the construction of socialism by a pluralist means.

2.5   We recognize that one of the spheres in which manifestations of uncontrolled leftism have most disturbed public life in our country is that of education. Thus the MFA restates its determination to support the Ministry of Education in restoring a normal productive climate in which, within democratic rules of management, students and pupils can fulfill their duty towards our society by training themselves and making ready for their functions as the workers of the future.

We must not forget that it is desirable that, in intellectual circles, there should be a strong revolutionary awareness. Intellectual workers--which includes students--have an obligation to prevent their political activities from so harming their specific forms of work that they become potential parasites on society.

3.   Economic and financial policy
3.1   The current economic situation of our country is characterized by the following three basic critical factors.

A)   Very marked imbalance of the balance of payments, the deficit on which is reckoned to be likely to reach, by the

end of this year, a deficit far higher than that for 1974,
which was about 17,000 m. escudos.

B)   A high unemployment figure, about 250,000 workers,
     that is, 8 percent of the working population.

C)   Falling internal production, endangering national inde-
     pendence; if present production trends are not altered,
     it is forecast that this year will show a fall of 6 percent
     on the GNP for 1974.

3.2   All Portuguese people must, therefore, be quite clear about
        the economic and financial situation of our country, which
        can be summed up in the following facts:

3.2.1   Imports: These, mainly of foodstuffs, are far higher than
        exports, and the excess may well be as high as a figure of
        50,000 m. escudos by the end of 1975. This figure is largely
        due to the high prices of foodstuffs and of oil in supplier
        countries.

3.2.2   This deficit is attenuated by foreign currency earned in Por-
        tugal by the remittances sent by emigrants and the sum spent
        here by tourists. (In the latter, as is well-known, there is
        a crisis at the moment.)

3.2.3   At the end of this year it is forecast that Portugal will be
        showing a deficit on the balance of payments of some 30,000
        m. escudos, which will have to be met from the currency
        reserves of the Bank of Portugal, which will almost exhaust
        them, leaving only our gold reserves.

3.2.4   This financial situation is part of an economic context in
        which the wealth produced in the country will fall, unless the
        current trend is changed, this year by some 6 percent in
        relation to 1974, even taking into account the rise in agri-
        cultural output.

3.2.5   This panorama is a very serious one, but not alarming, be-
        cause it corresponds to a socio-political phase of the elimi-
        nation of the errors of capitalism, based on monopoly and
        major landowning, which characterized our country and also
        the crisis of international capitalism. But if this crisis is
        not to become irremediable, the Portuguese people have no
        alternative but to take upon themselves the construction of a
        new socialist economic system and the working classes must
        take a conscious decision to opt for either socialism, and
        the relative, temporary sacrifices its construction entails,
        or capitalism, with all the oppression and exploitation in-
        herent to it.

3.2.6   The point is that if the destruction of capitalism calls for the
        removal of the exploiting power of the rich monopolist bour-
        geoisie, the big landowners and the major financiers, the
        building-up of socialism calls for work, sacrifices and

political awareness from the working classes to create a
future society free of classes and of exploitation; but this
does not mean, over the short term, that all the forms of injustice permitted or encouraged under the previous regime
can be rectified and that, all at once, we can start paying
every Portuguese worker a wage corresponding to his just
desires and real needs.

3.2.7   This being the case, the policy of truth that has at all times
been put before the Portuguese people makes it imperative
to adopt certain realistic measures, if the working people do
in fact, wish to build up a socialism. These are:

a) Reductions in imports, especially more superfluous
goods, or those which can be produced in our own country.

b) Policy of austerity in consumption.

c) Increase in home output, especially of such products
as, for example, foodstuffs, can replace those formerly imported, or those which can increase the value of our exports.

3.3   In view of this grave economic situation, it is a matter of
urgency to adopt the following:

a) Immediate prompt measures.

b) A strategy of economic development, defined on the
basis of three critical areas: the balance of payments, unemployment, and economic independence.

The future panorama of the politico-economic situation
and system, including discussion of the following aspects:

- organized control of output by the workers;
- local mobilization for development;
- organization of the planning system;
- qualitative and subsystems of the transitional economy
  (state sector and private sector).

Policy of foreign economic cooperation.

3.4   The two basic topics, strategy of economic development and
future layout of the economic system; will be discussed as a
matter of urgency by the economic team of the provisional
government and by the four ministers without portfolio representing the parties of the coalition, in connection with the
Council of the Revolution; the corresponding decisions should
be taken by the end of July, thus making it possible to draw
up a transitional plan for 1976-1978.

The discussion of these topics and the immediate prompt
measures will provide a far-reaching test of the political via-
bility of the present coalition and its capability of carrying
forward the united progress towards the real aims of socialism.

4.   Government and administration
4.1   The Provisional Government: The provisional government
       will work in the present circumstances as a unified govern-
       ment, meeting rapidly and efficiently the national and patriotic
       aims of the construction of socialism, as defined above.
           The MFA considers that the grave economic and financial
       situation of the country calls for the present coalition govern-
       ment to set aside natural divergences and to achieve a common
       solution for the problem of economic development.
           The MFA believes that the Portuguese people, the over-
       whelming majority of whom are represented by the parties
       forming the coalition, have a right to demand that these parties
       shall prove to be up to their historical duty, on pain of being
       considered unsuitable in relation to the objective needs of the
       country.
           Thus the MFA thinks that the discussion of the strategy of
       economic development and of the economic model of society to
       be begun at once by the provisional government, and which
       should be concluded by the end of July 1975, will be an extreme-
       ly important test that the Portuguese people are entitled to see
       settled.
4.2   Inertia of the machinery of state. The present state machinery
       is extremely heavy and bureaucratic, and is clearly unsuitable
       to the dynamism of the present revolutionary process. It can
       only respond slowly and incompletely to the demands made of
       it. To meet this problem the MFA thinks it is essential to:
           a) Decentralize the administration;
           b) Gradually set up a new state apparatus, non-party, or-
       ganized on dynamic patterns around basic programmed points,
       and endowed with staff sufficiently identified with the demands
       of revolutionary dynamism. As a parallel to this we shall
       start work to effect administrative reform in depth.
           c) Lay down a correct policy of re-classification and recuper-
       ation of the work of civil servants, making use of the weapon of
       dismissal in cases where recovery is clearly out of the question.
           d) Accept the pressure for dialogue between the organs of the
       state power, at the various levels, and the unitary popular or-
       ganizations which correspond to the same scales and levels,
       and which will be progressively given powers to control the
       activities of such organs of the state machinery.
           e) Eliminate excessively bureaucratic and complex procedures
       within the state machinery, replacing them by rapid, revolu-
       tionary methods able to meet the pressures of demand, at-
       tributing full responsibility to those who execute such a policy
       and such measures.

4.3   Administrative decentralization. Although this topic belongs
       to the domain of the future political constitution, the dynamism
       of the people in setting up associations to look after their com-
       mon interests has made it necessary for the Ministry of Home
       Administration to adopt measures, which the MFA considers
       justified, for regional decentralization of various state ser-
       vices and departments, thus making possible, at the regional
       level, the drafting of plans more suited to local circumstances
       and to their execution, with the progressive participation of
       local people's organizations, although maintaining the neces-
       sary links and coordination with the central organs of the state.
           The essentially pragmatic criterion adopted has consisted
       in the setting-up, at the level of a given region, of a planning
       bureau and a regional employment committee, to bring together
       representatives of the various ministries concerned, as well
       as a representative of the MFA. In collaboration with the plan-
       ning bureau there are assemblies of the representatives of the
       various administrative committees of the local authorities, the
       latter, in their turn, in close contact with the already numerous
       committees of local inhabitants, trade unions, and other unitary
       organizations. This initiative has already been launched in the
       Algarve, with good results; it will soon be extended to the re-
       gions covered by the military zones of the north, center and
       south so as to permit a better coverage and support by the MFA
       of local unitary people's organizations; it will be sufficiently
       flexible to permit a later adjustment to the decisions taken by
       the Constituent Assembly on the matter.
4.4   Link-up between the MFA and the unitary people's basic struc-
       tures. The MFA considers that in the present phase of the
       revolution it is extremely important and perhaps decisive to
       strengthen and dynamize these structures as a determinant
       factor of popular unity and of the overcoming of the contradic-
       tions existing at the level of summit political structures.
           This new power in the revolution does not seek to question
       the legitimacy of the existing political parties but rather to ob-
       tain an additional impulse towards unity and coherence through
       the dynamism of their basic structures based on the concrete
       everyday situation, thus causing an upsurge of energy from
       bottom to top. The future association of these unitary people's
       organs may set up the embryos of representative local organs
       or assemblies, reflecting the interests of the population, which
       gradually, through dialogue with the local organs of public ad-
       ministration, will dynamize them and identify themselves with
       the true local popular interests. The guidelines of this form of
       political orientation are now being studied by an MFA working-

party appointed specially; their conclusions, formulated on the
basis of real existing data, will shortly be publicized.

5.   Dynamization and information

5.1   It is recognized that the desired construction of a socialist
      society by the pluralist path already defined cannot be done
      without a mobilization and indoctrination of the whole Portu-
      guese people, to put them positively and consciously on the
      transitional path to socialism.

      It should be noted that the implementation of a real social-
      ism implies in essentials a development of mentalities so as to
      transform most of the almost purely materialist motivation,
      characteristic of capitalist societies, into a spiritual motiva-
      tion to persuade individuals to leave a selfish, individualist
      attitude towards their fellows in favour of an altruistic, col-
      lectivist attitude, centering their attention and concern on the
      common weal.

      This work will only be possible through a suitable policy
      of information which must be begun forthwith by a far-reaching
      transformation of the structures of the organs and services of
      social and mass communications. This does not mean that in-
      formation and the media should be monolithic or propaganda-
      oriented, for this would not be, in our view, in accordance
      with the pluralist principles followed by the Portuguese revo-
      lution.

      But this information must be at once a form of true educa-
      tion, to inform and enlighten the people, instead of as hitherto,
      exciting and confusing them, as has so often been the case.
      The MFA sincerely believes that freedom and the socialist op-
      tion are not incompatible, but the exercise of one must not limit
      the existence of the other.

5.2   One of the practices necessary to the attainment of the aims
      defined above is to transform one or more dailies, at present
      practically under state ownership, into official organs, whose
      presentation of news and comment will naturally reflect the
      positions of the MFA.

      It is hoped that by this step the Portuguese people will have
      at their disposal non-controversial dailies, without any party
      line or associations, following a general policy of truth and
      enlightenment of the people, the daily practice of which should
      make them eminently respected.

5.3   With the same aim it is necessary to control state radio and
      TV to bring to the public ear and eye, systematically, the
      position and views of the MFA on political events and the
      events of national life.

5.4   The mobilization of public opinion for aims of the national in-
        terest should be done through the rational use of publicity in
        the media, which will naturally imply the utilization of nation-
        alized publicity organizations.

5.5   Free information has a right to exist in Portugal but very often
        it has been misused, giving rise to the diffusion through the
        press, on radio, and over the TV of news items deliberately
        distorted to cause confusion or alarm among public opinion.
        The same is true of certain foreign correspondents, who have
        misused the hospitality granted them and have sent to the papers
        for which they work false or biased news items, intentionally
        distorting and worsening the image of Portugal received in other
        countries. The Press Law does not permit any decisive rapid
        measures against these prevaricators, who abuse that Law to
        carry out--so far with impunity--activities perfectly well de-
        finable as counter-revolutionary; so the MFA is determined to
        proceed directly and effectively against them by publishing, if
        necessary, revolutionary legislation on this topic.

5.6   The major Portuguese communities spread about the world,
        whose feelings of nationality remain unchanged, have been the
        victims of systematic campaigns of defamation about events in
        Portugal, the intention being to estrange them from the feeling
        of national liberation and, sometimes, to make use of them as
        a weapon of the forces of reaction through friends or relatives
        living in Portugal.
            The MFA hopes that all the Portuguese nation, including
        those who were forced to emigrate because of the lack of free-
        dom or decent living conditions in their own country, will feel
        proud of their nationality, and to this end they must be informed
        truthfully and opportunely of the revolutionary process.
            For this purpose the Foreign and Mass Communications Min-
        istries will put into practice suitable systems and measures.

5.7   The mobilization of the Portuguese people for the socialist path
        demands not only a new policy of information but also a constant
        policy of dynamization which, by its presence and in practice,
        will make the recommendations and the programs drafted by the
        central organs both visible and effective.
            To this end there must be an intensive, effective campaign
        of dynamization by the military, in joint efforts with the people's
        basic structures, which can, better than anyone else, reflect
        and represent the most just hopes and needs of the population
        as a whole. To effect this work, the suitable human and ma-
        terial means should be made available, not forgetting that the
        revolution of April 25, 1974 was carried out for the people and
        that from the people will come its force, its continuity, and its
        justification.

RONA M. FIELDS is Associate Professor, Department of Sociology, Clark University. She visited Portugal several times during the first 18 months following the revolution, and has frequently lectured at European universities on revolutionary movements and social conflict. In 1975 she was a Fellow at the Peace Research Institute in Oslo, Norway. Her articles on a wide range of political and social issues have appeared in numerous academic and professional journals. Her books include A Society on the Run and a forthcoming title, Psychological Genocide: The Case of the Irish People. Dr. Fields earned her Ph.D. at the University of Southern California.

SMALL STATES AND SEGMENTED SOCIETIES:
National Political Integration in a Global Environment
edited by Stephanie Glicksberg Neuman

DEVELOPMENT IN RICH AND POOR COUNTRIES:
A General Theory with Statistical Analyses
Thorkil Kristensen

THE FATE OF THE ATLANTIC COMMUNITY
Elliot R. Goodman

SPAIN IN THE 1970S: Economics, Social Structure,
Foreign Policy
edited by William T. Salisbury
and James D. Theberge

ALLENDE'S CHILE
edited by Philip O'Brien

FOREIGN POLICY AND U.S. NATIONAL SECURITY:
Major Postelection Issues
edited by William W. Whitson

DILEMMAS OF THE ATLANTIC ALLIANCE:
Two Germanys, Scandinavia, Canada, NATO,
and the EEC
Peter Christian Ludz, H. Peter Dreyer,
Charles Pentland, and Lothar Ruhl

DATE DUE